W9-AVH-504

Social Psychology
An Applied Perspective

P. Wesley Schultz

Stuart Oskamp

Prentice Hall
Upper Saddle River, New jersey 07458

Library of Congress Cataloging-in-Publication Data

Schultz, P. Wesley.
   Social psychology : an applied perspective / P. Wesley Schultz,
Stuart Oskamp. — 1st ed.
     p. cm.
   Includes bibliographical references and index.
   ISBN 0-13-096248-1
   1. Social psychology. I. Oskamp, Stuart. II. Title.
HM1011.S38 2000
302--dc221   99-30974
                                               CIP

Editor-in-Chief: *Nancy Roberts*
Executive Editor: *Bill Webber*
Assistant Editor: *Jennifer Cohen*
Managing Editor: *Mary Rottino*
Production Liaison: *Fran Russello*
Project Manager: *Patty Donovan (Pine Tree Composition)*
Prepress and Manufacturing Buyer: *Lynn Pearlman*
Art Director: *Jayne Conte*
Cover Designer: *Bruce Kenselaar*
Cover Art: *Lisa Henderling/SIS, Inc.*
Photo Research Supervisor: *Melinda Lee Reo*
Image Permission Supervisor: *Kay Dellosa*
Photo Researcher: *Anthony Arabia*
Marketing Manager: *Sharon Cosgrove*

This book was set in 10/12 Minister light by Pine Tree Composition, Inc.,
The cover was printed by Phoenix Color Corp.

© 2000 by Prentice-Hall, Inc.
Upper Saddle River, New Jersey 07458

Printed in the United States of America
10   9   8   7   6   5   4   3

Printed with Corrections 12/99
ISBN: 0-13-096248-1

Prentice-Hall International (UK) Limited, *London*
Prentice-Hall of Australia Pty. Limited, *Sydney*
Prentice-Hall Canada Inc., *Toronto*
Prentice-Hall Hispanoamericana, S.A., *Mexico*
Prentice-Hall of India Private Limited, *New Delhi*
Prentice-Hall of Japan, Inc., *Tokyo*
Pearson Education Asia Pte. Ltd., *Singapore*
Editora Prentice-Hall do Brasil, Ltda., *Rio de Janeiro*

To my children, Jordan and Sierra, and the future they will inherit. *PWS*

To Catherine, our children, and our grandchildren, and their promise. *SO*

TABLE OF CONTENTS

Preface

As an undergraduate student sitting in Professor Rosenberg's social psychology class at the University of California, Irvine, I (*PWS*) was fascinated to learn that people had actually used science to study social behavior. I was intrigued by theories of attraction, self, helping, aggression, stereotypes, conformity, and the like. At the same time, I was plagued by questions of how to find practical ways to use this knowledge. It is my sense that many of the undergraduates sitting in my classes 15 years later share these feelings—they are fascinated by the theories, but left searching for the applications. This book attempts to fill that gap—to provide an applied perspective to social psychological theory.

On a similar note, as a young assistant professor at the Claremont Graduate School, I (*SO*) was gratified to find that my teaching and research in psychology could be directed so as to be relevant to momentous issues of the time, such as the cold war and the civil rights movement of the 1960s. That relevance became a central theme for the rest of my career, and it is illustrated in this book.

Social problems are caused by human behavior, and applied social psychology is an attempt to understand and change the behaviors associated with different problems. We have tried to select issues that are relevant to students, as well as pressing national or international social problems. The applications we have selected include teenage pregnancy, physical health and longevity, prejudice and discrimination, divorce, aggression and violence, school failure, AIDS, and environmental problems. Clearly, this is just a sampling of the applied work being done, but it reflects most of the major areas of research and some of the most pressing social problems facing us today.

The book is divided into four main sections. The first section provides an introduction to applied science, and a framework for an applied perspective. An important part of this framework is a reliance on rigorous scientific research to evaluate the effectiveness of both theory and application. The second, third, and fourth sections have two or three chapters that cover the broad areas of social cognition, social relations, and social influence respectively. Each of these chapters contains an extended illustration of a study that has used social psychological theory either to understand the causes of a social problem or to change the behaviors that contribute to the problem. The final chapter discusses the crucially important but rarely presented topic of achieving social change, and the roles that social psychologists (both students and professionals) can have in promoting change.

This book is written for students with little or no background in psychology or sociology. It is our hope that the book will be used in tandem with class lectures to integrate an applied perspective into undergraduate courses in social psychology, applied psychology, or social problems.

Many people helped make this book possible. For providing a collegial and supportive atmosphere in which to write, we thank the faculty and staff at our home institutions: California State University, San Marcos, and the Claremont Graduate University. Many social psychology classes at St. Lawrence University and CSUSM have provided useful suggestions for topics. To help make the book student-friendly, several undergraduates read and commented on chapters: Pamela Brown, Quincie Douglas, Lisa Lukoski, Karen Roslie, Erik Ruzek, and Christianna Wolf. Three students in particular, Quincie Douglas, Lisa Lukoski, and Christianna Wolf, were instrumental in pulling together the necessary materials and editing the final manuscript. The reviewers who took the time to provide thoughtful, constructive feedback include Elliot Aronson, Eugene Borgida, Amy Marcus-Newhall, and Thomas Pettigrew. The staff at Prentice-Hall, Bill Webber, Jennifer Cohen, and Tamsen Adams, were helpful in all phases of writing. Most of all, we thank our families for their support and love.

We hope that readers will feel the sense of hope and excitement that went into writing this book. Please feel free to send us your comments and suggestions via email: *psch@coyote.csusm.edu* or *oskamps@cgu.edu*

P. Wesley Schultz
San Marcos, California

Stuart Oskamp
Claremont, California

PART ONE

Introduction
and
Methodology

Applying Social Psychology: Typical Features, Roles, and Problems

All science must be applied science, the goal of which is to lighten the toil of every-day life.

—Galileo

From the earliest days of science, people have hoped that the knowledge gained through research would improve their lives. For many scientific disciplines, this ideal has been realized. Computers, cars, air travel, cellular phones, the internet, modern medicine, compact discs, and so on are applications of biology, chemistry, and physics. Although applications of social science have been slower in coming than applications in the physical sciences, psychologists, sociologists, and political scientists are becoming increasingly interested in solving social problems. This book provides a glimpse into some of the areas to which scientific knowledge in social psychology has been, and is being, applied.

Consider the following four social problems. For each, think about what causes the problem, and what could be done to solve it.

Teenage Pregnancy. In the United States, 53% of teenagers between the ages of 14 and 16 report having had sexual intercourse (CDC, 1998a). Of sexually active students, 43% report not using a condom during their last sexual intercourse, and among sexually active females aged 15 or older, 20% report having been pregnant (Kann et al., 1998). Of these pregnancies, 80% are unwanted, and nearly 40% end in abortion (Center for Population Options, 1992). Teenage pregnancies have negative consequences for the adolescent mothers, their children, their parents, and society (DeRidder, 1993). It has been estimated that the public cost of teenage pregnancy through welfare payments (e.g., food stamps) and Medicaid is nearly $20 billion each year. How do you think we should go about reducing the number of teenage pregnancies?

Acquired Immune Deficiency Syndrome. An issue closely related to teenage pregnancy is AIDS. The deadly AIDS virus continues to spread. As of 1998, an estimated 11.7 million people worldwide had died from AIDS (World Health Organization, 1998). To date, there is no cure or vaccine for AIDS, and once contracted, AIDS is eventually fatal. Unlike other viruses, HIV (the virus that causes AIDS) can only be spread through the exchange of body fluids. Nearly 60% of the AIDS cases documented in the United States were contracted through sexual relationships—i.e., men having sex with men or women having sex with infected men (CDC, 1998). Clearly, it is of paramount importance that people protect themselves from this deadly disease—but how can we convince them to do so?

Violence. Violent behavior has been increasing in recent years—especially in the United States. Among young people aged 15 to 24, homicide is the second leading cause of death, and among young Black and Hispanic males, it is the leading cause of death (Bureau of Justice Statistics, 1990). Other violent behaviors like assault, bullying, and sexual abuse are also serious problems (Guerra,

Tolan, & Hammond, 1994). How can we use social psychological theories of violence and aggression to prevent these behaviors?

Environmental Destruction.   Human behaviors are destroying the natural environment. The earth's human population is nearly 6 billion. Many experts estimate that over the long term, the earth can support no more than 3 billion people (Pimentel et al., 1994). The large human population means more pollution and fewer natural resources. Indeed, we are rapidly depleting the earth's supply of oil, metals, and fresh water (Brown, 1995). The necessary changes required to prevent ecological disaster are *behavioral* in nature, and social psychology can play an important role in designing effective programs to promote change (Oskamp, 1995).

THE SCIENCE OF SOCIAL PSYCHOLOGY

Psychology is the scientific study of human thought, feeling, and behavior. Social psychology is a subdiscipline within psychology that focuses on human interaction. More formally, **social psychology** *is the scientific study of how the thoughts, feelings, and behaviors of an individual are influenced by other people* (Jones, 1998). *Applied* social psychology, stated very simply, takes some aspect of the knowledge base of social psychology and applies it systematically for some purpose. The purposes for which social psychological knowledge is used vary widely, and this book is intended to provide a glimpse into some of them.

Social problems like teenage pregnancy, AIDS, violence, and environmental destruction are complex issues that require analysis on a variety of levels, ranging from the individual level to group and societal levels. However, they all have human behavior at their core. Teenage pregnancy is caused by sexual behavior, as is AIDS. Human actions also cause violence, environmental destruction, and all other social problems. The social psychological contribution to understanding and solving these problems stems from the theories developed to understand and change human behavior. For instance, as one approach to reducing violence in public schools, social psychologists can work to change the behavior of individual students. In past research, social psychologists have identified variables that predict the students who are most likely to act aggressively, studied the factors that lead to violent behaviors, and worked with students to prevent aggressive behaviors from occurring. One finding from this research is that students who act aggressively often lack the social skills necessary to manage conflicts with others. Based on this research, social psychologists have worked to develop *competence training* programs to teach students these important relationship skills (Beelmann, Pfingsten, & Losel, 1994; Deffenbacher et al., 1996). We examine this area of research in Chapter 6.

Social psychologists also work at the level of group interactions. For instance, the social problems of prejudice and racism have concerned social psychologists for most of this century. Over 40 years ago, social psychological research was cited in the Supreme Court's *Brown v. Board of Education* decision, which outlawed racial segregation in schools (Cook, 1979). In subsequent years, many social psychologists have worked toward improving interracial relations in desegregated schools, for example by introducing theory-based systems of small-group cooperative learning (e.g., Aronson et al., 1978). We examine this issue in Chapter 4.

Social psychologists have also been active at the level of complex organizations. Notable examples include *team-building* approaches in businesses to foster cooperative work-team efforts toward common goals; innovative organizational procedures, such as *quality circles*, participative management, and employee ownership; and emphasis on humanizing the work environment and improving the *quality of working life*. A critical issue in recent years is how to handle increasing ethnic, cultural, and gender diversity among organizational members (cf. Chemers, Oskamp, & Costanzo, 1995).

TYPICAL FEATURES OF AN APPLIED PERSPECTIVE

In the preceding section, we stated that applied social psychology uses the knowledge obtained from social psychological research for some social purpose. As a more formal definition, **applied social psychology** is the *application of social psychological methods, theories, or principles to understand or solve a social problem.*

A Problem Orientation

Our definition stated that the aim of the field is to understand or solve social problems. This highlights one of the key features of applied social psychology: the fact that it typically begins by focusing on some kind of problem in society. For example, an applied social psychologist might start with a concern about violence in our society. From there, he or she might (a) design a study to learn more about the phenomenon, or (b) analyze the already available research knowledge and use it to plan an intervention or social program that would try to reduce some aspect of violence. In either case, the focus would be on the problem—violence.

In contrast, the approach of traditional "basic" science would choose a topic for study because of its relevance to some theory in the field, and would focus on finding evidence to support or refute the theory in question. A traditional basic scientist who chose to study a topic like violence would typically consider it as a special case of a theoretical concept—for instance, as an example of the frustration-aggression theory. Basic scientists would be less likely to plan an intervention to reduce societal violence, but if they did, it would be mainly for the purpose of providing support for the theory they were using. That is, basic research tends to be *process-oriented*, whereas applied research is *problem-oriented* (Aronson, Wilson, & Brewer, 1998).

Despite the differences in focus, there is often considerable overlap between the activities of basic and applied scientists. Both may plan studies to gather new information. Both may stress *theories* as ways of understanding a social phenomenon, though that is more apt to be the central focus of interest of a basic scientist. Both may carry out interventions designed to change some social phenomenon, but that is more likely to be the main goal of an applied scientist. The key difference is in the scientists' goals rather than their activities: Are they interested primarily in developing, supporting, or refuting a theory, or are they hoping to contribute toward solving a social problem?

Of course, many studies and many scientists are both basic and applied. The same person can switch back and forth between the two types of scientific work. And some studies—often the most valuable ones of all—seem quite clearly to be both problem-oriented and process-oriented. Such dual-purpose studies provide good examples of applied research on social problems at the same time that they contribute new theoretical knowledge about the world we live in (Deutsch, 1980). It is also important to note that applied work can contribute to fundamental psychological theory, just as theory should form the basis for application.

A Value Orientation

The common claim that conventional science is value-free has often been challenged (e.g., Myrdal, 1944). However, there is no controversy about the status of

Figure I–I   What one person sees as a social problem is not neccessarily a problem to someone else.

applied science—it definitely is *not* value-free. The classification of some topic as a social problem obviously requires a negative value judgment, which is, in the final analysis, always a personal one by the investigator. In some societies, killing another person is not considered reprehensible, whereas in our society murder is strongly condemned. Even in our society, some people see the more than 20,000 murders committed in the United States every year as a social problem requiring strenuous action, such as handgun registration and control, whereas other people see the murders as merely "a price we pay for freedom" (a quote from congressional testimony by an official of the National Rifle Association).

The above example illustrates an important point about value orientations. Our complex, pluralistic society contains many groups, and each has its own system of values. Similarly, as individuals, we often find ourselves in situations where two positive values are in conflict and we have to choose between them. For instance:

- the freedom to bear arms versus the desire to reduce murders
- the value of better medical care for developing nations versus the wisdom of investing the same funds in birth control assistance to reduce overpopulation
- the right of parents to discipline their children versus the right of children to be protected from abuse

These are value conflicts where no general consensus is likely. Yet applied social scientists who want to work on such problem areas must start with a value position that will help them determine for themselves what circumstances constitute a social problem that needs solving (Opotow, 1990).

However, just because applied science is not value-free does not mean that the methods used to study the problems are not value-free. That is, although the investigator may have a belief about what is a problem, or about a behavior that should be changed, s/he does *not* let these beliefs influence the way it is studied. In any science, and psychology is no exception, decisions about the effectiveness of a program or the validity of a theory are made on objective, empirical data (we will return to this issue in Chapter 2). In essence, values influence the topics that are studied, but not the methods used to study them.

The Importance of Theory

Recall that our definition of applied social psychology included the use of both theories and principles. What is the difference between a theory and a principle? In general, principles are smaller in scope than theories. A psychological **principle** is a statement of an underlying cause for a psychological event. Psychological principles describe the basic processes by which humans think, feel, and act. In contrast, a **theory** is an integrated set of principles that describes, explains, and predicts observed events. A principle describes a psychological process that leads to certain types of behavior, whereas a theory integrates this process with other processes.

Theories and principles are useful in everyday life as well as in science. People operate, whether they know it or not, on the basis of principles that were first suggested and later verified by theorists. For instance, the "simple" act of driving a car involves the use of many scientific principles, including gravity, centrifugal force, friction, inertia, peripheral vision, human reaction time, and size constancy of objects. Even though we may not think about the concepts themselves, we still depend on our essential understanding of them to get us safely home. A theory is: "the net [we] weave to catch the world of observation—to explain, predict, and influence it" (Deutsch & Krauss, 1965, p. vii). Just as in basic scientific research, valid theories are also useful in solving social problems. Fifty years ago, Kurt Lewin stressed this point in an often-cited quotation:

> Many psychologists working today in an applied field are keenly aware of the need for close cooperation between theoretical and applied psychology. . . . There is nothing so practical as a good theory. (1944/1951, p. 169)

Scientific theories vary widely in their scope or range of applicability. A few, such as the theory of relativity in physics, are broad, encompassing a tremendous range of phenomena. Psychological theories typically do not have such a broad scope; Freud's psychoanalytic theory was probably the broadest psychological theory to date. At the other extreme are theories dealing with smaller sets of events and circumstances. One example in social psychology is Latane and Darley's (1970) theory of the diffusion of responsibility among bystanders in emergency situations. **Diffusion of responsibility** is the theory that people often act as if they expect others to take the responsibility for helping a person in need. Thus, as the number of people who witness an emergency increases, the likelihood that any one of them will intervene decreases. This theory, in turn, spawned a broader theory of social loafing—the tendency for people to be less motivated and to exert less effort when working in a group than when working alone (Karau & Williams, 1995).

Between the broad, general theories and the smaller theories are many midrange psychological theories with varying degrees of scope—for instance, cognitive dissonance, normative influence, prototype perception, self-fulfilling prophecies, and attribution theory. Any or all of these diverse theories can be useful to the applied social psychologist who is trying to solve a practical problem.

A Broad Approach

To be as useful as possible, applied social psychology needs to be comprehensive and inclusive in its approach to social problems. This means, for instance, considering the whole range of variables that might influence a particular area of concern. In studying a topic like the expression of racial prejudice, for example, we need to know not only individual attitudes and experiences and immediate stimulus events, but also the social norms and expectations people have learned during their lives, and the characteristics of the overall social system within which they live (Lott & Maluso, 1995). Often such considerations will lead to an interdisciplinary approach, in which sociological, economic, and political factors are considered in addition to psychological ones.

Field Settings

It is clear that applied social psychologists are more inclined than most psychologists to do research in **field settings**—that is, natural settings where people live, work, or play, and consequently feel comfortable and behave in their usual ways. This naturalness is in marked contrast to the artificial atmosphere of most laboratory experiments.

   In traditional social psychology, the well-controlled laboratory experiment has been the research method of choice. As we will see in the next chapter, this approach allows a few variables to be selected for study out of the multitude of factors that may influence a behavior of interest. These variables can then be carefully controlled or manipulated, and their effects can be precisely measured. In contrast to controlled experiments, a less prominent research tradition in social psychology is the use of nonmanipulative or correlational methods. Though correlational studies can be conducted in field settings, most such research is done in laboratory settings, using undergraduates as the research participants (Sears, 1986; Taylor, 1998).

Practical Considerations

Applied social psychology, and applied science in general, has to pay attention to practical considerations. To start with, much applied research is reactive—that is, it is done in response to the needs or formal requests of a client or sponsoring agency. As a result, it must often be done under severe time constraints in order to be useful to the client or sponsor. These characteristics are quite different from the typical course of basic research in academic settings, in which investigators have relatively complete freedom to choose the topic, method, and pace of their work.

   When research results are reported, often the first question is: How strong are the effects? It is not enough for the results to be statistically significant, for if they are to be applicable in solving social problems, they must also be strong enough to have practical importance. For example, if a new program is developed that reduces substance use among adolescents, an applied social psychologist would not only be interested in whether or not it worked, but also in how *much* it worked. Imagine that a new program is found to reduce the rate of smoking among high school students by 1% (current estimates show that 36% of high school students reported smoking a cigarette within the past 30 days; Kann et al., 1998). Clearly the program works, but the effects are small. In contrast, an alter-

native program may reduce smoking by 5%; both programs can produce significant reductions in smoking, but the second program produces a stronger effect.

If the results are strong, the second question is: How far will they generalize
to other situations—that is, to different tasks, measuring instruments, types of individuals, organizations, and subcultures? This issue has been termed **external
validity**, and it is much more crucial in applied science than in basic scientific research (Cook & Shadish, 1994). For example, Head Start (discussed in more detail in Chapter 7) is intended to give economically disadvantaged children a
better change of succeeding in school. The data indicate that the program is effective, and that it can produce large effects. However, recent data suggest that
the effects are more pronounced for White children than for Black children. That
is, the effects of Head Start might not generalize across ethnic groups. We will
return to the issue of validity in the next chapter.

Another practical consideration that has received increasing attention is
cost-benefit comparisons. Even if research results are strong and able to be generalized, they may be too expensive to implement in a practical social program. For
instance, the U.S. national 55 mph speed limit, initiated during the energy short-
ages of the 1970s, was shown to have saved many lives and much gasoline, yet
many truckers and motorists strenuously objected to it because they felt its benefits did not compensate for its personal costs to them. As a result, the national 55
mph limit was finally terminated in 1996. In recent years the computation of
benefit-to-cost ratios has become common in decision-making about governmental programs and industrial and commercial investments. This approach requires
applied social scientists to develop quantitative estimates about both the costs
and the expected benefits of the social programs they hope to implement. Since
program benefits are often previously unquantified concepts like job satisfaction
or improved mental health, workers in the field have had to develop and test new
techniques for estimating their dollar value. An interesting example is the calcula-
tion that every dollar spent on high-quality preschool programs would save the
nation seven dollars in later costs for special education, school dropouts, welfare,
delinquency, and other social problems (Barnett, 1992).

A final practical factor that applied scientists must consider is the political
feasibility of programs. For example, every year in the United States, handguns
are used in approximately 15,000 of the nation's 20,000 murders and in a half-
million other crimes. Research results have shown that major handgun registration and control laws could decrease these totals significantly (e.g., Podell &
Archer, 1994). For decades, a large majority of the U.S. population, including
gun owners, has been in favor of stricter handgun control laws (Moore & Newport, 1994). Yet, with the exception of Massachusetts, New York, and Washington, D.C., most states and cities found it politically impossible to pass handgun
control laws until very recently. The reason is that very powerful lobbying organizations, such as the National Rifle Association, have shot down previous attempts to pass gun restriction or gun control laws (Kleck, 1991).

ROLES AND ACTIVITIES

Turning from the use of theories and other typical features of applied social psychology, let us consider the possible roles of people working in this field. We will discuss them roughly in the order from traditional to newly developing roles and activities.

Research

The traditional role of scientists has been to do research. In applied social psychology, at least as much as in other scientific fields, many unanswered questions still require investigation. In addition to the collection of empirical data, there are several other aspects of the research role. Scientific scholarship often involves searching through many scattered sources in the literature in order to find relevant facts and hypotheses. It may also involve culling these facts, integrating conflicting information, and building theories about the topic. An occasional aspect of the research role is serving as an expert witness before courts or legislative committees. All of these aspects of research will continue to be a key function of applied social psychologists.

Evaluation

Evaluation is another aspect of research, and one that has been growing greatly in recent years. Like other scientists, evaluation researchers frequently state hypotheses and collect and analyze systematic data to support or reject them. However, they have a specialized topic of study—the success or failure of particular experimental interventions or social programs. In the last 25 years, the laws or regulations initiating many government programs have mandated an evaluation research component to help determine the program's success or failure. There has also been an increasing demand for evaluation of other kinds of programs, such as businesses' capital investment decisions. In these activities, there are important roles both for outside evaluators and for employees of the organization, who function as inside evaluators.

Consultation and Change Agentry

Another kind of role for applied social psychologists is consultation with organizations, aimed at accomplishing desired changes in their operational methods or results. Often these organizations are businesses, or they may be civic organizations or government agencies. Such organizations hire many different kinds of consultants—lawyers, financial advisors, and advertising agents—as well as social psychologists, who can help them apply the theories and findings of psychology and sociology to their organizational goals and problems. Social science consultants operate under many different names: organization development (OD) specialists; management consultants; marketing, communications, public relations, job training, human resources, and personnel selection experts.

Policy Advice

Another role for applied social psychologists is to provide policy advice. The recipients may be either public, governmental agencies or civic or business organizations of many different types. In this role, a person simply gives advice to organizational managers, rather than work in or on the organization to bring about change. Of course, policy advice must be based on a study of the particular organization or agency, as well as on the application of general scientific principles and findings. A particularly fascinating example of policy advice was reported by Hammond and Adelman (1976): applied social psychological knowledge on human judgment, public opinion measurement techniques, and analysis of expert ballistic information were combined to help the Denver city council decide what kind of bullets the city's police officers should be authorized to use.

Management of Organizations

Usually a social scientist's most influential role is offering advice to organizational managers. Occasionally, however, applied scientists become managers themselves. Particularly in this era of limited academic job possibilities, many more social scientists are taking jobs in business organizations or in government agencies, where they may eventually assume managerial responsibilities. In such situations, of course, they do not shed all their scientific knowledge and skills, and one hopes that they use their scientific background to perform relevant aspects of their job better than they could without that training.

Thus, though it is an unusual activity for social scientists, management is a legitimate role for them. A few examples of psychologists who have attained high government positions are John Gardner, Secretary of Health, Education, and Welfare under President Lyndon Johnson; Richard Atkinson, head of the National Science Foundation under President Jimmy Carter and more recently president of the nine-campus University of California system; and clinical psychologist Leonard Haber, who was elected mayor of Miami Beach. Numerous social psychologists have reached high positions in business and educational organizations, such as Judith Rodin, the president of the University of Pennsylvania, and Alexander Gonzalez, the president of California State University, San Marcos. A particularly unusual example was Pat Carrigan, who became the first woman and the first psychologist to manage a General Motors auto assembly plant.

Social Activism

Whereas managers work on the inside of organizations, social activists typically try to influence them from outside. Though some social activists attempt to work from the inside to change organizations, that is usually a difficult (and often short-lived) position. A more typical kind of social activist "works to change systems from the outside through the application of pressure using such tactics as mass demonstration, civil disobedience, and violence" (Hornstein, 1975, p. 218).

Figure 1–2 Social activists attempt to change systems by influencing them from the outside, using such tactics as mass demonstrations and civil disobedience.

There are also social activists who apply outside pressure through less extreme techniques, such as legislative lobbying, media publicity, legal suits, grass-roots organizing, and effective marshaling of research evidence to get organizations and government agencies to change their ways. An outstanding example of this sort is Ralph Nader, whose organization called Public Citizen has spawned other social action groups in the fields of consumer affairs, environmental protection, and health care. Nader himself, like many other activist group organizers, is a lawyer, but many of the staff members who work in his several organizations are applied scientists—some in research roles, and some in social activist roles.

PROBLEMS FOR APPLIED SOCIAL PSYCHOLOGY

Many problems are implicit in the typical features and roles of applied social psychology. Here we will discuss the following major areas of potential problems in the field: the research evidence, the generalizability of the evidence, unintended consequences, and ethical questions.

What Is the Evidence?

A key problem in applying any science is to assess the available scientific knowledge. It is not enough to have theories, for there must be firm supportive evidence that the theories are correct before we can feel safe in using them to build a bridge or to design a social program. We need to ask: What studies have been done? What did they show? How were the data obtained? Unfortunately, the methods used in the social sciences are sometimes not appropriate to support the conclusions drawn, and in other cases the methods are appropriate but not powerful enough to demonstrate an effect. If the methods are acceptable, we should ask: How strong are the results? Are the effects large enough to be of practical importance as well as being statistically significant? If all these questions can be answered affirmatively, we have satisfied the criterion of **internal validity** of the research (Cook & Shadish, 1994). We will examine these issues in more detail in the next chapter.

Applying Theories Too Quickly and Too Easily

Throughout this chapter, and throughout this book, we have stressed the importance of theory in applied research. Theories of human behavior help social psychologists understand the causes of social problems, and suggest techniques by which the problem can be solved. Indeed, psychologists are often seen as experts who have insight into human behavior—insight that can help them to solve problems in applied settings. However, the emphasis on theory can sometimes lead to *over*application. As Claude Levy-Leboyer (1988) points out, it sometimes occurs too easily that "any theory that presents either a solution or suggestions on how to act in order to solve the problem is adopted without reservation" (p. 780). Thus, we should recognize the usefulness and importance of theory in conducting applied work, but also be mindful that a theory is never "proven" and should be used only as a guide for understanding human behavior. As Levy-Leboyer (1988) puts it, "we psychologists should not lament the difficulty of applying psychology, but rather protect both ourselves and our clients by standing as sentries at the door of our ideas and techniques to prevent their misuse."

Unintended Consequences

Even if research is internally valid and is applicable to the social situation in which the intervention is planned, unintended consequences of the intervention may arise. One notable case of this sort was a study in which aged residents of retirement homes were visited on various schedules by college students. After the study was completed and the visits ceased, the retirement home residents, who had initially benefited from the visits, exhibited unexpected precipitous declines in their mental and physical health (Schulz & Hanusa, 1978).

Another example of unintended consequences stemming from social programs is seen in various crime-control programs. These programs are often successful in decreasing crime rates in one locality, while apparently raising crime rates in surrounding communities (presumably because criminals are moving their activities elsewhere). On the other hand, some crime-control or educational-improvement programs may seem to have little success, whereas comparison of their results with appropriate control groups would show that their apparently small improvement was distinctly better than the worsening conditions in other communities (cf. Lipsey & Wilson, 1993).

The problem of unintended consequences often goes unnoticed because, if evaluation research is done at all, it is usually limited to the research participants or, at most, to the community in which the research was carried out. This fact highlights the importance, not only of appropriate control groups and research designs, but also of an even broader *systems approach* to understanding the effects of social programs. Social interventions are not discrete, isolated programs; they are embedded in a whole social system of related events and processes. As such, they are bound to have some consequences beyond their stated goals and target populations. Applied social scientists need to recognize and consider these possible unplanned effects.

SUMMARY

The many fascinating examples of the application of social psychology to practical problems range from individual concerns, such as reducing aggressive behavior, through group and organizational problems, to issues of governmental policy. A suggested broad-gauge definition of applied social psychology is: the application of social psychological methods, theories, or principles to understand or solve a social problem. Applied work can contribute usefully to fundamental psychological theories, principles, and methods, as well as the other way around.

Applied social psychology differs from other fields of psychology in several key ways. It typically starts with a concern for a particular social problem, and this starting point makes explicit its value orientation toward improving people's quality of life. It aims to have social utility and to adopt a broad, comprehensive approach to social problems. Most of its work is done in field settings, and applied researchers need to be especially concerned about the strength and generality of their findings, as well as about considerations of benefit-to-cost ratios. Theories are useful in applied work, just as in basic science, to help explain, predict, and influence the events and variables of interest.

Six different roles can be performed by various individuals working as applied social psychologists. The most traditional is the role of researcher. Recently developing roles are evaluator of social programs, organizational consultant or change-agent, and policy advisor to administrators or legislators. Rarer social scientist roles include organizational manager and social activist.

Among the major potential problem areas in this field are the adequacy of research methods and findings, the generalizability of the evidence to other settings and individuals, and the unintended consequences of social interventions.

KEY CONCEPTS

Applied social psychology   application of social psychological methods, theories, or principles to understand or solve social problems.

Competence training   programs that attempt to reduce aggressive behavior by teaching social skills necessary to manage conflict with others.

Evaluation   research designed to assess the success or failure of an intervention.

External validity   the extent to which research findings generalize across time, settings, and groups.

Field settings   natural settings where people live, work, or play, and where they behave in usual ways.

Internal validity   the extent to which a study can determine causal relationships between variables.

Principle   a statement of an underlying cause for an observed event.

Problem-oriented research   applied research focused on finding the causes or solutions to a social problem.

Process-oriented research   basic research focused on finding evidence to support or refute a theory.

Social activism   working to change a social system by applying outside pressure.

Social psychology   the scientific discipline focused on how the thoughts, feelings, and behaviors of an individual are influenced by others.

Theory   an integrated set of principles that describes, explains, or predicts observed events.

REVIEW QUESTIONS

1. Define social psychology and applied social psychology. Elaborate on the key aspects of each field.
2. Compare and contrast process-oriented and problem-oriented research.
3. What role do theories have in applied social psychology?
4. Describe the basic features of applied social psychology.
5. One social problem mentioned in this chapter was teenage pregnancy. Discuss at least three roles that a social psychologist could take to understand or solve this problem.

Science, Research Methodology, and Teenage Pregnancy

"Over the summer, I went from being a child to having one." At age 14, Wylita gave birth to a daughter, Monica. "Initially, after I learned of the first pregnancy, I tried to raise money for an abortion. But by the time I had enough money I was 16 weeks," Wylita recalls.

"I was already working part-time cleaning movie theaters. After my daughter was born, I continued to work. I also received support for my daughter from her father and his family. My grandparents supported me with advice, child care, and money when needed. Shortly after the birth of my daughter, I moved in with my mother for three months, then with my aunt, then with another aunt, and finally I got my own apartment. I worked cleaning theaters seven days a week to pay $260 a month rent. I'd pay biweekly at $130 and the alternating weeks I paid child care, bought groceries, and paid utilities. I did this while I continued my education at a magnet school. This lasted until I graduated from high school at 17 years old—and pregnant again."

At age 17, Wylita had her second daughter, Do'Nissa. "To use one word, I felt utterly stupid because I felt that I did not learn from my first mistake. I didn't believe it had happened to me. My self-esteem was tainted because I felt that I was labeled as "fast," or "hot," so I chose not to socialize with my peers. Instead, I concentrated on changing my image by engrossing myself as a respectable caregiver."

What factors do you think contributed to Wylita's pregnancy? What could have been done to prevent it?

The question of evidence is central to any science. For any observed event, there are a variety of possible explanations about its causes, and choosing between alternative explanations can be a difficult task. For instance, consider the issue of teenage pregnancy, as illustrated by the case of Wylita. The central question is: What causes a teenage girl or boy to engage in sexual behaviors that could lead to pregnancy? Some possibilities might include poor relationships with parents, low self-esteem, low achievement goals, values, little knowledge about human sexuality, intentions to engage in sexual intercourse, intentions to use condoms, cultural background, social support, and so on. From an applied perspective, if we can understand which factors lead teenagers to engage in risky sexual behavior, then we can develop interventions to prevent it from happening.

Research shows that teenagers are having sexual relationships earlier today than they were 20 years ago. A study of 12,118 randomly selected students in grades 7 through 12 found that nearly half of high school kids reported having sexual intercourse. Among sexually experienced females between the ages of 15 and 17, nearly 20% reported having been pregnant (Resnick, 1997). Teenage pregnancies have negative consequences for the adolescent mothers, their children, their parents, and society (DeRidder, 1993). For instance, research indicates that only 60% of teen mothers graduate from high school by age 25, compared to 90% of females who do not get pregnant (Ventura et al., 1992).

In this chapter, we will examine the process of conducting scientific research. Although the focus of the chapter is on research methodology, we will use studies on risky health behavior (both sexual behavior and smoking) to illustrate each type of methodology. After a brief overview of the scientific method, we will discuss three types of research methodologies: the correlational method, the experimental method, and the quasi-experimental method.

THE PROCESS OF SCIENCE

In any science, the procedure for determining the causes of an event is based on systematic observation. As an educated and critical thinker, you should continually ask yourself: "How do you know that?" Looking back at the case of Wylita presented at the beginning of this chapter, we can wonder what caused her to get pregnant, and whether it could have been prevented. School administrators may claim that Wylita's pregnancy was due to permissive parenting. Her parents, on the other hand, are likely to attribute her behavior to rebelliousness. Wylita herself says, "I had absolutely no knowledge about the reproductive system. I had no

Figure 2–1   Wylita, age 17, and her two daughters Do'Nissa and Monica. Among sexually experienced females between the ages of 15 and 17, nearly 20% report having been pregnant.

idea about how babies were conceived." Which of these explanations is right? To answer this question, we need to collect data through systematic observation.

Science is a four-step process. As shown in Figure 2–2, the process begins with a theory (step 1). As we discussed in the previous chapter, a theory is an integrated set of principles that describes, explains, and predicts future events. For example, Gibbons and his colleagues have recently developed a **prototype theory** for health risk behavior (Gibbons & Gerrard, 1995; Gibbons, Gerrard, & McCoy, 1995). According to this theory, our decisions to engage in such behaviors as smoking, drinking, or unprotected sex are a reflection of our attempts to acquire the image (termed a *prototype*) that we associate with groups of individuals who engage in favorable behaviors, and to distance ourselves from images (prototypes) we associate with negative behaviors. Clearly, this is a broad theory that can be used to explain a variety of behaviors.

The second step in the scientific process is to derive specific predictions from the theory. Applying the prototype theory to the topic of teenage pregnancy, we would predict that adolescents who have a relatively favorable perception of the typical unwed teenage parent would be more willing to engage in unprotected sex than adolescents who view this image negatively. For example, many young women see being a mother in a positive light—playing with the infant, hugging, being independent, having someone to care for and who will care for them. This is a testable **hypothesis**—a prediction that is derived directly from a theory.

The third step in the scientific process is to test the hypotheses. To test our hypotheses, we make systematic, objective, and usually quantified observations. *Systematic observation* means that our procedure for obtaining data could be reproduced by someone else. *Objective* means that we attempt to remain removed from the situation and to make accurate measures of events—that is, not to let our values or expectations influence our observations. *Quantified* means that our observations are recorded on a numeric scale. Quantification is not absolutely required for science, and there are instances where phenomena can be measured

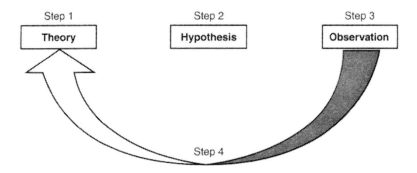

Figure 2–2   The Four-Step Process of Scientific Research.

without a numerical scale (Judd & McClelland, 1998). There are also many qualitative methodologies that do not use numeric scales to measure variables (e.g., various types of interviews). However, social psychologists have been skeptical of a sole reliance on such methodologies, and the bulk of social psychological knowledge is based on quantitative methodologies. In this book we will focus almost entirely on quantitative methods.

Once researchers have collected their data, they must decide whether the evidence supports or refutes their hypotheses. The decision of whether or not to reject a hypothesis is made through statistical analysis. People differ on a multitude of variables, and it is impossible to measure them all. After carefully measuring key variables, researchers use statistics to calculate the probability that their hypothesis is false (or stated differently, that the null hypothesis is true), given the measurements obtained in the study. If the probability is low (e.g., less than 5%), they report that the research hypothesis is supported. Note that scientists do not attempt to *prove* that their hypotheses are correct. The difference is a subtle one, but an important logical consideration. Typically, and for our purposes in this book, a research hypothesis that has a 95% probability of being correct is not rejected, while hypotheses that have a probability less than 95% are rejected. In practice, these values are expressed as p-values (i.e., probability values)—the probability that the researcher's hypothesis is false. Research hypotheses that are supported have p-values of less than .05, while those that are not supported have p-values greater than .05.

The final step (step 4) in the scientific process is to evaluate the theory based on the results. If our observations are consistent with the hypothesis, it *suggests* that the theory may be correct. If the observations are inconsistent with the hypothesis, it indicates that the theory is incorrect, at least in some of its aspects. Note that even if the observations are consistent with the theory, it does not mean that the theory has been proven. In fact, for the same reason that a hypothesis cannot be proven correct, a theory can never be proven in any absolute sense. Any theory could be wrong—which is why it is called a theory and not a fact.

TESTING HYPOTHESES

As we have seen, hypotheses are testable derivations of a theory; they are sets of predictions that are logically consistent with a theory. To test a hypothesis, we obtain measures that will show whether or not our predictions are wrong; the process of systematically obtaining these measures is called **research methodology**. Although there are a variety of research methodologies, most social psychological research can be classified as either correlational, quasi-experimental, or experimental. We will discuss each in the sections that follow. These are quantitative methodologies—procedures where the variables of interest are measured using a numeric scale (e.g., a Likert scale measuring attitudes from 1 = strongly disagree to 5 = strongly agree).

The Correlational Method

In a correlational study, the researcher measures two or more variables and assesses the relationships between them. In this approach, the researcher makes no effort to manipulate or change any aspect of the situation, but instead measures what is already there.

The most common statistic used to describe the association between two measures is a *correlation coefficient*. The correlation coefficient is represented by the symbol r and can range from -1 to $+1$. If there is no relationship between two variables, the correlation coefficient is 0. The + and − signs denote the direction of the relationship. A positive relationship indicates that as one variable increases, so does the second; a negative relationship indicates that as one variable increases, the second decreases. Coefficients that are farther from zero indicate stronger relationships. As a general rule, correlations around .10 are small effects, correlations of .30 are considered medium effects, and correlations larger than .50 are considered large effects (Cohen, 1992). It is important that you understand correlation coefficients, because we will use them throughout the book to describe research findings.

An Example of Correlational Research.   To illustrate the correlational method, let us consider a study by Gibbons and his colleagues (1995, study 2). As mentioned, the prototype theory of health risk behavior states that risky health behavior (e.g., pregnancy, smoking, drug use) is caused by a person's desire to be like his or her positive prototypes and to attain distance from negative prototypes. Based on this prototype theory, Gibbons et al. (1995) predicted that students with more favorable perceptions of teenagers who get pregnant would be more willing to engage in unprotected sexual intercourse. Thus, the researchers hypothesized a positive correlation between favorable prototypes and willingness to engage in risky sexual behavior.

Participants in the study were 244 male and 256 female junior high students ages 13 to 15. Each student completed a short questionnaire about his or her attitudes and past behaviors. Questionnaires were mailed to each student's home and were completed while other family members completed other questionnaires. Although the students' responses were not anonymous, the researchers stressed that responses were confidential, and family members were asked not to discuss their answers with one another.

Items on the questionnaire asked about age, gender, favorable perceptions of prototypes, and willingness to engage in unprotected sex. Favorability of prototypes was measured by asking each student to rate the extent to which several positive adjectives described the "type of girl who gets pregnant" (question for females only) or the "type of boy who gets a girl pregnant" (question for males only). A sample of the adjectives included: intelligent, popular, "cool," self-confident, and independent.

Willingness to engage in sexual activity was measured with a question that asked:

> Suppose you were out on a date with your boy/girlfriend and s/he wanted to have sexual intercourse. Neither of you have used or have available a contraceptive method. Under these circumstances, how likely is it that you would do each of the following? (a) not have sex; (b) go ahead and have sex anyway without birth control.

Both questions were rated on a scale from 1 (not at all likely) to 7 (very likely). Scores on the first item were reversed so that higher scores indicated a greater likelihood of having sex, and the responses to the two items were summed to produce a "willingness index" that ranged from 2 to 14. The average score on the willingness index was 4.26 ($SD = 2.96$). Because one of the central questions in the survey asked about willingness to engage in sexual activity, students who identified themselves as virgins were removed from the study. Of the 500 students in the sample, 65 were excluded because they were virgins and 3 neglected to answer one of the questions.

The results from the survey showed a significant correlation coefficient of $r = +.33$ ($N = 432$; $p < .05$) between positive prototypes and willingness to have unprotected sex. This statistic indicates that students with more positive perceptions of teenagers who get pregnant are more likely to engage in unprotected sex—a finding which is consistent with the prototype theory of health risk behavior.

Identifying Cause and Effect.   The results from Gibbons et al. (1995) showed a positive relationship between favorable prototypes and willingness to engage in risky sexual intercourse. Does this finding mean that having a positive prototype of pregnant teenagers *causes* students to engage in risky sexual behavior? The answer is an emphatic *no*; just because two variables are correlated with each other does not necessarily mean that one caused the other. Although it *is* possible that prototypes cause risky sexual behavior, it is also possible that risky sexual behavior causes increased prototype favorability. Perhaps after engaging in risky sexual behavior, a student's prototype becomes more positive. A third possibility is that another, unmeasured, variable caused both favorable prototypes and risky sexual behavior. For instance, perhaps students with lower self-esteem are more likely to engage in risky sexual behavior and also more likely to have favorable prototypes of other people (including pregnant teenagers).

In order to establish a causal relationship between two variables, we would need to control prototypes and observe the effect of differing prototypes on sexual behavior. That is, we would need to create positive prototypes for some students but not for others, and then observe the effect of this manipulation on sexual behavior.

The Experimental Method

Experiments are studies in which there is a high degree of *planned manipulation* by the investigator, and research participants are randomly assigned to groups (Aronson et al., 1998). Experiments have three core aspects: random assignment to one or more conditions, a manipulated variable, and an outcome measure.

1. Random Assignment.   Random assignment is central to an experiment because it creates separate groups of research participants that are statistically indistinguishable on *any* dimension. Groups produced through random assignment should be nearly identical on any variable: height, weight, self-esteem, intelligence, aggressiveness, and so on. If participants are assigned to one group or another on a completely random basis, there is no reason to expect one group to differ from another (provided that the groups are large enough). The random groups of participants in an experiment then receive one of several possible treatments.

2. Independent Variables.   The experimenter manipulates (regulates the levels of) one or more variables and controls or holds constant other variables that might otherwise have an effect. These manipulated variables are called *independent variables.* Each level of the independent variable is referred to as a *condition.*

3. Dependent Variables.   The final aspect of an experiment is the measured outcome. *Dependent variables* are ones that are expected to be affected by the manipulation of the independent variable. If the predictions are correct, the experimental conditions should differ on one or more dependent measures.

Because the groups assigned to different conditions were indistinguishable to begin with (due to random assignment), any difference in the dependent variable observed between the conditions must have been *caused* by the manipulation. This conclusion, however, is based on the assumption that all other aspects of the setting were controlled. Experiments typically exceed all other research methods in their degree of *control* of conditions and in the *precision* of measurement possible. As a result, experiments are better than other methods for *determining the direction of causal relationships.* Because the researcher establishes and controls all the experimental conditions, the obtained results are likely to be due to the experimental condition rather than to some unknown or uncontrolled factor.

When conducting an experiment, we are rarely interested in the descriptive differences between the participants in the two conditions. Instead, we want to use the findings from a study to infer that the same effect would be found in a larger population. However, although random assignment produces groups of research participants that are similar, there is always the possibility that any difference found between the groups was due to chance. That is, if we observed a difference between a control group and an experimental group, it is possible that this difference was due to chance fluctuations between the two conditions, and not to any systematic manipulation on our part. A **significance test** provides a statistical assessment of the probability that the results of a study are due to chance. As with the correlation coefficient discussed above, psychologists typically set a 95% confidence level for our findings; we are willing to accept a 5% probability that our results are due to chance.

A second issue that arises in examining the results from an experiment is, How big is the effect? There are several commonly used statistics that represent the size of the effect. In the preceding section we learned that correlation coefficients of .1 are considered small, .3 medium, and .5 large. For experiments, the *effect size* is a measure that indicates the standardized difference between two conditions—typically between an experimental and a control condition. One widely used index of this difference is Cohen's *d*. A *d* value of zero indicates no difference, and larger *d* values indicate larger differences. Unlike correlation coefficients (*r*), *d* values do not range from –1 to +1, and in fact *d* values can be considerably larger than 1.0 or smaller than –1.0. As a general rule, *d*-values around .20 are considered small, *d*-values around .50 are considered large, and *d*-values around .80 are considered large (Cohen, 1992). Note that *d* values can be both positive and negative, with negative *d* values indicating lower scores in the experimental group relative to the control. We will be reporting *d* statistics throughout the book, so it is important that you remember how to interpret them.

An Example of Experimental Research.   Recall that the prototype theory suggests that risky health behavior (e.g., pregnancy, smoking, drug use) is *caused* by a desire to be like positive prototypes and to distance oneself from negative prototypes. This theory would lead to the hypothesis that changing a person's prototypes should cause a change in the corresponding behavior.

A study by Blanton, VandenEihnden, Buunk, Gibbons, Gerrard, and Bakker (1998) tested this hypothesis. Participants in the study were 120 undergraduates (60 male and 60 female) attending the University of Michigan. Participants were randomly assigned to one of three conditions—two experimental conditions and a control condition. In the two experimental conditions, participants read a bogus newspaper article that described the results from a study on "Sexual Behaviors and Personality." The first experimental condition was a negative-prototype condition which described people who engage in unsafe sex as "less responsible" and "more selfish" than people who engage in safe sex. The second experimental condition was a positive-prototype condition in which people who engaged in unsafe sex were described as "more responsible" and "less selfish." In the control condition, participants read a bogus newspaper article in which the typical person who did not vote was described as "less responsible" and "more selfish."

The dependent variable in the study was a person's willingness to engage in unprotected sex. Participants read a scenario in which they were told to imagine an opportunity to engage in sexual intercourse with a desirable romantic partner. Participants were then asked four questions about their willingness to use a condom; for instance, "Do you think you would use a condom?" and "Do you think you would use a condom if this new partner told you that he/she prefers not to use a condom?" Each question was rated on a scale from 1 (absolutely not) to 7 (absolutely). These four items were reversed and averaged to produce an overall index of a person's willingness to engage in unprotected sex.

Results for this study are shown in Figure 2–3. As predicted, the negative-prototype condition produced significantly less willingness to have unprotected sex compared to the control condition ($d = -.60$; $p < .01$). The p-level indicates that there is less than a 1% likelihood that this result was due to chance factors. The positive prototype condition was not significantly different from the control condition ($d = +.09$; $p = .37$). Note that the p-value of .37 is not less than .05, and so the researcher cannot conclude that the positive prototype condition is significantly different from the control condition.

Identifying Cause and Effect.   These results suggest that prototypes *cause* behavior. Unlike the correlational study discussed above, participants in this study were randomly assigned to one of three conditions. The only difference between these three groups was the type of information they received—either positive prototype, negative prototype, or information about the typical person who does not vote. Therefore, assuming that everything else in this experiment was held constant, the only possible explanation for the difference between the conditions is that the information received (i.e., the negative prototype experimental manipulation) caused the decreased willingness to have unprotected sex.

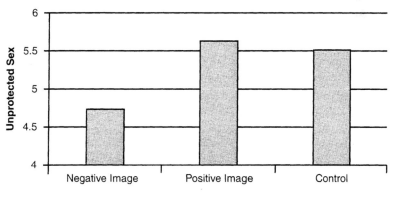

Figure 2–3 Willingness to Have Unprotected Sex. *Source:* Blanton et al. (1998).

From the Lab to the Field.   The studies cited above support the use of prototype theory to understand teenage pregnancy. The results clearly show that teenagers with a negative prototype of a pregnant teenager are less likely to engage in unprotected sex. How could we use this knowledge to *prevent* teenagers from becoming pregnant? That is, how can we create more negative prototypes of pregnant teenagers?

One approach is to have teen mothers and fathers speak to teenagers about what it is "really like" to have a baby. Many such programs are currently in place. An example, is the Teen Choices program organized by the Child Abuse Prevention Center in California. The Teen Choices program consists of a panel of 10 teen parents who describe their experiences to groups of high school students. Dino Mayorga, one of the panelists, explains that raising his 4-year-old daughter makes "everything much harder." Jayme Ritche, also a panelist with the Teen Choices program, described the sleepless nights, the middle-of-the-night feedings, and the screaming at 2 A.M. "It isn't any easier now," she says. "He's all over the place and getting into everything. I look forward sometimes to just putting him to bed. I want to let you know that being a teen mom isn't all cute. It's not walking around the mall with a baby stroller" (Bold, 1998).

This type of program illustrates how social psychological theories can be used to solve a social problem. The process began with the formation of a theory, followed by empirical investigation of the theory, and then application. However, the process does not end there. As the data from this program become available, they will be used to assess both the accuracy of the prototype model and also its applicability to the real world.

The Quasi-Experimental Method

Random assignment to condition is a requirement for an experiment. However, in many field situations it is impractical or impossible to use random assignment. In *quasi-experimental* studies, the researcher cannot randomly assign participants to conditions and relies instead on existing or nonrandom groups. There are a large number of possible quasi-experimental designs, ranging from simple ones with many problematic aspects to more complicated ones. For our purposes, we will only discuss quasi-experimental studies in which two or more intact groups of people are compared.

For instance, we could compare teenagers who were pregnant with teenagers who were not pregnant (cf. Sheaf & Talashek, 1995). Such comparisons would tell us about differences between these two groups, but would not tell us about the *causes* of those differences. As an example, let us say that we measured teenagers' prototypes about the "type of girl who gets pregnant" or the "type of boy who gets a girl pregnant"—measures similar to those reported by Gibbons et al. (1995) in the correlational study. From other responses, we identified those females who had ever been pregnant, along with the teenage fathers. If our results showed that pregnant teenagers had less favorable prototypes than teenagers who had not been pregnant, would this indicate that prototypes *caused* the students to engage in risky sexual behavior? The answer is no; there are a variety of other possible explanations, and because we did not randomly assign the research participants to either a pregnant or not-pregnant condition (which would clearly not be ethical or practical), we cannot draw any solid conclusions about causality. We might conclude that the data *suggest* a possible causal relationship, or that the evidence supports the possibility of a causal relationship, but we cannot conclude that prototypes cause risky behavior.

An Example of Quasi-Experimental Research.   As we have seen, there is considerable evidence, both correlational and experimental, supporting the prototype theory of risky health behavior. We will briefly mention a study by Gibbons et al. (1991) which illustrates the use of quasi-experimental research. Gibbons and his colleagues examined differences in prototypes between smokers who were successfully able to quit and smokers who were not successfully able to quit. Based on the prototype theory, the researchers hypothesized that smokers who are able to quit should have less-favorable prototypes of the average smoker than smokers who are not able to quit.

Participants in the study were 120 smokers who responded to an ad placed in a local newspaper. On average, the respondents smoked 29 cigarettes per day, and each expressed a desire to quit. All participants went through a nine-week smoking cessation program. In the fourth week of the program, 111 of the participants agreed to quit (9 did not make the commitment to quit), and by the end of the nine-week program, 86 were still not smoking. Participants completed questionnaires, including the prototype measurement at the beginning of the study (Time 1), four weeks into the study (the quit date), at the end of the study, and six months after the end of the program. Of the 96 participants who responded to the questionnaire at the six-month follow-up, 38 reported that they were still not smoking. A biochemical test verified that these 38 subjects were telling the truth.

Prototypes were measured by asking participants to "Describe the typical smoker on the following dimensions . . ." Participants rated seven adjectives (e.g., friendly, considerate, hard-working, self-assured, outgoing) using a Likert scale. Responses to these adjectives were summed to produce a measure of prototype favorability—higher scores indicated more positive perceptions of the average smoker.

The prototype of the nonsmokers was compared to the prototype of the smokers at each stage of the study. The overall pattern of results is shown in Figure 2–4. The figure shows that the prototypes for both groups became more negative over time, and that the abstainers' prototypes were more negative than the relapsers' at the six-month follow-up. Abstainers and relapsers did not differ significantly in the favorability of their prototypes at the pretest, quit date, or last session. However, at the six-month follow-up, the mean prototype rating for the abstainers was 28.8, whereas the mean prototype rating for the relapsers was

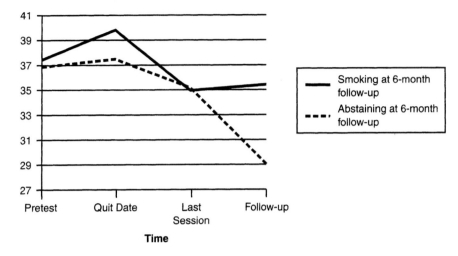

Figure 2–4   Comparing Evaluations of the Typical Smoker among Abstainers and Relapsers over Time. *Source:* Gibbons et al. (1991, p. 248).

35.3. This difference was statistically significant ($p < .01$). Cohen's d showed the effect size to be $d = .60$.

These results clearly show that smokers who were able to quit had less favorable prototypes of the average smoker than smokers who were unable to quit. However, this is a quasi-experimental study—people were not randomly assigned to abstinence or relapse. Because the study lacked random assignment, it is impossible to know for sure whether changing prototypes caused the abstinence.

DRAWING VALID CONCLUSIONS

Recall that a major goal in doing research is to reach conclusions about cause-and-effect relations between variables. We reach such conclusions by using all the available relevant information to help us interpret the results of research studies. In the process, many threats to valid inference may arise—factors that would lead us to incorrect causal conclusions. The better the research design, the fewer such threats will be present, but even the best research designs can have some aspects that are not fully controlled or are open to differing interpretations. In general, experiments have relatively few threats to valid inference, while correlational studies have more. Quasi-experiments are in-between, and, depending on the particular design involved, they may range from very poor to very good in their safeguards against invalid conclusions.

There are three major types of validity: internal, external, and construct validity. No study is perfect, and in evaluating the quality of a study, it is important to recognize its possible limitations in all these aspects of validity.

Internal Validity

If statistical tests show a significant effect, the next major question in research is: Is the demonstrated relationship a causal one? Another possibility is that confounding variables created the appearance of a causal relationship between two variables when in fact the two were unrelated. Alternatively, if the results are nonsignificant, the next question is whether there were factors that prevented a causal relationship that actually exists from being demonstrated. These issues are central to the **internal validity** of the study—that is, whether the independent variables really had a causal effect in this particular study.

Threats to the internal validity of a study arise when the researcher fails to control *all* aspects of the experimental setting. When this happens, it is possible that something in the environment which is irrelevant to the independent variable affected the outcome.

Construct Validity

After we have determined what causal conclusions we can reach in any specific study, the next question is: What do these particular research results mean in conceptual terms? For instance, did the researchers really measure what they intended to measure? As Cook and Campbell (1979, p. 38) expressed it, **construct validity** refers to "the fit between operations (i.e., what was actually measured) and conceptual definitions." In order to have construct validity, the research operations must correspond closely to the underlying concept that the investigator wants to study.

Threats to construct validity come from **confounding**—"the possibility that the operational definition of a cause or effect can be construed in terms of more than one construct" (Cook et al., 1990, p. 503). For instance, is it the pill or the *placebo effect* (belief in the pill and the doctor) that causes the sick person to improve? One important way of assessing construct validity is to use **manipulation checks**. Manipulation checks assess the degree to which participants perceived crucial aspects of the study in the way the experimenter intended. For instance, in the study by Blanton et al. (1998) about prototypes of people who have unsafe sex, did the subjects notice and remember the positive or negative adjectives used to describe people who have unsafe sex? Manipulation checks can verify whether the treatment actually created differences in the intended constructs and left unchanged other features that it was not intended to affect.

External Validity

The final question in assessing research findings is: To what extent can the findings be generalized to other persons, settings, and times? This question defines the **external validity**, or generalizability, of the research findings. When samples of participants are chosen because they are conveniently available (such as introductory psychology students), it is difficult to know what underlying population they represent, and even more difficult to know whether the findings apply to specific other groups.

We can increase external validity by choosing research samples that are either *representative* of an important population or else as *heterogeneous* as possible. Since obtaining a representative sample is often impossible in applied settings, a very useful model is to select settings for study that differ widely along important dimensions. For instance, in research on an innovative educational method, the treatment should be tried out in one or more of the "best" schools available, and in some of the "worst" problem schools, and in some "typical" schools. Racial composition and other important dimensions might be varied using a similar procedure. Though this procedure does not guarantee generalizability to other schools in other geographic areas, it certainly increases its likelihood.

ETHICAL ISSUES

Many ethical issues can arise in applied research, and applied scientists need to be constantly aware of them. A fundamental question at the outset of any applied project is whether or not to intervene in a given social situation. The issue is not just a pragmatic one of whether we have useful methods or knowledge, but also an ethical one of whether they should be used. If we decide to participate in the project, then we will have to be ready for a later decision about when and how to terminate the intervention. "Intervention entails both taking responsibility and letting go of it" (Mayo & La France, 1980, p. 91).

The American Psychological Association has had a strong ethical code ever since 1953, and it has been updated every few years to include new concerns and developing areas of research and practice. For applicable formulations, see publications by the American Psychological Association (1982; 1992) and Box 2–1. A volume edited by Bersoff (1995) has elaborated on many specific topics of ethical concern.

Fortunately, it is rare for psychological experiments to pose any real risk of **harmful consequences** to participants, and most psychologists are sensitive to their responsibility to protect participants from any such risks. However, some experiments have used noxious situations that were physically or psychologically stressful to subjects (cf. Greenberg & Ruback, 1992). An extreme example involved some post–World War II military studies of stress, which exposed unsuspecting soldiers to highly realistic simulations of radioactive contamination, aircraft engine failure in flight, or false information that their own errors with explosives had injured other soldiers (Berkun et al., 1962). Such stressful experiments would probably not be allowed under the federal regulations that have been in effect since the early 1970s. Since then, because of the ethical and legal issues involved, all proposed research procedures using human participants must be approved by an *institutional review board* (IRB).

Box 2–1 Examples of Ethical Guidelines for Psychologists

The following are very brief extracts from the latest revision of the *Ethical Principles of Psychologists* (American Psychological Association, 1992). In the complete document each of these general principles is elaborated; they are followed by eight sections on ethical standards, including over 100 subsections stating specific ethical resposibilities (e.g., avoiding harm, explaining assessment results, avoiding false statements, avoiding sexual intimacies, maintaining confidentiality, accuracy in teaching, compliance with law, reporting ethical violations).

Preamble. Psychologists work to develop a valid and reliable body of scientific knowledge based on research . . . and, where appropriate, to apply it pragmatically to improve the condition of both the individual and society. . . . Psychologists respect and protect human and civil rights and do not knowingly participate in or condone unfair discriminatory practices.

A. Competence. Psychologists strive to maintain high standards of competence in their work. They recognize the boundaries of their particular competencies and the limitations of their expertise. They provide only those services and use only those techniques for which they are qualified by education, training, or experience.

B. Integrity. Psychologists seek to promote integrity in the science, teaching, and practice of psychology. . . . In describing or reporting their qualifications, services, products, fees, research, or teaching, they do not make statements that are false, misleading, or decptive. . . . Psychologists avoid improper and potentially harmful dual relationships.

C. Professional and Scientific Responsibility. Psychologists uphold professional and scientific standards of conduct, clarify their professional roles and obligations, accept appropriate responsibility for their behavior, and adapt their methods to the needs of different populations.

D. Respect for People's Rights and Dignity. Psychologists accord appropriate respect to the fundamental rights, dignity, and worth of all people. They respect the rights of people to privacy, confidentiality, self-determination, and autonomy.

E. Concern for Others' Welfare. Psychologists seek to contribute to the welfare of those with whom they interact professionally. In their professional actions, psychologists weigh the welfare and rights of their patients or clients, students, supervisees, human research participants, and other affected persons, and the welfare of animal subjects of research . . . they do not exploit or mislead other people during or after professional relationships.

F. Social Responsibility. Psychologists are aware of their professional and scientific responsibilities to the community and society in which they work and live. They apply and make public their knowledge of psychology in order to contribute to human welfare. Psychologists are concerned about and work to mitigate the causes of human suffering. When undertaking research, they strive to advance human welfare and the science of psychology. Psychologists try to avoid misuse of their work.

Most researchers in recent years have recognized their obligation to obtain **informed consent** from research participants, and the federal government has promulgated instructions about the way this should be done—for example, telling participants the essential facts about the study, and informing them that they can refuse to take part or can withdraw from participation at any time (U.S. Department of Health, Education, and Welfare, 1971). However, in field experiments, such as studies of door-to-door solicitation, obtaining informed consent is generally considered unnecessary if the experimental conditions are relatively natural situations to which the residents might be exposed in everyday life. Though allowing participants' consent to be implied rather than explicit is somewhat controversial, it is similar to the situation in survey research, where informed consent is considered to have been given by the respondent's act of answering an interviewer's questions.

The two most common ethical problems in experiments are deception and debriefing. Because of the need to avoid experimental artifacts and to keep the participants ignorant of the research hypotheses, **deception** has often been used in social psychological experiments. A recent survey of the prevalence of deception in social psychological research showed that it is still widely used (Sieber, Iannuzzo, & Rodriguez, 1995). In the *Journal of Personality and Social Psychology*, deception was used in 66% of the research reports published in 1969, 47% in 1978, 32% in 1986, and 47% in 1992. Undoubtedly, deception has been overused and misused at times, and the practice has been severely criticized (Kelman, 1967). In recent decades, the scrutiny of proposed research procedures by IRBs has made investigators more careful to avoid unnecessary deception. Only where deception is necessary for the completion of the research and justified by the potential value of the research findings is it considered ethical, and there is still vigorous debate about this degree of permissiveness (Soliday & Stanton, 1995).

Debriefing, on the other hand, is considered an ethical requirement for laboratory experiments. Even if a study involves no deception, it is still important to answer the participants' questions afterward and to be sure that they do not leave with any anxieties or misconceptions (Gurman, 1994). However, research has shown that the false impressions instilled in deception experiments can survive the traditional type of debriefing, and correcting them, therefore, requires much more thorough discussion with the research participants about the processes which cause false impressions to persist. In field experiments, debriefing is normally carried out only if the participants are aware that they have been in a study. In studies involving unobtrusive observation of public behavior, where the subjects are unaware of being studied and might become more upset from learning about it than from remaining ignorant of it, both informed consent and debriefing are usually omitted.

Finally, like atomic scientists after World War II, social researchers must face the ethical question of the **use of their findings**. Our research results are fortunately not so deadly, but they can certainly have major effects on some people's lives. Knowing that, what is our responsibility to the people who will use them, to the people on whom they will be used, and to the advancement of scientific knowledge? To take a mild example, if you were a researcher, would you be just as content to have your research findings on prototype perception used by a cigarette company to promote smoking as you would be to have them used to prevent smoking? Or if, like Milton Rokeach (1979), you developed a strong method of changing people's values, would you be willing to have it used by the Ku Klux Klan or the American Nazi Party? If not, should you give up experimental research and turn to some less controversial occupation? Obviously there can be no final answer to these questions; all investigators must decide for themselves. However, the ethical code of the American Psychological Association (1992, p. 1600) reminds us:

> Psychologists are aware of their professional and scientific responsibilities to the community and the society in which they work and live. They apply and make public their knowledge of psychology in order to contribute to human welfare . . . [and] try to avoid misuse of their work.

SUMMARY

In this chapter, we have examined the process of science and the types of research methodologies that are used in scientific research. Science is a four-step process which begins with a theory. Hypotheses are generated from the theory, and these hypotheses are then tested through systematic, objective observations. Finally, the results of the study are interpreted as supporting or refuting the theory. The major types of research methods are correlational, experimental, and quasi-experimental research designs.

In a correlational study, the researcher measures two or more variables and calculates the relationship between them. For instance, a study by Gibbons et al. (1995) found a correlation coefficient of +.33 between prototypes and behavior. In contrast, experimental studies have three core aspects: random assignment to conditions, a manipulated independent variable, and a measured dependent variable. Unlike correlational studies, experiments can demonstrate cause-and-effect relationships. For example, a study by Blanton et al. (1998) showed that experimentally changing prototypes *caused* a change in participants' willingness to engage in unprotected sex.

Quasi-experimental studies are similar to experiments in that two or more groups of people are compared. However, unlike experiments, quasi-experiments do not use random assignment to conditions, and in some instances (as in the smoking-cessation study discussed in the chapter) the independent variable might not be manipulated. Instead, intact groups of people are compared; for instance, smokers and nonsmokers, or pregnant teenagers versus nonpregnant teenagers.

One of the goals of doing research is to reach conclusions about cause-and-effect relationships between constructs. In assessing the quality of a study, readers should consider issues of validity. Internal validity is an assessment of the likelihood that the independent variable caused a change in the dependent variable. Construct validity is the appropriateness of the study's measures as indices of the concepts of interest in the study. External validity refers to the extent to which the results can be generalized to other people, settings, or times.

In conducting research, psychologists must be mindful of the ethical issues involved in studying people. The use of deception, informed consent, and debriefing are important considerations in designing an effective, yet ethical, study.

KEY CONCEPTS

Cohen's *d*   a standardized measure of the difference between two groups: small (.20), medium (.50), and large (.80).

Construct validity   the degree to which the measures used in a study accurately assess the variables being studied.

Correlation coefficient   a numeric value ranging from +1 to –1 that represents the strength of the relationship between two variables: small (.10), medium (.30), large (.50).

Correlational design   a study in which the relationship between two or more variables is assessed.

Debriefing   a procedure conducted at the end of a study in which participants are provided with the full information about all aspects of the study.

Deception   intentionally misleading participants in a study.

Dependent variable   in an experimental study, any variable that is affected by the manipulation of an independent variable.

Experimental design   studies in which participants are randomly assigned to two or more conditions that differ along a manipulated variable.

External validity   the degree to which the results from a study apply to different groups of people or different settings.

Hypothesis   a prediction derived from a theory.

Independent variable   in an experiment, those aspects of the setting that the researcher can manipulate.

Informed consent   a procedure for making potential participants in a study aware of all of the requirements and risks involved before they decide to take part in the study.

Internal validity   the degree to which a study can demonstrate a causal relationship between two variables.

Objective—observations made without bias.

p-value   the probability that the null hypothesis is true (i.e., that the research hypothesis is incorrect). Research results that have *p*-values of < .05 are considered statistically significant.

Prototype   the most typical member of a category.

Quasi-experimental design   a study in which existing or nonrandom groups are compared.

Random assignment   the process of assigning participants to different conditions in such a way that each participant has an equal opportunity of being in any condition. This is one of the distinguishing features of an experiment.

Research methodology   the process of systematically obtaining measures to test hypotheses.

Science   a procedure, based on systematic observation, for identifying cause-and-effect relationships.

Significance test   a statistical assessment of the probability that the results of a study are due to chance.

REVIEW QUESTIONS

1. Summarize the prototype theory for risky health behavior. Generate three hypotheses for sexual behavior based on this theory.
2. What is random assignment, and why is it so important in conducting research?
3. Describe the *r* and *d* measures of effect size. For each, what is a large, medium, and small effect?
4. Suppose that you were interested in knowing whether sex education programs decrease the chances that an adolescent girl would become pregnant.
   a. Can you think of a theory that would lead to this prediction?
   b. Describe a correlational study that would test this hypothesis.
   c. Describe an experimental study that would test this hypothesis.
   d. Describe a quasi-experimental study that would test this hypothesis.
5. Assess the internal, external, and construct validity of the three studies by Gibbons and his colleagues discussed in this chapter.
   • The correlational study (Gibbons et al., 1995)
   • The experimental study (Blanton et al., 1998)
   • The quasi-experimental study (Gibbons et al., 1991)

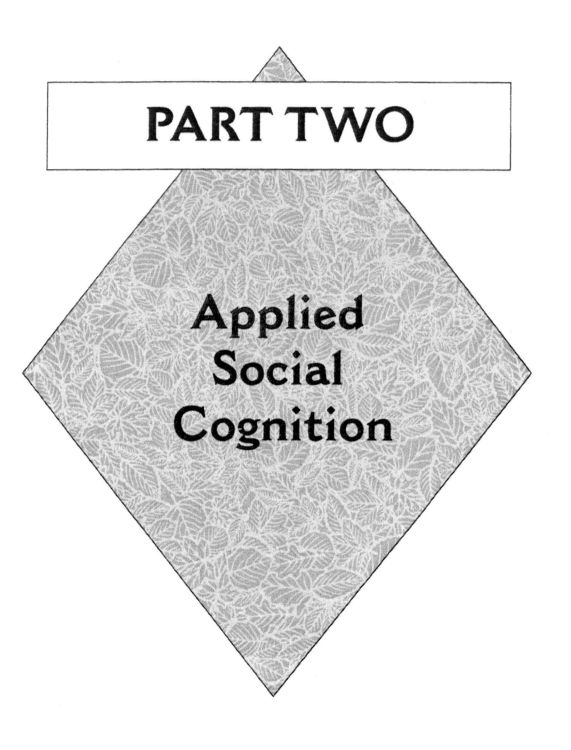

PART TWO

Applied Social Cognition

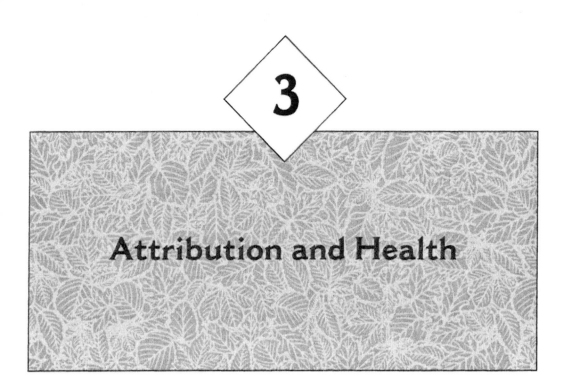

Attribution and Health

> *Tom and Jerry were old friends. In their late 50s, each of them had been feeling weak and breathless for several months, and suffering from a persistent bronchial infection and cough. Recently they had both begun to experience some sharp chest pains. After consulting their doctor, each learned that he had an early stage of lung cancer and needed immediate surgery.*
>
> *Both Tom and Jerry had been regular smokers for many years. Their doctor's conclusion and their own judgment agreed that smoking was one of the main causes of their cancer, and that they would have to kick the habit if they were to have a favorable future prognosis.*
>
> *But the two men differed in the attributions they made for the fact that they had continued smoking for so long in spite of the clear medical evidence that it was dangerous to their health. Tom lamented, "I just didn't try hard enough to quit," whereas Jerry felt, "The pressures from my job and my family problems made it impossible for me to quit."*

Do you think the explanations they gave can suggest which man will be more likely to succeed in giving up smoking in the future? Can they tell us anything about their probable future health—or about their likely longevity?

The reasons Tom and Jerry stated for their not giving up smoking and for getting cancer are examples of attributions. In general, **attributions** are inferences that people make about the unobservable characteristics of other people, themselves, objects, or events. More specifically, the main class of attributions that psychologists have studied are the *causal explanations* that people give for the occurrence of events, such as what caused an argument or why someone gets a disease. These causal explanations help people make sense of their world. In the last 30 years, the study of attribution processes has been one of the most dominant theoretical and empirical topics in the field of social psychology.

ATTRIBUTION THEORY

Social cognition is a field of study within social psychology that focuses on how people think about other people and themselves. One example of social cognition is the study of how people think about the causes of events. Attribution theory consists of systematic sets of ideas about how, when, and why people make attributions. There is not just one attribution theory, but a large collection of theoretical and empirical contributions, each of which deals with some aspect of attribution processes. In the next few paragraphs we will summarize some of their key principles, and later we will show how these principles apply to the areas of mental and physical health and help us to understand some surprising health outcomes. We begin with an overview of attribution theory.

Causal attributions can be either internal or external. **Internal** (or **dispositional**) **attributions** ascribe the causes of events to something within a person—for instance, she smiled at me because she is a friendly person. Note that the cause of the behavior (smiling) was attributed to an internal quality (friendliness). In contrast, **external** (or **situational**) **attributions** focus on the situation outside of the person, to which he or she is responding. For example, he ignored me because he was watching TV. In this instance, the cause of the behavior (ignoring me) was attributed not to the person, but to the situation (watching TV).

In deciding whether to attribute an event to an internal or external cause, we consider several pieces of information. Two such pieces of information are the ability and motivation of the individual in question (motivation includes both intentions and degree of effort; Heider, 1958). A person may fail on a task because of poor ability, lack of intentions to succeed, limited effort, or a combination of these factors. A very common tendency of human beings is to overemphasize internal factors and largely ignore external influences when making attributions about another person's behavior. This tendency is so common that it has been called the **fundamental attribution error** (Ross, 1977).

Another piece of information used to make attributions is the *social desirability* of the behavior. Socially desirable or expected behavior is not very informative about the person's true characteristics, whereas unexpected or socially devalued behavior is likely to lead us to make a dispositional inference. For instance, if a bank teller is friendly toward us at the bank, it doesn't necessarily mean that she is a friendly person (most bank employees are generally cordial). In contrast, if she was rude to us, we would likely conclude that she is an arrogant or insolent person (an internal attribution). A similar factor is whether the observed behavior is part of a social role, which is not very informative, or is out-of-role, which more strongly suggests underlying personality characteristics. For instance, a woman's hospitable manner is less revealing if she is the hostess at a party than if it is exhibited in an unexpected encounter.

Another factor in determining whether we will make an internal attribution is the *noncommon effects* of two possible actions that a person might have taken (e.g., going to a party or seeing a movie alone). The common effects (e.g., having a recreational evening) are uninformative, but the noncommon effects of the chosen alternative (being sociable vs. unsociable) suggest clear inferences about the individual's personality characteristics. Finally, as observers, we are more likely to make a dispositional inference if the person's behavior helps or hurts us (termed "hedonic relevance") and if it seems to be intentionally directed at us (Jones & Davis, 1965).

The strength of our causal inferences is influenced by the principles of **discounting** and **augmentation**. People discount any given causal attribution when there are two or more plausible causes for a particular behavior that they have observed—for example, your roommate may have complimented you because he is a generally appreciative person or because he is "buttering you up" before asking a favor. On the other hand, people augment the strength of a personal attribution if they observe an effect occurring together with a plausible opposite cause—for example, if your roommate failed a test in spite of having studied hard for it, she must be really poor in that subject area (Kelley, 1972).

Up to this point, we have been focusing solely on internal versus external attributions. However, these are not the only types of attributions that people make. Weiner (1979) suggested that there are three types of attributions that people will make about the causes of success and failure: internality, stability, and controllability of the cause:

- **Internality** vs. externality (also called *locus*) was discussed above: Is the cause within the person or the situation?
- **Stability** refers to the consistency of the cause over time: Will it probably continue, or is it changeable?
- **Controllability** concerns whether or not the cause is under the person's control.

In considering success and failure in achievement situations, Weiner classified many different possible causal factors in this three-dimensional scheme (see Table 3–1). Among the internal factors, ability or aptitude is stable and uncontrollable, whereas mood is unstable (changeable) but perhaps uncontrollable by the person. Typical effort exerted on the task is both stable and controllable, while temporary effort exerted on this particular task is unstable but controllable. Examples of external factors affecting academic success or failure are the difficulty of the task (stable and uncontrollable) and luck (unstable and uncontrollable). Among the controllable external factors are teacher preferences or bias (possibly stable) and unusual or special help received from others (unstable).

Later in this chapter, we will see a fourth type of attribution that people can make, termed *globality*.

Consequences of Attributions

So far, we have primarily been considering the *process* of making attributions and the *types* of attributions that people make. But what are the *consequences* of making particular attributions? In the fields of health and mental health, the effects of

Table 3–1   Possible Causes of Success or Failure, Classified According to Locus, Stability, and Controllability

	Internal		External	
Controllability	*Stable*	*Unstable*	*Stable*	*Unstable*
Uncontrollable	Ability/aptitude	Mood	Task difficulty	Luck
Controllable	Typical effort exerted	Temporary effort exerted(for this particular task)	Teacher bias	Unusual help from others

Source: Slightly modified from Weiner (1979, p. 7).

attributions provide prime examples of the value of applying psychological theories to real-world social problems.

A detailed analysis of the effects of the above dimensions of attribution on people's emotions, expectations, and likely future performance was made by Weiner (1986). It applies to issues of health and health care, as well as to other situations involving achievement goals, such as school or sports. Here are some of its main principles:

As a starting point, the usual result of success is feelings of happiness, whereas failure usually produces feelings of sadness. If the attributed locus of success or failure is internal, these emotions are modified into self-esteem-related feelings of pride or shame, but if the cause is external, self-esteem is less likely to be affected. Attributions of controllability also affect these emotions and evaluations of oneself and others. Negative outcomes that you see as controllable by yourself are likely to cause guilt feelings. Your own positive or negative outcomes that are seen as controllable by someone else are likely to induce feelings of gratitude or anger, respectively. Observing another person's failure that is perceived as uncontrollable is likely to elicit offers of help, whereas if it is seen as controllable, it may produce condemnation and/or efforts to motivate the other person.

The stability dimension is the one most closely tied to future expectations and future performance. If you view the cause of your success or failure as stable (e.g., ability or task difficulty), your expectations for future success or failure should shift in the direction of your past performance, whereas if the cause is seen as unstable (e.g., luck or temporary effort) and therefore likely to change, your expectations for the future should not be affected.

Actual future performance, in turn, is generally influenced by your expectations and your emotions in combination. You are likely to try harder and do better in future situations if you have high expectations for success (attributing past failures as unstable and controllable) as well as some guilt over past deficiencies. On the other hand, if you have low expectations for success and are feeling hopeless about the future, both your future effort and performance are apt to be dismal.

Quite similar theoretical propositions can be derived from Bandura's (1986, 1997) social cognitive theory, in which self-efficacy is a central concept. **Self-efficacy** is defined as "people's judgments of their capabilities to organize and execute [particular] courses of action" (Bandura, 1986, p. 391). It is conceived of as specific to a particular domain of action, rather than being a generalized expectation. It is also differentiated from outcome expectancies, which are beliefs that a given behavior will have the desired consequences. That is, it is possible to be confident about one's ability to perform an action (e.g., pass a football accurately) while at the same time being unconfident about the probability of a related outcome (e.g., that the pass will be caught and result in a touchdown). Attribution theory and self-efficacy theory are related because causal attributions for past success or failure are some of the main determinants of self-efficacy feelings about future actions, and both theories have been used extensively in the field of health psychology.

Applications to Health Psychology

People are especially likely to make causal attributions about factors affecting their health because health events and outcomes are important to them and are often negative, unexpected, and/or ambiguous in their implications (Salovey, Rothman, & Rodin, 1998). In making these attributions about health questions, people typically consider the factors mentioned earlier, such as the social desirability of their past behavior, the hedonic relevance of their symptoms, and the noncommon effects of possible remedies.

In the field of health psychology, the same causal dimensions discussed above are relevant to attributions about success or failure in one's health care—that is, to explaining why one did or did not get a disease or recover from a disease. For instance, among internal factors, a genetic predisposition would be stable and uncontrollable, whereas lowered immune system protection due to seasonal overwork demanded by one's job would be unstable and uncontrollable. An unhealthy diet or lack of exercise would be stable but controllable, while occasionally going outside in frigid weather without adequate clothing would be unstable but controllable.

Among external factors, living in a community where factories constantly spew toxic products into the air would be a stable and uncontrollable situation, whereas living with a person who caught a severe communicable disease would be unstable but probably uncontrollable. Habitually spending time as a volunteer in a hospital's communicable disease ward would be a stable but controllable situation, but occasional exposure to an acquaintance with flu would be unstable but potentially controllable.

ATTRIBUTIONAL STYLE

Many researchers have built on the above classification of attributional dimensions to study the effects of a person's typical **attributional style** or **explanatory style**—that is, the kind of causal explanations individuals typically give for events that happen to them. In particular, Peterson and Seligman (1984) and their colleagues have identified pessimistic explanatory style as a personality pattern that is stable across time and has negative implications for a person's mental and physical health.

Pessimistic Explanatory Style

Pessimistic explanatory style has close parallels to Weiner's attributional analysis of success and failure situations, discussed above. To begin with, it deals with people's reactions to *uncontrollable* bad events that happen to them. Its measurement assesses three dimensions of the causes that are attributed: stability vs. instability, internality vs. externality, and globality vs. specificity. The first two dimensions have meanings like those in Weiner's analysis, while **global attributions** describe causes as pervasive and broad in the number of life outcomes they affect—"it's going to ruin everything I do" rather than "it only affects a small part of my life" (Peterson, Seligman, & Vaillant, 1988).

In keeping with the focus of each attributional dimension, internal attributions are expected to affect their holder's self-esteem, stable attributions are expected to produce longer consequences in future-related situations, and global attributions should produce more pervasive consequences. People who are fairly extreme on all three of these dimensions (i.e., are internal, stable, and global) demonstrate a pattern of helplessness in responding to bad events. As a result, they are expected to be vulnerable to low self-esteem and psychological depression, as illustrated in Table 3–2.

Measuring Attributional Style

Two standard procedures have been developed to measure attributional style. One is a paper-and-pencil measure called the Attributional Style Questionnaire (Peterson et al., 1982), some items from which are shown in Table 3–3. The other is a method that analyzes the content of natural speech or writing, called the CAVE technique (Content Analysis of Verbatim Explanations—Peterson, Schulman, Castellon, & Seligman, 1992).

In the CAVE technique, transcribed statements are coded by judges who do not know the characteristics of the author. The judges note causal explana-

Table 3–2   Possible Perceived Causes of Uncontrollable Bad Events, and Their Emotional Consequences

	Global		Nonglobal	
	Stable	*Unstable*	*Stable*	*Unstable*
Internal	Pervasive, stable, low self-esteem; potentially serious depression (e.g., "I am unlovable")	Temporary, but pervasive loss of self-esteem (e.g., "1983 was a really bad year for me")	Loss of self-esteem but confined to limited aspect of one's life (e.g., "I cannot do athletics to save my life")	Some short-lived loss of self-esteem (e.g., "I look terrible today")
External	Pervasive and long-term ennui or displeasure but no loss of self-esteem (e.g., "The economy is lousy, and there are no jobs")	Temporary, but pervasive ennui with no loss of self-esteem (e.g., "It's a wretched day, the electricity is out, and there's nothing to do")	Long-term ennui or displeasure confined to limited aspect of one's life (e.g., "My tennis partner has moved out of town and now I have no one to play with")	No depression, little emotional disruption (e.g., "He's in a bad mood today. Better wait until tomorrow")

Source: Fiske & Taylor (1991, p. 90), derived from Abramson, Seligman, & Teasdale (1978).

Table 3–3   Items from the Attributional Style Questionnaire

Directions:

Please try to vividly imagine yourself in the situation that follows. If a situation happened to you, what would you feel would have caused it? While events may have many causes, we want you to pick only one—the *major* cause if this event happened to *you*. Please write this cause in the blank provided after each event. Next we want to ask you some questions about the cause. . . .

- Is this cause due to something about you or something about other people or circumstances?
- In the future will this cause again be present?
- Is this cause something that just influences this situation or does it also influence other areas of your life?

[These ratings are made on seven-point scales that indicate the following aspects]

internality (7) vs. externality (1)

stability (7) vs. instability (1)

globility (7) vs. specificity (1)

1. You have been looking for a job unsuccessfully for some time.
2. A friend comes to you with a problem and you don't try to help.
3. You give an important talk in front of a group and the audience reacts negatively.
4. You meet a friend who acts hostilely toward you.
5. You can't get all the work done that others expect of you.
6. You go out on a date and it goes badly.

Source: Peterson et al. (1982).

tions for events and rate them for their stability, internality, and globality on 7-point scales. These ratings are then averaged across events and across judges, and they can be combined into a single composite score across the three dimensions. The great virtue of this technique is that it can be used to obtain explanatory style scores for people who are unavailable to answer questionnaires (e.g., corporate executives or high government officials) or who lived in different eras (e.g., people who are now dead)—provided that sufficiently long verbatim statements or writings from them are available.

Studies have shown that judges' ratings on the dimensions of the CAVE technique are highly reliable (e.g., Cronbach alpha coefficients of .77 to .90). Moreover, people's explanatory-style scores obtained in this way are quite stable over long periods of their lives (e.g., a correlation of .55 over a period of 52 years—Peterson et al., 1988, p. 24).

PESSIMISTIC EXPLANATORY STYLE AND MENTAL HEALTH

It seems logical that a negative explanatory style could influence our emotions and feelings about life, and therefore our adjustment to life events—that is, mental health. In particular, it has been proposed that a pessimistic explanatory style is closely related to depression. Depression can range from normal sadness over misfortunes or losses to a full-blown psychotic condition characterized by most or all of the following groups of symptoms:

- a miserable mood—feeling downhearted, sad, despairing, anxious, irritable, worthless
- thought disturbances—poor concentration, illogical reasoning, obsessiveness, self-blaming, thoughts of death or suicide
- behavioral deficits—passivity, indecisiveness, fatigue; or agitation, suicidal actions
- physiological changes—diminished appetite, insomnia, impaired immune system functioning

Many studies have investigated the link between depression and a pessimistic explanatory style. The theoretical connection between them is due to the dimensions involved in the pessimistic style. It is normal to be sad if bad events have happened to you, but the sadness and despondency usually go away after awhile. However, if you interpret the bad events as being due to your own failings (i.e., internal), likely to continue persistently (stable), and affecting most areas of your life (global), these attributions lead logically into a depressed state. If the depression is not counteracted by appropriate treatment or by improved events, it may become serious and prolonged.

Evidence for the connection between a negative attributional style and depression comes from a variety of sources. The most impressive evidence on an issue such as this is usually a **meta-analysis**, which is a statistical summary of the results of many studies on the same general topic. In this case, the results of 104 studies were statistically summarized (Sweeney, Anderson, & Bailey, 1986). In this meta-analysis, individuals' levels of depression were correlated with their scores on each of the three attributional dimensions. Across the whole group of studies, the findings were clear and dramatic. For bad events, attributions to stable, internal, and global causes were all highly significantly related to depression. The correlations of depression with each of the three dimensions were very similar (mean $r = .36$), and the correlation for a composite score combining the three dimensions was $r = .44$.

These effect sizes were essentially the same whether the participants involved were college students, normal adults, or clinical patients. Similarly, several other potential moderator variables, such as whether the bad event considered in the study was a hypothetical one or a real-life outcome, did not affect the findings. Moreover, another overall relationship pattern, which we have not discussed before this, was also significant: Attributions for *good* events that were *unstable, external, and specific* were also significantly correlated with depression, though the strength of this relationship was somewhat lower (correlation coefficients ranged from $r = .12$ to $r = .36$).

All of the studies reviewed in this meta-analysis were cross-sectional ones, where data were collected at a single point in time. With this type of design, it is difficult to know which came first, depression or explanatory style. One way to address this limitation is to conduct **longitudinal studies** where data are collected at two or more points in time. This design will tell us whether attributional style predicts a person's level of depression several months or even years later. Several longitudinal studies have been conducted to examine whether a pessimistic explanatory style leads to depressive symptoms, or vice versa. One of the strongest of these studies followed 352 third-graders over a five-year period, with nine waves of measurement (Nolen-Hoeksema, Girgus, & Seligman, 1992). This study combined the measures of a pessimistic explanatory style for both bad and good events, and used them in combination with depression scores to predict the students' responses on the next succeeding wave. It found that, from the fifth grade onward, the explanatory-style measure at each earlier wave did significantly help to predict depression at the next later wave, even after controlling for the level of depression at the earlier wave. In like manner, and starting as early as third grade, depression at each earlier time significantly helped to predict a pessimistic explanatory style at the next time, even after controlling for explanatory style at the earlier time. These results suggest *reciprocal causation*—being depressed leads people to become more pessimistic, just as being pessimistic leads them to become more depressed.

Rather similar results were reported in a short-term longitudinal study with 94 college students that examined their reactions to a real-life setback—getting a midterm exam grade that they were dissatisfied with (Metalsky, Halberstadt, & Abramson, 1987). For students who got poor grades, their pessimistic style before the exam significantly predicted increases in depressed mood two days after receiving the exam grade.

PHYSICAL HEALTH EFFECTS
OF A PESSIMISTIC EXPLANATORY STYLE

Though studies such as these have clearly linked explanatory style to mental health, it is a more far-reaching and controversial notion that it could also influence a person's physical health. In the health area, a thought-provoking finding showed that people who explained bad events pessimistically made more visits to the doctor than did people who gave optimistic explanations (Peterson, 1988). This finding could have two opposite implications for future health. On the one hand, seeing the doctor more often might prevent serious illness and lead to better health in the long term. On the other hand, it is possible that a pessimistic explanatory style might lead to *more* physical illness over the years, despite any preventive effects of seeing the doctor.

Which prediction do you think is more likely? Or do you think that explanatory style would be unrelated to later physical health? One remarkable investigation of this topic was done with participants who were part of a 40-year longitudinal study of adult development which started when they were undergraduates at Harvard (Peterson et al., 1988). In this research, the investigators made the second prediction—that a pessimistic explanatory style would be associated with more physical illness in later years.

A 40-Year Longitudinal Study

In this study, members of the Harvard classes of 1942 through 1944 were carefully screened to select only students who were successful in their studies, in good physical and psychological health, and nominated by college deans as independent and healthy. Over 250 of these students were selected and given extensive physical, personality, and intelligence tests. After graduation, they filled out annual questionnaires about their employment, family, health, and so on, and every five years the study obtained the results of a full physical exam conducted by the participant's own doctor. After the age of 50, these exams were supplemented with a full battery of health tests of blood, urine, X-rays, and so on.

At approximately age 25, the participants filled out an open-ended questionnaire about difficult experiences they had had in World War II:

> What difficult experiences did you encounter (we want details)? Were they in combat or not, or did they occur in relations with superiors or men under you? . . . How were they related to your work or health? What physical or mental symptoms did you experience at such times? (Peterson et al., 1988, p. 24)

The CAVE score of explanatory style was derived from these responses, using a 1–7 scale. Examples of fairly extreme scores are as follows (p. 25):

- I cannot seem to decide firmly on a career . . . this may be an unwillingness to face reality. (rating = 5.75, where 7 = most pessimistic)
- Accused of violating a confidence . . . because the officer involved had not bothered to get all the facts. (rating = 1.83)

This study analyzed long-term data for 99 of these participants in the Harvard study of adult development. The results of their every-five-year physical exams were studied by a medical internist and rated on a 5-point scale from normal good health (1), through irreversible chronic illness without disability (e.g., hypertension or diabetes (3), to deceased (5). Correlations were computed between their explanatory style at age 25 and their physical health at each subsequent five-year period through age 60. Since all of the participants were originally in good physical and mental health, these correlations were initially close to zero.

Results. By age 45, a strong correlation developed between a pessimistic explanatory style at age 25 and later poor physical health. Moreover, this correlation remained strong even when the participants' initial level of physical and emotional health was controlled for ($r = .37$). In subsequent years through age 60, this correlation remained significant, though not quite as high as at age 45 (e.g., it was $r = .25$ at age 60).

Another set of analyses made a particularly stringent test by holding constant the participants' health status at the *previous* five-year period, rather than at age 25. All of these correlations were also positive, though smaller than the first set, and the one at age 45 was highly significant ($r = .42$). This showed that explanatory style at age 25 influenced health at age 45 even after controlling for health levels at age 40. Finally, when the three dimensions of pessimistic explanatory style (stability, internality, and globality) were examined separately, each of them displayed the same positive relationship with illness levels.

These long-term results over 40 years of life are highly dramatic, but to many people they may seem unlikely. That is, it may be hard to understand how a cognitive style of explaining events could really be responsible for influencing a person's illness and even death several decades later. Thus it is an important question whether these results are replicable, or whether they might perhaps be just a statistical accident. Therefore let us examine a recent study on a very similar topic.

Another Very Long-Term Study of Explanatory Style

In 1998, members of the same research group published another long-term study linking explanatory style and, in this case, untimely death (Peterson et al., 1998). This study used a longitudinal design over a *55-year* period, conducted with a famous group of participants—members of the Terman Life-Cycle Study of over 1,500 intellectually gifted children in California. On average, they were born around 1910 and first given the Stanford-Binet intelligence test in the early 1920s when they were in public schools around San Francisco or Los Angeles. All of them had IQs of 135 or greater, most were white, and most were middle-class or above. They were not originally screened for good health, but in later years they were generally healthy, successful, and productive citizens.

In 1936 and 1940, when they were in their late 20s or early 30s, the questionnaires that they answered contained open-ended questions about difficult life events. For instance:

- Have any disappointments, failures, bereavements, uncongenial relationships with others, etc., exerted a prolonged influence upon you?
- What do you regard as your most serious fault of personality or character? (Peterson et al., 1998, p. 128)

If responses to these questions included causal explanations, they were written down and blindly rated by eight independent judges using the CAVE technique. A total of nearly 3,400 attributions was obtained from 1,182 different respondents. The analysis of rater agreement showed a high level of consistency (Cronbach's alpha ranged from .73 to .94 for the three dimensions).

The whole sample from the Terman Life-Cycle Study has been followed up to the present—a period of 80 years or more—so some surviving participants are now in their 90s. Consequently, age of death and the dichotomous variable of death vs. continued life were the dependent variables of the study, rather than a rating of health status. By 1991, 489 of 1,179 participants had died, and the cause of death was known for all but 38. The mortality data were predicted by a statistical equation including sex (since women generally live longer than men) and the three dimensions of explanatory style.

Results.   In this study, global explanatory style turned out to be the only one of the three dimensions that significantly predicted early death. Participants with a high globality score (i.e., those who explained bad events in terms that were pervasive—"it's going to undermine everything") had about a 25% higher chance of early death than participants with low globality scores. This effect was greater for males, producing a three-year-shorter lifespan on average. The globality effect was shown most clearly for deaths by accident or violence (including suicide), and for deaths from unknown causes; in both of these categories a global explanatory style approximately doubled the odds of an early death. By contrast, it had no noticeable effect on deaths from heart disease, the most common cause of death. The above findings concerning the globality effect remained unchanged when scores on mental health and psychological adjustment were controlled for, indicating that these control variables were not causing the findings.

The authors of this study refer to the global explanatory style as **catastrophizing**—a tendency to see bad events as affecting one's whole life. They suggest that this style's link to untimely death stems from its relationship to an incautious lifestyle that may lead to being the victim of an accident or violence.

Comparison of Research Findings

In comparing the two longitudinal studies, it is noteworthy that only globality was a significant predictor of early death in the Terman study—and not the other dimensions of a pessimistic explanatory style, as was found in the Harvard study. Other studies of various health effects of explanatory style have also found somewhat different patterns of relationships. A thorough meta-analysis of depression as a health outcome showed that all three explanatory dimensions were significantly related to depressive symptoms (Sweeney et al., 1986). In partial contrast, a review of studies on poor physical health found that globality and stability, but not internality, were consistently significant predictors (Peterson & Bossio,

1991). Thus, different patterns of significant predictors may hold for different health outcomes.

Outside of the health realm, other research has shown that explanatory style can help to predict good or bad performance in other arenas as well, including academic, athletic, and work settings (e.g., Nolen-Hoeksema, Girgus, & Seligman, 1986; Rettew & Reivich, 1995; Seligman & Schulman, 1986).

WHAT MECHANISMS UNDERLIE PESSIMISTIC STYLE EFFECTS?

If we conclude, despite some differences in findings, that a pessimistic explanatory style has significant health effects, an important question is: What is (are) the **mediating variable(s)** through which this style has its effects? A number of possible mediators have been suggested. The most general process involved is that a pessimistic style influences feelings of helplessness, and helplessness is a predictor of failure or difficulties in many spheres of human activity.

In the health field, several hypotheses have been offered about more specific mediators (e.g., Peterson, Maier, & Seligman, 1993). One is that individuals with a pessimistic explanatory style may become passive when faced with illness—they may neglect basic health care procedures, avoid getting medical advice, or fail to follow it, thus exacerbating their medical problems. Evidence for this view was found in a longitudinal study that followed college students over time and investigated what curative steps or treatments they took when they developed colds or flu. Pessimistic students were less likely than optimistic ones to take recommended measures, such as trying to sleep more, drinking more fluids, seeing a doctor, and following the doctor's advice (Peterson, Colvin, & Lin, 1992).

A second, more general hypothesis is that pessimistic individuals tend to be poor problem solvers. As a result, they may fail to face and resolve problems early and therefore may experience more numerous and severe bad life events, many of which have inevitable impacts on health. A cross-sectional study by Peterson (1988) found a relationship between a pessimistic explanatory style and the number of stressful life events that respondents experienced, as well as their reports of unhealthy habits, and their feelings of low self-efficacy to change these habits to healthier ones. In a separate, longitudinal study of the resulting health effects, respondents with a pessimistic explanatory style experienced more days of illness in the following month and consulted doctors more times in the following year than did optimistic respondents (Peterson, 1988). Similar results have been reported in several other studies.

A third hypothesis is that people who make negative explanations for bad events are apt to be socially withdrawn, lonely, and lacking in social support. This relationship has also been supported by empirical research (Anderson, Horowitz, & French, 1983). Such social isolation is likely to have negative health consequences, for a great deal of research has shown that having a strong network of social support is a protective factor when people are confronted with negative life events, such as health problems (e.g., House, Landis, & Umberson, 1988).

Finally, at a physiological level, a connection has been found between a pessimistic explanatory style and lowered immune system functioning, which in turn would make illness and death more likely. A study with elderly adults in their 60s through 80s showed that individuals with a pessimistic style had a lower ratio of helper T-cells to suppressor T-cells, which would make their immune systems less effective in warding off disease. This result held even after controlling for many other possible factors, such as the influence of current health, depression, medication, alcohol use, and so on (Kamen-Siegel, Rodin, Seligman, & Dwyer, 1991). A similar effect of attributions on decline in helper T-cell levels was found over an 18-month period in patients with a positive HIV diagnosis (Segerstrom et al., 1996).

Conclusion. These hypotheses about the various mechanisms by which a pessimistic explanatory style may affect health outcomes are not mutually exclusive, and all of them are probably correct in some situations. Each of them helps to explain some aspects of health problems, and the several mechanisms may sometimes operate in conjunction and reinforce each other's effects. The overall picture they present is that people who give stable, internal, and global explanations for bad events are at serious risk for later negative health outcomes.

Related results from other research paradigms are also supportive of this general picture. For instance, another research approach has defined **optimism** as a global belief that one will usually experience good outcomes in life, and measured it in ways quite different from the Attributional Style Questionnaire. In many studies with various groups of patients, this approach has shown that optimism predicts lower distress over time, controlling for the seriousness of the initial medical condition and the initial levels of distress. For instance, such results were found with men followed for five years after coronary bypass surgery (Scheier et al., 1989), with women being treated for early-stage breast cancer (Carver et al., 1993), and with patients whose positive HIV status would lead them to develop AIDS (Taylor et al., 1992). Moreover, several such studies have shown that initial optimism also predicted better physiological and medical outcomes over time, for instance with the coronary bypass patients.

Looking at the other side of the coin, among AIDS patients a variable called "realistic acceptance," which involved accepting what might happen to them and preparing for the worst, was associated with a markedly *shortened* survival time after diagnosis with AIDS (Reed et al., 1994).

Is Optimism Always Desirable?

Over the years, a debate has developed in the research literature as to whether *all* optimism is health-promoting, or only when the optimism is justified. That is, is *false* optimism really healthy? One group of researchers has proposed that "positive illusions" are generally helpful, even if unrealistically positive (e.g., Taylor & Brown, 1988, 1994). Critics of this view have questioned the desirability of "unrealistic optimism" (Weinstein & Klein, 1996) and pointed out its potentially harmful effects (Colvin & Block, 1994). For instance, people who underestimate their health risks are less likely to adopt health-protective behaviors.

A resolution to this dispute has been suggested by Schwarzer (1994), who distinguished between defensive optimism and functional optimism. *Defensive optimism* is a belief that one is less likely than others to suffer harm, and such feelings of invulnerability may encourage people to avoid taking self-protective measures. In contrast, *functional optimism* is a belief in one's own personal control and self-efficacy in dealing with situations which may involve risk, and it logically should encourage taking reasonable precautions. Though optimism can have these opposing effects, there is widespread agreement that a pessimistic attributional style is generally detrimental to mental health, and often to physical health as well.

REATTRIBUTION TRAINING

Several questions follow from the above discussion: What can be done about a person's pessimistic explanatory style? Can it be changed so as to reduce the person's health risk? If so, how? These questions have led to the development of a process termed **reattribution training**.

Following from the research of Weiner and Peterson and their colleagues, two basic principles in reattribution training are that:

- Under conditions of success, stable, global, and internal causal attributions for desirable outcomes are to be reinforced.
- Under conditions of failure, unstable, specific, uncontrollable, and external causes are to be reinforced. (Lewis & Daltroy, 1990, p. 98)

In addition to this process of altering incorrect attributions to more correct ones (in terms of their several dimensions), other related goals may be included in reattribution training regarding health and illness. Two important ones are altering the focus of attributions (e.g., shifting a patient's attention from an uncontrollable disease to his or her own attitudes and activities that are controllable), and attributing desirable characteristics to the individual, such as personal effectiveness in making behavioral changes.

More concrete examples of some typical goals and procedures in reattribution training are shown in Box 3–1. Such training is most often incorporated as part of a broader program of cognitive psychotherapy, and thus the unique effects of the reattribution aspects may be confounded with those of the other elements in the psychotherapy program (Metalsky et al., 1995). Since clear-cut research findings cannot be obtained from such confounded situations, we will primarily report the results of narrower studies of reattribution training, rather than those done in a therapeutic setting.

A review of studies in this area concluded that "attributional retraining methods have been consistently successful in increasing persistence and performance" (Forsterling, 1985, p. 509). Most of these studies focused on achievement situations and taught participants to attribute their unsuccessful outcomes to lack of effort rather than lack of ability. They used a variety of methods, including persuasion (e.g., presenting arguments that participants' outcomes were due to effort), modeling of desirable behavior (e.g., persistence), provision of relevant information (e.g., that college students' grades go up over time), and operant conditioning through reinforcing the desired attributional statements. One limitation of these studies is that they taught participants to make attributions to

Box 3–1   Examples of Reattribution Strategies to Combat Depression

1. Change the estimated probability of the relevant event's occurrence:
    a. Reduce estimated likelihood for aversive outcome (e.g., provide better medical care to relieve pain), and
    b. Increase estimated likelihood for desired outcomes (e.g., environmental manipulation by social agencies, such as help with rehousing, nursery care).
2. Make the highly preferred outcomes less preferred:
    a. Reduce the aversiveness of unavoidable outcomes (e.g., "Failing to be the top of your class is not the end of the world; you can still be a competent teacher") or
    b. Reduce the desirability of unobtainable outcomes (e.g., encourage a disappointed lover to find another boy or girlfriend).
3. Change the expectation from uncontrollability to controllability when the outcomes are attainable:
    a. Train necessary skills (e.g., child management skills), or
    b. Modify distorted expectations (e.g., teach more appropriate goal-setting and self-reinforcement).
4. Change unrealistic attributions:
    a. For failure: toward external, unstable, and specific causes (e.g., "The system minimized the opportunities for women. It's not that you are incompetent") and
    b. For success: toward internal, stable, and global causes (e.g., "He loves you because you are nurturant, not because he is insecure").

Source: Slightly modified extracts from Abramson, Seligman, & Teasdale (1978, pp. 69–70).

effort, ignoring the issue of whether or not the attribution was realistic or correct. Nevertheless, all of the methods showed highly promising results, affecting both cognitions and behaviors in the intended direction, and sometimes also improving related objective outcomes, such as students' GPAs.

A few studies have used similar methods in clinical treatment situations and reported similarly positive results. For instance, in a smoking-cessation program, instructional procedures that stressed intrinsic self-regulation were more successful in maintaining participants' smoking abstinence over time than were procedures using external aids, such as nicotine gum (Harackiewicz et al., 1987). Focusing on internal attributions has also proved successful in persuading women over age 40 to have a mammogram screening for cancer (Rothman et al., 1993).

Despite the success of such health reattribution programs, some warnings have been offered about the difficulties of implementing them. It is often surprisingly hard to get adults to change their attributions simply by providing contrary information. In part, this is because in many situations people rely heavily on their **schemas**, which are cognitive organizations of their past experiences, beliefs, and knowledge (e.g., about types of persons, events, roles, or causal relationships). If the schemas conflict with the information provided by the reattribution program, the new information may be disregarded, misunderstood, or distorted. Thus, reattribution therapy needs to be integrated with people's schemas and to be sufficiently thorough and prolonged to have a fundamental, continuing effect (Metalsky et al., 1995).

SUMMARY

Attribution theory focuses on the causal explanations people give for the occurrence of events. Four key dimensions of causal attributions—their internality, stability, controllability, and globality—can be measured with questionnaires or through content analysis of people's explanatory statements. In many situations, such as those involving health and achievement, these dimensions of people's attributions can have important effects on their emotions, expectations, and future performance.

Much research has studied the consequences of a pessimistic explanatory style—that is, one that makes internal, stable, and global attributions for bad events. This style has been found to be a major contributing factor to psychological depression, physical illness, and even to death. These findings come from both cross-sectional research and longitudinal studies that tracked people's mental and physical health over periods ranging from weeks to more than 50 years.

Research findings suggest that the effects of a pessimistic style occur through a variety of mediating processes that can affect people's thinking, emotions, behavior, and physiology. Processes that have been proposed include passivity, helplessness, depression, poor problem-solving, social isolation, a reckless lifestyle, and lowered immune system functioning.

Because of the seriousness of these problems, many strategies of reattribution training have been proposed to make pessimistic people's attributions more optimistic and/or valid, and these approaches are often incorporated in broader programs of cognitive therapy. Research on reattribution strategies has generally shown them to be quite successful in increasing people's persistence and performance levels in achievement situations, as well as in inducing some desirable health-protective actions.

KEY CONCEPTS

Attributional style or **explanatory style**   the kinds of causal explanations people typically give for events that happen to them.

Attributions   inferences people make about the unobservable characteristics of other people, themselves, objects, or events. Most often, these are causal explanations.

Augmentation   increasing one's confidence in the strength of a causal attribution when one observes an effect occurring together with a plausible opposite cause.

Catastrophizing   a global explanatory style; a tendency to see bad events as affecting one's whole life.

Controllable attributions   causal explanations of events or behaviors in terms of causes that are under a person's control (opposite of uncontrollable).

Discounting   decreasing one's confidence in a particular causal attribution when there are two or more plausible causes for a particular behavior one has observed.

External (or situational) attributions   causal explanations of a person's actions in terms of the situation outside of the person, to which he or she is responding.

Fundamental attribution error   the common tendency to overemphasize internal factors and largely ignore external influences when making attributions about another person's behavior.

Global attributions   explanations of events in terms of causes that affect many areas of one's life (opposite of specific).

Internal (or dispositional) attributions   causal explanations of a person's actions in terms of characteristics within the person.

Longitudinal study   research in which data are collected from the same participants at two or more points in time.

Mediating variable (or mediator)   an intervening variable that accounts for the relationship between two other variables.

Meta-analysis   a statistical summary of the results of many studies on the same general topic.

Optimism   a global belief that one will usually experience good outcomes in life.

Pessimistic explanatory style   a general tendency to explain bad events with internal, stable, and global attributions, and to explain good events with external, unstable, and specific attributions.

Reattribution training   systematic strategies to change individuals' attributional patterns from pessimistic to optimistic and/or realistic.

Schemas   cognitive organizations of a person's past experiences, beliefs, and knowledge about types of persons, events, roles, or causal relationships.

Self-efficacy   people's judgments of their capability to carry out a particular type of behavior.

Social cognition   the field of study that focuses on how people think about other people and themselves.

Stable attributions   explanations of events in terms of causes that are expected to continue relatively unchanged (opposite of unstable).

REVIEW QUESTIONS

1. In the vignette about Tom and Jerry at the beginning of this chapter, which man will be more likely to succeed in giving up smoking, and why? Entirely apart from their smoking, is there a basis for predicting which one is likely to have better health in the future? If so, which one will?

2. Give examples of the various combinations of types of attributions (internal, stable, and global) that a team member might give for losing a basketball game. Which one(s) would constitute a pessimistic explanatory style?

3. You observe a student shouting at a janitor on campus. What kind of attributions (about whom?) would be examples of the fundamental attribution error? Give examples of some alternative attributions that you might make.

4. What do you think is (are) the most plausible mechanism(s) by which attributions can influence a person's long-term health? Why?

5. Give a concrete example of the ways in which causal attributions can lead a college student to become depressed.

6. If you were trying to help that student by reattribution training, what would you do or say?

7. Do you think it is healthier to be overly optimistic or to be realistic in one's expectations and attributions? Cite research evidence that supports your viewpoint.

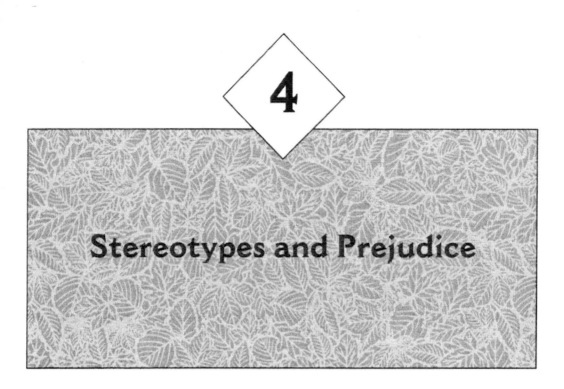

Stereotypes and Prejudice

My first victim was a woman—white, well dressed, probably in her early twenties. I came upon her late one evening on a deserted street in Hyde Park, a relatively afflu-ent neighborhood in an otherwise mean, impoverished section of Chicago. As I swung into the avenue behind her, there seemed to be a discreet, uninflammatory distance between us. Not so. She cast back a worried glance. To her, the youngish black man—a broad six feet two inches with a beard and billowing hair, both hands shoved into the pockets of a bulky military jacket—seemed menacingly close. After a few more quick glimpses, she picked up her pace and was soon running in earnest. Within seconds she disappeared into a cross street.

That was more than a decade ago, I was twenty-two years old, a graduate stu-dent newly arrived at the University of Chicago. It was in the echo of that terrified woman's footfalls that I first began to know the unwieldy inheritance I'd come into. It was clear that she thought herself the quarry of a mugger, a rapist, or worse. Suffering a bout of insomnia, however, I was stalking sleep, not defenseless wayfarers. . . .

In that first year, my first away from my hometown, I was to become thor-oughly familiar with the language of fear. At dark, shadowy intersections, I could cross in front of a car stopped at a traffic light and elicit the thunk, thunk, thunk *of the driver—black, white, male, or female—hammering the door locks.*

Another time I was on assignment for a local paper and killing time before an interview. I entered a jewelry store on the city's affluent Near North Side. The propri-etor excused herself and returned with an enormous red Doberman pinscher straining at the end of a leash. She stood, the dog extended toward me, silent to my questions, her eyes bulging nearly out of her head. . . .

Such episodes are not uncommon. Black men trade tales like this all the time.
(Quoted from Staples, 1997.)

The passage above was written by Brent Staples, a writer for the *New York Times*. What characteristics do you think that people used to form perceptions of Sta-ples? How do you think these people's perceptions and behavior affected his self-image? Do you think that people can act in prejudiced ways without being aware of it?

Prejudice and discrimination are tragic aspects of social interaction. Exam-ples range from Biblical times, when there was hostility between Jews and Samar-itans, to present-day Yugoslavia, where Christian Serbs have been systematically killing, raping, and torturing Muslim Albanians. In the United States, beatings and lynchings of Black Americans were commonplace from the end of the Civil War and well into the 1900s. In the depression years of the 1930s, over 100 Black men were lynched in the South (U.S. Bureau of the Census, 1975). Similar waves of violence, atrocities, and murder have been perpetrated against Native Ameri-cans, Asians, and Hispanics in the United States, and also against other ostra-cized groups, including foreigners, homosexuals, and peace marchers.

Prejudice and discrimination in intergroup relations have been studied since the earliest days of social psychology (Fiske, 1998). A sample of topics studied in-cludes how children develop attitudes toward other ethnic groups, the content of racial stereotypes, how prejudiced attitudes are displayed in hostile, racist behav-ior, and also how prejudiced beliefs and behavior can be changed to tolerance and acceptance of other groups in society. In this chapter, we will focus on two topics. First, we will examine theoretical concepts and empirical research on how negative stereotypes affect members of the stereotyped group, and second, we will examine how this knowledge can be used to reduce the social problem of prejudice and discrimination.

INTERGROUP RELATIONS: BELIEFS, ATTITUDES, AND BEHAVIOR

First, some definitions. **Stereotypes** are overgeneralized sets of beliefs about members of a particular social group. Example of stereotypes include beliefs that Blacks are athletic, Jews are greedy, athletes are dumb, Asians are smart, or immigrants are lazy. By their very nature, stereotypes are highly simplified sets of beliefs, and thus they cannot fully describe the group's characteristics. Typically they have clear evaluative aspects and are rather rigidly resistant to change (Oskamp, 1991).

One reason that stereotypes about other groups are resistant to change is because they are *useful* to the people who hold them; stereotypes are useful in the sense that they reduce the complexity of the world into a few simple guidelines that suggest how members of certain groups should be treated. When similar stereotypes are *shared* by many people, they have a powerful influence on patterns of intergroup behavior. For instance, the Nazis promulgated the stereotype that Jews were unclean and subhuman, and Germans were pressured to treat them accordingly. Stereotypes help to make our world predictable and easily understandable. However, not all stereotypes are negative. For instance, I may believe that Hispanics are family-oriented, or that Asians are smart, and I may also value these qualities.

It is when stereotypes include negative evaluations that they become harmful. **Prejudice** can be defined as an irrational unfavorable *attitude* toward a person or group of people. Literally, it means "prejudgment" of others, which could be positive or negative, but in current use it generally means negative attitudes and beliefs that are not justified by the facts. Prejudice involves a negative attitude toward a stereotyped group. **Discrimination** can be defined as unequal or unfair behavior toward an individual based on his or her membership in a particular group. In essence, stereotypes are cognitions, prejudice is an emotion, and discrimination is a behavior (Fiske, 1998).

When prejudice and discrimination are directed at an ethnic group, they become aspects of **racism**, which includes both negative attitudes and hostile behavior. Racist behavior also inevitably has an ideological element—belief in the superiority of a particular race and its right to domination over others (Zuckerman, 1990). Racism can be *individual*, as in cases where a person organizes much of his or her life around opposition to another racial group. An even more powerful form is **institutional racism**, which includes both formal laws and regulations as well as informal, but powerful, social norms that limit the opportunities and choices available to certain ethnic groups. Examples are segregated school systems, laws prohibiting interracial marriages, racial or religious restrictions on hiring or promotion, "White only" country clubs, and tests or other qualification requirements that unfairly discriminate against particular groups (Briggs & Paulson, 1996). Individual and institutional racism can act separately, but generally they are mutually reinforcing. Institutional racism cannot develop or survive without support from many individual racists, and individual racism is much less likely to be expressed and to spread without strong societal support.

The most extreme form of discrimination is **hate crimes**, such as spray-painting swastikas or racial epithets, burning down or vandalizing property, personal beatings or murder. Violence against individuals from stigmatized groups increased substantially in the United States in the 1980s and 1990s. *Thrill* hate crimes are the most common type, according to research by Levin and McDevitt (1993). They are usually committed quite randomly by small groups of young males who are looking for "excitement" and find it by bashing a stranger who appears different from them. *Defensive* hate crimes are responses by highly prejudiced individuals to perceived "intrusions" by some stigmatized person into their neighborhood or workplace or campus. They are often committed by a single individual and frequently involve an escalating series of assaults. *Mission* hate crimes are the rarest but most serious category. They are committed by members of hate groups, such as the Ku Klux Klan or Skinheads, who view them as attempts to rid the world of all members of some "inferior" or "treasonous" group. Examples include lynchings and the 1995 bombing of the federal building in Oklahoma City.

Institutionalized norms and practices frequently contribute to or form patterns of institutional racism. For instance, cultural customs, such as clothing patterns, can act as stimuli that provoke prejudice or violence by others. An extreme example was the Nazi requirement for all Jews to wear yellow stars on their clothing. Some discriminatory practices may be required by law, such as Jim Crow segregation in the American South up until the 1950s, which mandated separate schools, bus and railroad waiting rooms, and even separate drinking fountains for Blacks and Whites. Informal means can also be used to accomplish similar outcomes. Examples include *redlining* of housing neighborhoods by realtors, which has kept ethnic minorities out of desirable residential neighborhoods, or the *glass ceiling* that prevents most women employees from reaching higher managerial levels.

SOME IMPACTS OF PREJUDICE AND DISCRIMINATION

The terms "race" and "ethnic group" have often been used interchangeably. However, as far back as 1950, scientists began to emphasize the inadequacies inherent in the concept of race (Montagu, 1951; Yee et al., 1993). Consequently, we will avoid that term and refer to ethnic groups instead.

An **ethnic group** is made up of people who share a language, culture, and traditions, as well as some physical similarities. Examples include European Jews, Eskimos, the British, Sioux Indians, Koreans, and the Amish religious group. Though ethnic groups are often referred to as racial groups, scientists have long realized that there are no pure races. There are tremendous variations in genetic and physical characteristics among persons who are nominally classified as of the same race (e.g., Blacks or Whites), and stating a person's race is not a biological fact, but a social and linguistic convention (a "folk taxonomy"—Fish, 1995). In fact, genetic studies of blood groups and other evidence indicate that, in the United States, about 70% of "Blacks" have some White ancestry and about 20% of "Whites" have some Black ancestry (Reed, 1969; Stuckert, 1964).

Research on Ethnic Groups

When ethnic group comparisons are reported in research, readers must understand that they do not involve pure groups with homogeneous biological and genetic backgrounds, but rather groups having varying degrees of biological, linguistic, and cultural similarity. In studies of psychological variables, such as temperament or personality characteristics, it is almost inevitable to find "much more variation within groups designated as races than between such groups" (Zuckerman, 1990, p. 1297).

Psychological research on ethnic group differences in the United States has focused mostly on African-Americans, the earliest and largest minority nationwide (Ackerman & Humphreys, 1990). A crucial aspect of the social and cultural history leading to their disadvantaged status is that most of their ancestors came to the United States as slaves. Their unique position as a minority group resulted from that background of slavery—the issue that ignited the Civil War—and from the legalized segregation imposed on them after their emancipation.

Though Hispanics have lived in the Southwestern states for nearly 400 years, and are now a rapidly growing minority group, they have received much less research attention. A key factor affecting their status in the United States is their linguistic uniqueness as Spanish-speaking; in addition, many Hispanics are recent immigrants, so length of time in this country is a crucial variable in understanding their adjustment and other characteristics. A third important minority group is Asian-Americans, who have only recently begun to receive any research attention. Like Hispanics, Asians have critical linguistic differences from the English-speaking majority. Because they come from many diverse countries with quite different languages and cultural patterns, they cannot meaningfully be lumped together on many variables. In addition, all the major Asian national groups in this country except the Japanese have a majority of foreign-born members, so they particularly experience the challenge of trying to understand a new culture and unfamiliar customs. Consider the case of Joyce Lee in Box 4–1.

Box 4–1   Joyce Lee, a Young Immigrant

Joyce Lee came to the United States from Hong Kong with her mother and two brothers in 1969.

"I was placed at an elementary school in a working class neighborhood. . . . I was five years old when I experienced for the first time in my life, that being different was not something to strive for. Acting different could alienate you, looking different could make you feel inferior. I remember in kindergarten standing next to the bathroom in front of the children's coat rack, immobile, for one school year. I had no friends, I didn't talk with anyone, including the teachers. . . . If a classmate gave me any attention, I stood as still as possible, wanting them to think I wasn't a real person. . . . I tried not to blink or move. . . . "

"[In high school], the refugees were hated and often targets of social violence. Sometimes, I would see other Chinese students get threatened and harassed. I felt sorry for them but at the same time relieved that, for the moment, it wasn't me. I hated myself for a long time and was ashamed of being Chinese. . . . For thirteen years, I endured the barrage of racial slurs."

Quoted from Lee (1997, pp. 212–214).

Stereotypes and Intergroup Differences

As with most past psychological research, we will focus here mainly on the situation of African-Americans. Stereotypes of Blacks in America have been studied empirically since the early years of social psychology. An influential early study, done with Princeton undergraduates, found that more than 75% of the students agreed that, as a group, "Negroes" were superstitious and lazy, and 25% or more agreed that they were ignorant, ostentatious, happy-go-lucky, and musical (Katz & Braly, 1933). Studies since then have shown a general fading of sharp ethnic stereotypes and a growing reluctance to attribute traits to whole ethnic groups. However, raters continue to show high levels of agreement when they are asked what traits *others* attribute to Blacks rather than about their own beliefs (cf. Lepore & Brown, 1997).

Because the topic is a pejorative one, national surveys rarely ask directly about ethnic stereotypes, so most studies in recent years have been done with samples of college students. One careful study showed that more than 50% of a college student sample considered each of the following characteristics as part of the stereotype of Blacks: musical, athletic, violent, and criminal (Lepore & Brown, 1997). Whether or not individuals endorse these stereotypic views, it is clear that most Americans are well aware of the negative stereotypes about Blacks, and of course that is true of Black Americans too (Devine, 1989). Similar evidence that people are generally knowledgeable about ethnic stereotypes has been found for Hispanics. Schultz et al. (1999) found a high degree of consistency in responses to "the words and images that *other people* think are associated with people of Hispanic descent." Hispanics were equally as knowledgeable as Whites about the content of the Hispanic stereotype. Some of the most common characteristics were: welfare, uneducated, gang, family, and traditional.

Returning to African-Americans, one of the most prominent stereotypes about U.S. Blacks is that they are intellectually inferior to Whites (and to Asians, who have recently gained a stereotype reputation as a "model minority"). Though this stereotype long predates organized mental testing, it has gained some empirical support from many studies of measured intergroup differences between African-Americans and other groups. On cognitive measures, such as standardized individual intelligence tests and group school achievement tests, it is common to find that the average score for Euro-Americans is as much as one standard deviation higher than the average for African-Americans (Ackerman & Humphreys, 1990; Neisser et al., 1996). We will briefly cite some of this research as background for the study described in the next section.

African-American students in most U.S. school districts score lower than their Euro-American classmates on standardized achievement tests in vocabulary, reading, and math. Although the gap has steadily narrowed since 1970, the typical African-American still scores below 75% of White Americans on standardized tests (Jencks & Phillips, 1998). In high school, the Black dropout rate is slightly higher than for Whites, and in college, 70% of Blacks who enter do not complete a bachelor's degree within six years, compared to 42% of Whites (American Council on Education, 1990; McMillen, 1997). Those Blacks who do graduate have an average GPA two-thirds of a letter grade lower than White graduates (Nettles, 1988, cited in Steele & Aronson, 1995).

The causes behind these educational differentials are a matter of great dispute. A highly controversial volume, *The Bell Curve* (Herrnstein & Murray, 1994), attributed them largely to genetic ability, as did an earlier widely debated overview by Jensen (1969). However, this viewpoint resurrects the old nature-versus-nurture argument, and it is undeniable that the differentials reflect huge discrepancies in the typical environments of Blacks and Whites (Neisser et al., 1996). In part, these are a function of lower social class or socioeconomic status (SES), which often prevents families from providing their children with many of the physical necessities of life, let alone the early experiences and advantages that stimulate motivation and achievement in academic areas. Consider the case of Dick Gregory (1997, p. 145) as he recalls his experiences in the second grade:

> The teacher thought I was stupid. Couldn't spell, couldn't read, couldn't do arithmetic. Just stupid. Teachers were never interested in finding out that you couldn't concentrate because you were so hungry, because you hadn't had any breakfast. All you could think about was noontime, would it ever come? Maybe you could sneak into the cloakroom and steal a bite of some kid's lunch out of a coat pocket. A bit of something. Paste. You can't really make a meal of paste, or put it on bread for a sandwich, but sometimes I'd scoop a few spoonfuls out of the paste jar in the back of the room. Pregnant people

get strange tastes. I was pregnant with poverty. . . . Paste doesn't taste too bad when you're hungry.

The same economic forces frequently lead students to drop out of school to make money, or to hold jobs that interfere with their continuing education.

Economic factors are just a part of the overwhelming differences in the environmental influences that shape the behavior and outcomes of Blacks, Whites, and other ethnic groups. There are also important *social psychological* influences on people's behaviors, and we discuss one of them—stereotype threat—in the next section of this chapter.

Reactions of Stigmatized Groups

Up to this point, we have focused on the stereotypes *about* ethnic minorities. But what are the reactions of members of ethnic minorities and other stigmatized groups to the prejudice and discrimination directed at them? Some psychological theories predict that they would suffer from low self-confidence and self-esteem because of their awareness that others devalue and reject them (e.g., Cooley, 1956). However, despite the negative social and economic consequences of prejudice and discrimination, empirical studies show that members of stigmatized groups often *do not* display lowered self-esteem (Crocker, Major, & Steele, 1998). In fact, they sometimes make a virtue of their stigmatizing condition, as in the "Black pride" movement.

Careful research on the general self-esteem of stigmatized or oppressed individuals has suggested that there are several mechanisms by which they protect themselves against the negative appraisals of others (Crocker & Major, 1989). First, they may attribute any negative feedback or poor outcomes to prejudice on the part of others rather than to their own inadequacies. Second, they may compare their own outcomes to those of other members of their ingroup rather than to those of advantaged outgroups, and thus feel relatively well-off. Third, when they recognize their less favorable position on some characteristic (e.g., mathematical ability, income), they are likely to minimize the size of the difference, selectively devalue the importance of that characteristic, or focus attention on other aspects where they feel superior.

STEREOTYPE THREAT

Influential research by Claude Steele has examined the largely unstudied question of what effect stereotypes have on *those who are stereotyped* (Steele, 1997, 1998; Steele & Aronson, 1998). For example, since Blacks as well as most other Americans know about the widespread negative stereotype concerning Blacks' intellectual ability, what effect does that have on Blacks' academic performance? Steele and Aronson (1995) proposed that it creates a stereotype threat to Blacks' self-evaluation, and they did several experiments to demonstrate the effects of this threat. **Stereotype threat** refers to being at risk of acting in a manner consistent with a negative stereotype about one's group. Steele predicted that stereotype threat would be particularly high in intellectual achievement situations that are difficult or frustrating, but not in situations that are less demanding, and that it would reduce performance in the demanding situations, *regardless of whether participants themselves believed the stereotype.*

Illustrative Experiments

The experiments Steele and Aronson (1995) conducted to test their hypotheses are models of creativity, rigorous design, and applied social importance. They recruited Black and White college students of exceptional ability (e.g., Scholastic Aptitude Test scores around 600 or higher) and gave them a 25-minute test of very difficult items taken from the Graduate Record Exam (GRE) study guides. In one representative experiment, half of 20 Black and 20 White students were randomly assigned to one of two conditions in which the instructions differed only in their stress on diagnosing the participants' abilities. In the *diagnostic condition*, they were told that the test involved "reading and verbal reasoning abilities" and that after the test they would be given feedback about their "strengths and weaknesses." In the nondiagnostic condition, they were told that the test concerned "psychological factors involved in solving verbal problems" and that the feedback would inform them about "the kinds of problems that appear on tests [you] may encounter in the future" (Steele & Aronson, 1995, p. 799). Both groups were told that the test was so difficult that they should not expect to get many items correct, and both were instructed to make a strong effort on the test despite its difficulty.

   A key dependent variable in this study was the number of problems answered correctly, adjusted by using SAT scores as a control or baseline measure of problem-solving ability. The results are shown in Figure 4–1, which shows a strong interaction effect ($p < .01$). In the diagnostic condition, the Black students performed significantly worse than any of the other three groups. In fact, their adjusted score was only a little over half of the number of items that the Black nondiagnostic group answered correctly. Similarly, the Black diagnostic group was lowest in accuracy score (the number of items correct divided by the number attempted—interaction $p < .05$), and also lowest in the number of items attempted. Thus, being warned that the test measured their abilities slowed down the Blacks, but not the Whites, and also worsened their performance. Further studies replicated this basic finding and demonstrated several of the processes involved in the stereotype threat effect (Steele & Aronson, 1995).

   Why would instructions that the test involved "reading and verbal reasoning abilities" lead Black students to try less and perform worse? Additional measures in the study showed that several processes were activated in Black participants by these diagnostic instructions. First, thoughts regarding their ethnic group membership were activated significantly more for Blacks in the diagnostic condition

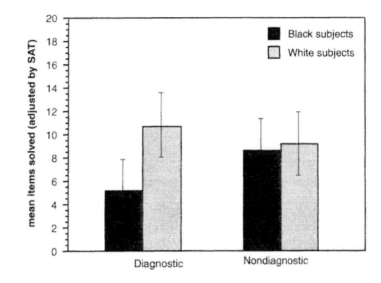

Figure 4–1   Mean Test Performance of Black and White Students. The diagnostic condition induced stereotype threat. Note: The vertical lines indicate the 95% confidence interval around each mean.

than for any of the other groups. Second, self-doubts were stimulated significantly more for that group—over twice as many as for any of the other groups. Third, on a self-report measure of activity preferences and personality characteristics, Blacks in the diagnostic condition *avoided* agreeing with ethnically stereotypic descriptions, significantly more so than any of the other groups. Fourth, only 25% of this key group indicated their race on a short self-description questionnaire given just before the test, whereas all members of the other groups did so (a huge and significant interaction—$p < .01$). In essence, these findings indicate that the diagnostic instructions created a heightened awareness of ethnicity, and of the negative stereotype about Blacks, and produced a strong feeling of **evaluation apprehension**. Apparently, the diagnostic instructions reminded participants that they were Black, and they then acted in a manner consistent with this cultural stereotype.

A final experiment demonstrated how easily this stereotype threat could be invoked. In this study, the same very difficult test was given to participants, but no mention was made of its testing their ability; instead, the nondiagnostic instructions from the previous studies were used. The key manipulation of stereotype threat was in a brief questionnaire given just before the test. It merely asked the participant's age, year in school, major, number of siblings, parents' education—and, for the threat group, it asked their race. Despite its simplicity and apparent triviality, this event clearly served to *prime* or activate the stereotype

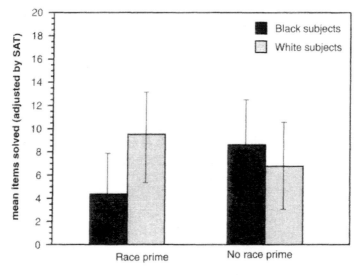

Figure 4–2   Mean Test Performance for Priming Study.

threat. This was shown by a significant interaction effect, in which the primed Black group had significantly lower SAT-adjusted scores on the test than the other three groups, and also significantly lower adjusted accuracy scores and lower numbers of completed items (see Figure 4–2). Yet the participants were not aware of this effect on their performance, and claimed not to have been distracted by recording their race. In postexperimental interviews, many stated that they had paid no attention to recording their race because it was a common event in their lives. The researchers concluded that "stereotype threat—established by quite subtle instructional differences—can impair the intellectual test performance of Black students, and . . . lifting it can dramatically improve that performance" (Steele & Aronson, 1995, p. 808).

One of the important implications of this research is the ease with which stereotype threat can be invoked by apparently innocuous or well-meaning actions or references. Think about the range of circumstances in which you are asked to "mark the box indicating your race." In addition, the research findings on stereotype vulnerability are not limited to ethnic stereotypes. Recent research has shown similar results for social class and for gender (Croizet & Claire, 1998; Spencer, Steele, & Quinn, 1997). How often do we find ourselves in situations in which we may be vulnerable to the stereotypes about the groups to which we belong?

Steele's (1997) theory goes further and proposes that many threatened individuals respond to evaluation apprehension by **protective disidentification**— that is, ceasing to identify with the threatening domain of activity or to use it as a basis of self-evaluation. This action protects their self-esteem, which is thus unlinked from achievement in that area. In addition, peer groups may apply pressure and threats of rejection to enforce this disidentification as a group norm. For instance, Black peers may say you're an "oreo"—white on the inside and black on the outside—if you try to do well in school (Cook & Ludwig, 1998).

On the other hand, the nondiagnostic-condition instructions in Steele and Aronson's research offer a model for ways to avoid stereotype threat—*describe a task as difficult and challenging, but not as an indicator of the participant's abilities.* This is a hopeful suggestion that ways can be found to remedy Black underachievement by making changes in the testing situation. Further, these results propose at least a partial explanation of the mechanisms leading to the pervasive finding of deficits for Blacks on standardized achievement and ability tests (e.g., IQ, SAT), as described above.

Application to Women Studying Mathematics

As we have pointed out, stereotype threat is applicable to individuals from any group on tasks where a well-known stereotype indicates that their group is inferior. An obvious example is women's performance in mathematics, and some past research findings are consistent with the theory's principles. For instance, a large-scale study of college women who were talented in math and science showed that they took courses intended for majors in those areas and underachieved in them, whereas less-talented women took easier courses intended for nonmajors and performed up to their predicted level there (Strenta et al., 1993). An intriguing finding by Dreyden and Gallagher (1989) showed that adding a time limit on a difficult math test—an apparently trivial change like asking one's race—sharply reduced the performance of talented girls in comparison to boys, whereas without the time limit girls took no more time but performed just as well as boys.

Steele has done experimental research on this topic as well, and his results support the theory of stereotype threat. In one study, mathematically talented men and women college students were given either a very difficult math test or one that was more within their skills. Women underperformed men on the difficult test but not on the easier one (Spencer, Steele, & Quinn, 1999). However, this result might be interpreted as consistent with the suggestions of some authors that there is a genetic limit on women's ability in very high levels of mathematics. To refute that interpretation, Spencer et al. (1999) conducted a similar experiment, using the same difficult math test as before for all participants. In this experiment, half of each gender group were told that the test generally displayed gender differences, while the other half were told that it did not do so. As predicted, women dramatically underperformed men in the first condition, but they performed as well as men when the stereotype threat was removed by the instructions that the test did not show gender differences (see Figure 4–3).

Stereotype threat has also been demonstrated for socioeconomic background, where students from low SES groups tend to perform worse on a test

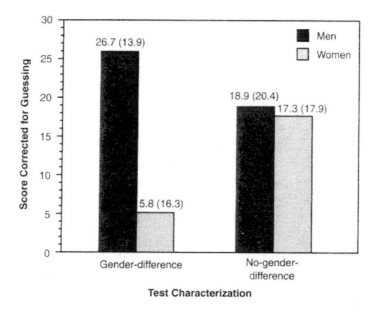

Figure 4–3   Performance on a Difficult Math Test as a Function of Sex of Subject and Test Characterization. Note: Means and standard deviations (in parentheses) for each condition are printed above the corresponding bar. *Source:* Spencer, Steele, & Quinn (1999).

when it is described as a measure of intellectual ability. However, high- and low-SES subjects do not differ on test scores when the test is presented as nondiagnostic of intellectual ability (Croizet & Claire, 1998).

REDUCING STEREOTYPE THREAT

Steele (1997) has built on these experimental findings to propose a system of "wise" education that will help stereotype-threatened individuals make the most of their academic potential. To remove the sense of stereotype threat and prevent threatened students from disidentifying with academic work, he suggested that teachers and other adults should use several techniques:

- Affirm that the students have good learning potential—i.e., openly attribute this ability to the students
- Present highly challenging assignments rather than remedial work to make up for past deficits
- Stress the expandability of human abilities

Figure 4–4   Who would be vulnerable to stereotype activation if this were a calculus class? What if it were an English class?

- Encourage students to work together in groups, which can overcome the feeling of threatened students that they are unique in experiencing frustration and difficulty in learning

As evidence that such approaches can elicit much-improved academic performance from minority students, Steele cited the success of Jaime Escalante in challenging urban ghetto high schoolers to outstanding performance in math and calculus. Similarly, Treisman (1985) developed a very effective challenge-oriented program to teach calculus to Black university students. To test these ideas further, Steele and his colleagues developed the 21st Century Program at the University of Michigan. Conducted each year since 1991, this program recruits 250 first-year college students (about 170 Whites, 40 Blacks, and 40 Latinos and Asians) who are representative of the incoming class. These students live together in one wing of a large dorm. The 250 students are encouraged to take classes together, and to develop a sense of community and shared experiences. The goals of the program are: challenge, academic engagement, student cooperation and learning, appreciation of diversity, and openness to difference (Steele at al., 1998).

The 21ˢᵗ Century Program

As we have seen, emphasizing minority status—a common practice among higher-education institutions—can lead to decreased performance. In recruiting students for the program, it was important that it not be presented as a "minority" opportunity because that would imply that the selected students were valued not for their academic ability and potential, but for their minority status. To avoid this problem, the 21ˢᵗ Century Program recruited students honorifically. Students were informed that their admission to the University of Michigan was based on academic potential, and that the program was intended to "facilitate development." The program was described as open to promising students, and not as a program for minority or underskilled students. Students recruited for the program were chosen randomly from the whole group of admitted freshmen, so that their later performance could be fairly compared with that of nonprogram students.

During the year, a range of *challenge workshops* were offered in writing, chemistry, physics, and math. Each met for four hours per week, and taking them was optional but strongly encouraged. The workshops stressed that ability was expandable, and that failure and frustration should be taken as a sign that students were being challenged, not that they lacked ability in the area. A major goal of the workshops was to encourage group study in mixed-race groups, which is a strong factor in reducing stereotype threat.

Weekly *rap seminars* were held each week in the evening. These informal session were intended to break down barriers between students and allow them to share their experiences. Oftentimes, students believe that their academic anxiety and difficulties in college are due to themselves, and that other students do not have these problems. These informal discussions were intended to change these beliefs. As Steele states, "knowing that people from other groups also feel pressured by the demands of college life disarms the interpretation that such pressures reflect something about you or your group" (Steele et al., 1998).

The University of Michigan, like many universities, has a strong commitment to retaining minority students, and it offers a variety of support and remedial programs that are are known for being "minority programs." Among the Black students who were not enrolled in the 21ˢᵗ Century program, many were participating in the university's minority programs. (Some of the Black students in the 21ˢᵗ Century program also participated in the university's minority programs, but we will not report their results. For more detail, see Steele et al., 1998.)

Results from the first four years of the 21ˢᵗ Century Program are very encouraging. Black students in this program performed much better in their first-semester courses than Black students who were not in the program. After one semester, students in the 21ˢᵗ Century Program showed higher grades (White students' GPA = 3.06; Black students' GPA = 2.81) compared to other first-year students in the university (White students' GPA = 2.90; Black students'

GPA = 2.64). The difference was significant for both Black students (d = .08; p < .05) and White students (d = .24; p < .01).

Black students in the program showed less underachievement in relation to White students across the whole university, and follow-ups showed that they continued to do well through their sophomore year—even though they were no longer in the program (it ended after the first year). Only 4% of the Black participants dropped out after their first year, compared 12% of those who were in no special program. For comparison, 5% of White students in the 21st Century Program dropped out after their first year, compared to 11% of those who were in no special program (Steele et al., 1998). Of the Black students who were in the university's minority program, 25% dropped out sometime in their first two years.

The 21st Century Program intervention only occurred during the first two semesters of a student's college career. Yet, even four to five years later, its effects were still evident. At that point, 33% of the Black program participants had dropped out of college, compared to 41% of Black students who were in no special program and 44% of Black students in the minority program. For White students, there was a 27% dropout rate for those in the program, compared to 29% of those who were in no special program. Cumulative GPAs after four years at the university were 2.55 for Black students in no special program, 2.37 for Black students in the minority program, and 2.66 for Black students in the 21st Century Program. For White students who were in the 21st Century Program, the average GPA was 3.19, while for White students not in the program, the average GPA was 3.05.

The overall results of the program provide impressive support for the use of psychological theory to address a very difficult and important social problem. In attempts to help minority students succeed in college, many schools create well-intended programs that are remediational and segregating. However, both theoretical views and applied research findings indicate that such programs perpetuate negative stereotypes about minority students and increase stereotype threat. Steele's applied social psychological research suggests an alternative type of program—one that is not a minority program, or remediational, but which can reduce the likelihood that ethnic minorities are vulnerable to cultural stereotypes.

PREJUDICE AND RACISM IN MODERN SOCIETY

Let us now return to the attitudes and actions of majority-group members that create the climate of inequality in our society. The widespread ethnic *stereotypes* discussed above are one important constituent of the phenomenon of ethnic prejudice. However, as defined earlier in this chapter, **prejudice** also includes *attitudes* that are intolerant, unfair, or irrationally unfavorable toward another group. And **discrimination** and **racism** constitute *actions* that are unfair or hostile toward another ethnic group. How common are such patterns within American society?

Many of us would like to believe that discrimination and racism have been largely eliminated in the United States. However, the era of slavery still has a legacy in current patterns of racism, and African-Americans live in a divided world, torn between their identification as Americans and their socially inferior status as Blacks (Gaines & Reed, 1995). Most African-Americans grow up in an environment where daily events emphasize their subordinate status, and to a lesser extent the same is true for other ethnic minorities. For example, teachers' expectations regarding academic performance are generally lower for Blacks than for Whites, and are especially low for Black males (Ross & Jackson, 1991). In Chapter 7 we will explore what effect such teachers' expectations have on children.

A major contribution to people's ethnic stereotypes and prejudiced attitudes comes from the mass media, where minority groups are most often ignored, but when presented are frequently depicted in negatively biased ways (Campbell, 1995; Dines & Humez, 1995). In 1968, the Kerner Commission's report on civil disorders indicted the news media for "repeatedly, if unconsciously, reflect[ing] the biases, the paternalism, the indifference of White America" (p. 66).

The prevalence and societal importance of ethnic prejudice is suggested by the fact that it is one of the most studied topics in social science. Many differing analyses of prejudice and racism have been made by psychologists in recent years. We will quickly sketch some of the most important approaches. **Traditional racist** attitudes in the United States involved support for segregation laws and belief in the moral and intellectual inferiority of Blacks. Since the civil rights movement of the 1960s, this blatant form of prejudice has been abandoned by most citizens except for a small percentage who are sympathetic to extremist groups such as the Ku Klux Klan or the White Aryan Resistance. For instance, 40 years after the (originally controversial) Supreme Court decision that racially segregated public schools were illegal, 87% of a national sample of Americans said they approved of that decision (McAneny & Saad, 1994).

In contrast, **modern racist** attitudes are more subtle, less extreme indications of negative attitudes toward Blacks (McConahay, 1986). They are measured, for instance, by endorsement of statements indicating that American racial problems have been largely solved, that civil rights groups' goals are too extreme, or that Blacks have gotten more respect and benefits than they deserve. As examples, in a nationally representative survey in 1993, 47% of Whites said that Black civil rights groups are asking for too much, whereas only 7% of Blacks agreed with that view. Similarly, 70% of Whites but only 30% of Blacks said that Blacks had as good a chance as Whites in their community to get a job for which they were qualified (Wheeler, 1993).

Similar concepts of current racism as being more subtle and disguised in form have been proposed using the concept of **symbolic racism**, which is defined as a blend of anti-Black attitudes with belief in traditional American values such as individualism, self-reliance, and the work ethic (Kinder & Sears, 1981). This concept highlights the symbolic importance of these values, and it explains people's opposition to welfare, busing, and government programs designed to help poor people and/or minority groups as being largely based on the belief that they violate these traditional values.

REDUCING PREJUDICE AND DISCRIMINATION

The well-established finding that prejudice and discrimination are still quite prevalent in our society leads us to the question of what techniques can be used to reduce prejudice and its expression. In this area, the **contact hypothesis** has a long history of theory and research. Allport (1954) predicted that intergroup contact would lead to decreased prejudice, but only under the following four conditions: (1) equal status between the groups in the situation, (2) common goals, (3) lack of competition between the groups, and (4) support by authorities for the contact.

Later researchers have suggested additional conditions, such as an intimate situation that allows personalized understanding of members of the other group, and contact situations that provide the participants with the chance to make friends (Brewer & Miller, 1984; Pettigrew, 1998).

The contact hypothesis, in its several variations, has received support in many studies conducted in various situations and with stigmatized social groups ranging from foreign students to the elderly (e.g., Ellison & Powers, 1994; Gaertner et al., 1994; Wittig & Grant-Thompson, 1998). Among the most successful applications of this principle have been cooperative learning programs for elementary and secondary school students, such as the approach that Aronson et al. (1978) termed the "jigsaw classroom."

In addition to intergroup contact, other methods have been used successfully to reduce intergroup prejudice. One approach is to provide majority-group members with a *planned, personal experience of discrimination*, such as minority-group individuals undergo every day. This experience should make them more empathetic and understanding of the problems of minorities, and this method has been used both in elementary classrooms and in sensitivity training for public officials, such as police officers (e.g., Pfister, 1975; Sata, 1975; Weiner & Wright, 1973).

Another approach to reducing prejudice is *spotlighting people's value conflicts*, which can motivate them to change their beliefs and behavior in the direction of consistency with their underlying values, such as fairness and equality. Rokeach and his colleagues demonstrated that long-lasting attitudinal and behavioral changes could be produced with the relatively simple technique of **value self-confrontation** (e.g., Ball-Rokeach, Rokeach, & Grube, 1984; Rokeach, 1971). Grube, Mayton, and Ball-Rokeach (1994) have summarized the results of 27 such studies, reporting that 96% of them demonstrate changes in the values that were targeted, and that large but lower percentages also show changes in relevant attitudes (73%) and behaviors (56%). For instance, Rokeach (1971) found behavioral changes that lasted as long as 21 months—specifically, increased enrollment in ethnic relations courses, and membership in civil rights organizations such as the NAACP. Thus, this method of value-confrontation is a promising intervention to use in attempts to reduce prejudice and discrimination. A recent series of studies by Altemeyer (1994) used similar procedures to increase sympathy for Indian-rights activism in Canada.

SUMMARY

Stereotyped negative beliefs about members of another group are important elements of prejudiced attitudes or feelings. Behavioral variables related to prejudice are discrimination (unequal or unfair treatment) and racism (a general pattern of negative actions toward an ethnic group), which may be either individual or institutionalized.

African-Americans' legacy of slavery and legal segregation makes their history unique, but Hispanic and Asian groups also have distinctive cultural and situational characteristics, and they too are targeted by prejudice and racism. Stereotypes about Blacks are largely negative, and are well known to most Americans. On average, Blacks tend to score lower than Whites on many cognitive measures, but there are scientific debates about how much of the difference is biological and how much is due to centuries of environmental impoverishment.

Claude Steele's creative research has shown that knowledge of a negative stereotype about one's social group can be a potent threat in performance situations relevant to the stereotype. Studies show that this stereotype threat can depress Blacks' test scores and also women's mathematics performance. It is very easy to arouse, and it encourages individuals to protectively disidentify from the threatening domain of activity. Steele's research has also shown that techniques of strong teacher support, challenging assignments rather than remediation, and group cooperative learning can help to avoid or lessen the impact of stereotype threat.

Patterns of prejudice and discrimination are still widespread in America, though now they are subtler and more indirect than in the era of segregation. Psychologists have done extensive research on modern racism, symbolic racism, aversive racism, and ways to break habits of prejudice. Intergroup contact, under favorable conditions, has been shown to increase understanding and reduce prejudice, especially in cooperative learning situations. Psychological research has also demonstrated other effective techniques for reducing prejudice and discrimination.

KEY CONCEPTS

Attitude   favorable or unfavorable evaluations of a person, object, concept, or event.

Contact hypothesis   notion that intergroup contact will lead to decreased prejudice when (a) the groups are of equal status, (b) there are shared common goals, (c) there is no competition between the groups, and (d) there is institutional support for positive interactions.

Discrimination   unequal treatment of an individual based on his or her membership in a particular group.

Ethnic group   people who share a language, culture, and traditions, as well as some physical similarities.

Evaluation apprehension   anxiety about how one's performance will be evaluated by others.

Hate crimes   extreme forms of discrimination often expressed in acts of violence.

Institutional racism   formal laws and regulations as well as informal social norms that limit opportunities and choices available to certain ethnic groups.

Modern racism   subtle, less extreme indications of negative attitudes toward an ethnic group.

Prejudice   irrational unfavorable attitudes toward a person or group of people.

Protective disidentification   ceasing to identify with a threatening domain of activity or to use it as a basis of self-evaluation.

Racism   negative actions expressed toward an ethnic group.

Stereotype   overgeneralized set of beliefs about members of a particular social group.

Stereotype threat   being at risk of acting in a manner consistent with a negative stereotype about one's group

Traditional racism   belief in the moral and intellectual inferiority of other ethnic groups, and support for segregation laws.

REVIEW QUESTIONS

1. What are the differences between stereotypes, prejudice, and discrimination?
2. Define the concept of stereotype threat, and give an example to show how it affects people.
3. Lety is a Hispanic-American who works as a bank teller. It has become apparent that several of her fellow employees view her as potentially dishonest, and whenever something is missing, they immediately look at her. Describe three

specific behaviors that would illustrate the process of protective disidentification in Lety.

4. Summarize the results from the 21st Century Program. What aspects of the
program do you think produced these effects, and why?

5. How are traditional racism and modern racism alike, and how do they differ?
Give two statements that a person could make that would illustrate traditional
racism and modern racism.

6. Imagine that you are the coordinator for disabled-student services at a small
liberal arts college. You have learned that many of the students on campus
have prejudiced attitudes toward disabled students and often act in subtle
ways to undermine the services that are offered. Using the material discussed
in this chapter, describe one strategy that could be used to reduce students'
prejudice. Be sure to link the aspects of your program to research on stereotyping, prejudice, and discrimination.

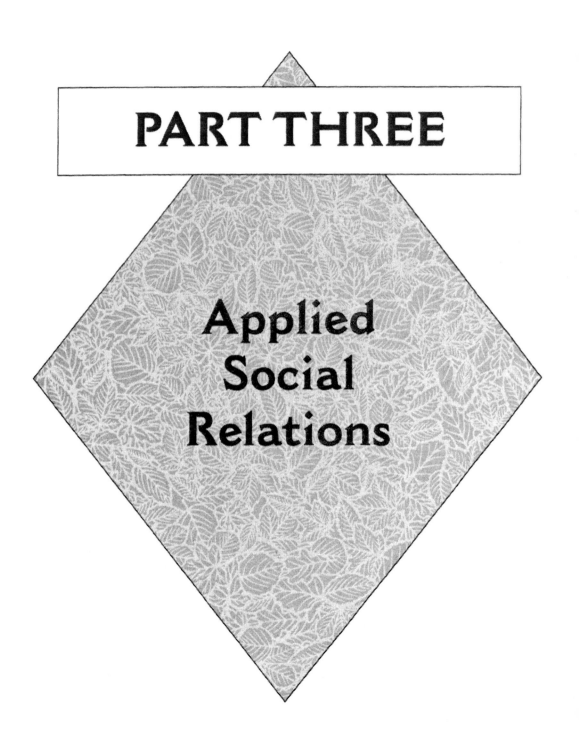

PART THREE

Applied Social Relations

5

Love, Intimacy, and Divorce

Mary Maxwell's marital problems did not begin early. She reported, "We've been married 12 years and I really feel as though the first 10 years were very good." Mary and Michael had moved many times in their marriage, because of Michael's work. Mary accepted the moves, though she found them painful, and devoted herself to child rearing and volunteer activities in each new town. After the last move, though, something seemed to give.

Mary started in therapy because she felt so depressed. She gradually realized that she was very angry at her husband about their most recent move and felt it was important for them to work together on their marriage. For a while they went to a therapist together. In one therapy session a couple of months later, Michael said:

You've got to get your act together and decide whether you want me the way I am, because this is the way I was 12 years ago when you married me, and this is the way I am now, and this is the way I'll always be.

Mary gradually came to the realization that "there just wasn't any way that I could stay in this marriage because he wasn't willing to work on it."

The Maxwells made every effort to dissolve their marriage in a way that would be relatively painless for their children. They hoped to spare them too much change. Nevertheless, they sold the house they had shared, and Mary bought a condominium in a more urban, active neighborhood. Michael searched for a job in the same area, without success, and ended up moving away. Their efforts to cooperate in making plans for the children quickly ran into trouble. They ended up in court. When the judge demanded that they come to an agreement, the pressure was great enough to force them to agree on temporary arrangements. Michael agreed to support Mary and the children while Mary completed her education. (Adapted from Stewart et al., 1997, pp. 6–7.)

What factors do you think led to the Maxwells' divorce? Could something have been done to prevent the divorce? What effects do you think the divorce will have on their children?

Our relationships with other people comprise some of the most important aspects of our lives. We spend much of our day in the presence of other people, and when we're not with others we are often thinking about them. Having positive relationships gives us joy. Losing a relationship makes us sad. In this chapter, we will examine theoretical and applied research on social relationships—focusing particularly on love, marriage, and divorce. We will address the following issues: Current views about marriage. How common is divorce? What effect does divorce have on adults and children, and can any potential harm be prevented? What factors lead to conflict in a relationship? And what can be done to keep relationships satisfying?

SOCIAL RELATIONSHIPS

We have many different kinds of relationships: Father. Mother. Friend. Companion. Spouse. Lover. Child. Each of these terms conveys a very distinct pattern of interaction and a different type of social relationship. For more than 30 years, social psychologists have been studying topics of interpersonal attraction, friend-ship, and love (Berscheid, 1992). Some of the topics studied in this area include interpersonal attraction, mate selection, first encounters, close relationships, at-tributions within relationships, communication patterns, social attachment, and trust. In their review of the research on attraction and close relationships, Berscheid and Reis (1998, p. 194) state:

> Along with developmental, clinical, and counseling psychology, social psychol-ogy is playing a central role in the development of a science of relationships. One important reason for its centrality is that social psychology focuses on the processes that underlie social behavior.

Of the many different kinds of relationships that people form, our focus in this chapter will be on close, loving relationships.

One widely cited approach to understanding love relationships is Robert Sternberg's (1988, 1997) triangular theory of love. From this perspective, love re-lationships can be characterized by three factors: passion, intimacy, and commit-ment. **Passion** is the physical attraction in a love relationship—a strong infatuation with the other person. **Intimacy** is the feeling of closeness in a rela-tionship—the degree to which a person can share feelings freely with another. **Commitment** is the strength of a person's intention to continue a relationship—a willingness to invest time and resources in a relationship. A graphical represen-tation of this theory is presented in Figure 5–1. Different types of love are characterized by varying levels of passion, intimacy, and commitment. High lev-

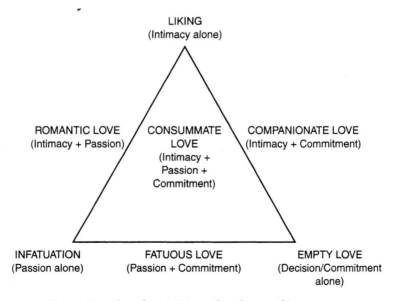

Figure 5–1   Sternberg's Triangular Theory of Love.

els of intimacy and passion make for a romantic relationship. In contrast, companionate relationships are characterized by high levels of intimacy and commitment.

Passion is exciting and intense; it is "a state of intense longing for union with another person" (Hatfield, 1988, p. 193). There is a difference between "loving" someone and being "in love." Passion is the type of feeling people report when they are "in love." However, passion is short-lived—usually only a few months or, at most, a year or two. For example, couples who are married for two years express affection toward each other only half as often as newlweds (Huston & Chorost, 1994). Does this mean that love is short-lived? Clearly, the answer is no. But if a lov-

Figure 5–2 Chris and Barbara have been dating for 6 months, and both say they are in love. However, for their relationship to endure, they must transition from passionate love to companionate love.

ing relationship is to last and be mutually satisfying, it must transition from passionate love to companionate love. As Sternberg (1988) stated:

> "Living happily ever after" need not be a myth, but if it is to be a reality, the happiness must be based upon different configurations of mutual feelings at various times in the relationship. Couples who expect their passion to last forever, or their intimacy to remain unchallenged, are in for disappointment.

One of the keys to a successful companionate relationship is *intimacy*. Feelings of intimacy often result from self-disclosure (Aron et al., 1997). **Self-disclosure** is the process of revealing important aspects of oneself to others (Derlega et al., 1993). As a relationship develops, people reveal more and more of themselves to one another. This knowledge about the other person produces a deep feeling of intimate knowledge, and of a close relationship. In fact, when someone discloses something in this way, the partner often feels obligated to disclose in return. This pattern of interaction is termed **disclosure reciprocity**—the tendency for one partner's level of self-disclosure to match that of the other partner. As each person discloses information, it produces reciprocation by the other, and a deepening spiral of intimacy (Aron et al., 1997; Hatfield & Rapson, 1993).

There are several keys to developing and maintaining intimacy with a partner. First, the disclosure must happen slowly. Disclosing too much too soon can drive away a person who is not yet ready to disclose comparable information. Likewise, failing to self-disclose in reciprocation for a partner's disclosure can leave the partner feeling vulnerable and cheated. Finally, disclosure necessitates good listening and communication skills (Shaffer et al., 1996). Good listeners are attentive to their partners, appear to be comfortable and enjoying themselves, and often utter supportive phrases while their partner is speaking. Several of the treatment programs we will discuss later in this chapter attempt to increase feelings of intimacy in a relationship by training partners how to listen and how to self-disclose.

Marriage

For many couples, marriage is the ultimate expression of their love and intimacy. Over the past 30 years, consistently more than 95% of the American public has expressed a personal desire for marriage. Almost three-quarters of adult Americans believe that "marriage is a lifelong commitment that should not be ended except under extreme circumstances." Even 81% of divorced or separated couples still believe that "marriage should be for life" (Blankenhorn, Bayme, & Bethke, 1990). In 1995, there were 2.4 million marriages in the United States and 160,251 marriages in Canada. In about half of these marriages, one or both partners were getting re-married (U.S. Bureau of the Census, 1997; Statistics Canada, 1998).

Consider the following statements. For each statement, decide whether you agree or disagree. The figures shown after each of the statements reflect the percentage of respondents who "agreed" or "strongly agreed" with each statement in a telephone survey (Wirthlin Worldwide, 1998).

1. Marriage is an old fashioned, outmoded institution. (11%)
2. Marriage should be considered a promise "till death do us part." (69%)
3. Marriage is for life. (93%)
4. All things being equal, it is better for children to be raised in a household that has a married mother and father. (92%)

The Effects of Marriage.   It is clear that people think marriage is important and worthwhile. In general, the available research confirms that being married has positive effects. Comparisons between married people and people who (a) have never been married, or who are (b) widowed, (c) separated, (d) divorced, or (e) cohabitating, consistently find married people to be happier than any of the other groups (Stack & Eshleman, 1998). In addition to being happier, married people also have better health, lower rates of suicide, and longer lives (Hahn, 1993; Stack, 1990; Tucker et al., 1997). Research evidence also suggests that the positive relationship between marriage and happiness is true for both men and women, and is consistent across many cultures (Stack & Eshleman, 1998).

So why are married people happier? In fact, given that many couples choose to divorce, it may be more logical to think that people who are married would experience more conflict and be more *un*happy than people who are not married. A considerable amount of research has addressed this issue, and some consistent patterns of results are beginning to emerge. In essence, this area of research is an attempt to find variables that mediate the relationship between marriage and happiness. Recall that a **mediator** is an intervening variable that accounts for the relationship between two other variables. Variables like education, income, smoking, exercise, and emotional support have been examined. In general, the research indicates that married people are happier primarily for two reasons: (1) they are more satisfied with their financial situation, and (2) they are in better health.

Unfortunately, many marriages end in divorce. In these cases, two persons who were once in love and wanted to spend the rest of their lives together may now look at each other with anger and bitterness.

DIVORCE AS A SOCIAL PROBLEM

You probably have heard the often-cited statistic that half of all marriages end in divorce. For example, in 1995 there were 2.4 million marriages in the United States. In that same year, there were 1.2 million divorces (Horner, 1998; U.S. Bureau of the Census, 1997). Does this mean that if you were married in 1995, there would be a 50–50 chance that your marriage would eventually end in divorce? In fact, this statistic can be misleading, because the two numbers (marriages and divorces) are based on two very different populations; most people who divorced in 1995 were married in a previous year. Historical trends show that today fewer people are getting married, those that do marry are waiting until later in life, and they are staying married longer. For example, in 1970 the median age of a woman at her first marriage was 21, and the median marriage lasted approximately six years. In 1990, a woman's median age at her first marriage was 24, and the median marriage lasted more than seven years. The same pattern holds for men, for whom the median age at first marriage was 22 in 1970, and 26 in 1990 (U.S. Bureau of the Census, 1997).

An alternative method for calculating the divorce rate is the number of divorces per 1,000 people (Guttmann, 1993). For example, in 1995, the divorce rate was 4.4 per 1,000 people in the United States. This is the highest rate of divorce in the world! Consider a sampling of divorce rates from other countries: Canada 2.8, England 2.5, France 1.96, Germany 2.04, Italy 0.48, and Japan 1.66 (United Nations, 1995). Historical trends in U.S. divorce rates show that they reached a peak in 1980 at 5.3. From 1900 through the mid 1940s, the divorce rate remained below 2.0. During World War II, the divorce rate surged to 4.3, and then slowly declined back to 2.0. During the 1960s, divorce rates increased steadily, finally reaching their peak in 1980. Since then, the divorce rate has remained high, but slowly crept downward (U.S. Bureau of the Census, 1997). These historical trends have led some authors to refer to divorce as an "epidemic" (Brehm, 1992).

What effects do all these divorces have on the people involved? On the couples? The children? The grandparents? This is a highly controversial and heavily researched question. At first glance, it would seem that divorce is harmful—especially for children. But the research evidence has been somewhat inconclusive. In part, this is because divorce is a complex issue. The age of the children, the length of the marriage, the family dynamics, the financial resources, the social networks, and the personalities involved all play a role in determining the effects of divorce. In the short section that follows, we will attempt to summarize, at a broad level, the effects of divorce on children.

The Effects of Divorce on Children

More than 1 million children are involved in a divorce in the United States each year. In fact, as of 1995, 32% of children under the age of 18 living in the United States lived in a single-parent household—usually run by the mother. There are several reasons to predict that divorce is likely to be harmful for the children involved. First, children of divorce usually live with their mother, and divorce typically leads to a decline in the standard of living for mother-custody families, often putting them below the poverty level. One of the consequences of fewer economic resources is lower rates of success in school. Poorer students tend to live in poorer neighborhoods, where schools are poorly funded, and children may be pressured to leave school early to earn money. Second, single-parent families provide fewer opportunities for child-parent social interactions. Often, single parents work full-time, giving them less time to spend with their children than two-parent households. Finally, divorce is emotionally stressful and often involves moving, changes in friends, losing contact with grandparents, and parental remarriage (Amato & Keith, 1991a).

Short-Term Effects.   From the above reasoning, we might expect to find large harmful effects of divorce on children. However, the research on this topic has been somewhat inconclusive—with some studies showing short-term harmful effects, and other showing no effects at all. This overall pattern of results has led some researchers to conclude that children are resilient and not easily harmed by divorce. A 1991 meta-analysis examined 92 studies that compared children living in divorced single-parent families with children living in continuously intact families (Amato & Keith, 1991b). The results showed that children of divorce scored lower than children from intact families across a variety of outcomes, with the median effect size being $d = -.14$. In general, research shows a small, short-term damaging effect of divorce on a variety of measures of psychological well-being in children, including increased aggression, increased anxiety, lower academic performance, lower self-esteem, and poorer relationships with peers (Wolchik et al. , 1993). These effects appear to be larger for boys than for girls.

Long-Term Effects.   Given that divorce can have some small, short-term effects on children, how long do these effects last? Several studies have examined adult children of divorced parents. A 1991 meta-analysis identified 37 such studies, which included 81,678 participants (Amato & Keith, 1991a). The combined results of these studies showed that parental divorce had broad negative consequences for adult quality of life. Outcomes associated with parental divorce included depression, low life satisfaction, low marital quality, increased divorce rates, less education, and less income. The size of these effects varied, but most were weak (average d-statistics between $-.10$ and $-.30$). However, given the amount of time that had passed since divorce, the fact that the results were statistically significant at all is noteworthy. Of all the dependent variables included in this analysis, 45% were significantly negative, 1% were significantly positive, and 54% were not significant. In addition, consistent with the short-term effects, the psychological damage of divorce tended to be stronger for boys than for girls.

In summarizing their findings, Amato and Keith (1991a) state, "These results lead to a pessimistic conclusion: the argument that parental divorce presents few problems for children's long-term development is simply inconsistent with the literature on this topic" (p. 56).

Protecting Children from the Harmful Effects of Divorce

We have seen that divorce can have harmful effects on some children. The largest of these effects are on problems in conduct and in parent-child relationships. However, most of the effects found in the research were small, which indicates that many children are not harmed by divorce. In a national longitudinal study, Zill et al. (1993) found that 34% of children from divorced families had adjustment problems in school, compared with 20% of children from intact families. This finding reemphasizes the potential harm that divorce can have on children, but it also shows that 66% of children from divorced families were not adversely affected. As Pedro-Carroll (1997) states, "whereas some children land deftly on their feet after divorce, for others there is a lifelong legacy of negative fallout" (p. 216).

A variety of intervention programs have been developed to help children "land deftly on their feet" and to reduce the harmful effects of divorce. Most of these programs aim to increase adjustment by working individually with children (Grych & Fincham, 1992), whereas some focus on parents (Wolchik et al., 1993; Weiss & Wolchik, 1998). One program that has produced positive effects is the New Beginnings Program (Wolchik et al., 1993), which is designed to change four aspects of parent-child interactions following divorce. Table 5–1 shows the four targeted variables and the specific intervention techniques used to produce change.

The program consists of eleven 1 3/4–hour group sessions and two 1-hour individual sessions. The group sessions are designed to teach single mothers spe-

Table 5–1   Theory of the New Beginnings Intervention: Proposed Mediators of Intervention Techniques

Proposed Mediators	Intervention Techniques
Quality of mother relationship	Family Fun Time One-on-One Time Catch 'Em Being Good Listening skills
Effective discipline	Clear expectations and rules Monitoring misbehavior and consequences Increased consistency
Contact with father	Education about importance of child's relationship with father Reduction of obstacles to visitation
Negative divorce-related events including interparental conflict	Anger management skills Listening skills

Source: Weiss & Wolchik (1998, p. 449).

cific skills to promote positive social interaction with their children, and to eliminate the negative patterns of communication between mothers and children that
often follow divorce (Weiss & Wolchik, 1998). A study on the effects of the New
Beginnings Program was reported by Wolchik et al. (1993). Participants in the
study were 70 women who had recently experienced a divorce. Of these, 36 were
randomly assigned to a delayed-treatment control condition, and 34 were assigned to the intervention condition. In a **delayed-treatment study** participants

Box 5–1   Case Study from the New Beginnings Program

Olivia is a 35-year-old married woman whose husband left her for another
woman. She has two children, Gary, 9, and Anna, 8, who have become increasingly quiet and distant since the divorce. She is concerned that Gary in
particular doesn't talk about his feelings and that he has become increasingly
rude and defiant to her. Olivia tried to get Gary to talk and also to mind her,
but the more she tried, the more withdrawn and defiant he became. She reports that he treats her "pretty much the way my ex-spouse does"—with little
respect and much belittlement. Olivia is self-effacing and believes that she
doesn't deserve much respect. She feels that she doesn't have control over
Gary. At times she becomes so frustrated with him that she resorts to spanking, which only escalates the negative cycle. Olivia's ex-husband calls her frequently and berates her in front of the children. Since he is a mental health
professional, she is convinced that he knows best and she allows him to berate
her.

   Although Olivia felt like a child herself, she recognized that she had to act
as the parent. She tried the program activities with her children—Family Fun
Time, One-on-One Time, and Catch 'Em Being Good. She was surprised that
Gary looked forward to these activities and that she was starting to change the
negative cycle of her relationship with him. She also started using her listening
skills when Gary expressed his anger, and Gary was able to express his feelings
about the divorce in more appropriate ways. Finally, Olivia learned some anger
management skills and refused to participate in verbal fights with her ex-
spouse in front of the children. Although Olivia alternated between being Pam
Permissive and Attila the Mom in her discipline style, she recognized that she
had to make some changes for the children's sake. Even though there was
some testing of limits and "things got worse before they got better," she was
able to become more consistent in managing her children's behavior, and her
relationships with them improved. Olivia didn't make these changes in her relationship overnight, and she needed a great deal of support and instruction from
group leaders and other mothers to effect these changes in herself and her children.

Source: Slightly adapted from Weiss & Wolchik (1998, pp. 470–471).

in the control condition receive the treatment *after* the intervention group. This allows for random assignment to conditions (the key ingredient of an experiment) without denying some participants the benefit of the treatment.

At the conclusion of the intervention program, mothers and children completed questionnaires that contained a variety of social-interaction measures. Children's reports showed significant increases in feelings of acceptance by their mothers, less interparental conflict, and fewer negative divorce events. Mothers' ratings showed increased consistency in the use of discipline, less interparental conflict, and fewer negative divorce-related events. A case description of a mother who went through the New Beginnings Program is provided in Box 5–1.

These results suggest that structured interventions to provide single mothers with specific social interaction skills can produce short-term changes in both children's and mothers' ratings of family dynamics. However, what remains to be seen is whether these changes will eliminate the harmful effects of divorce. That is, does producing positive mother-child interactions lead to fewer behavior problems among the children, better performance in school, or less depression? Based on the existing data, it would seem that the answer is yes. However, future research is needed to examine the long-term effects of these interventions on both family dynamics and social interactions with others.

PREDICTING DIVORCE

Among relationship researchers, no question has attracted more attention than why one close relationship ends and another endures (Bersheid & Reis, 1998). In the sections that follow, we will examine the research on marital satisfaction and divorce. However, it is important to note that not all unhappy marriages end in divorce, for many couples remain married even when the passion and intimacy are gone. Although marital dissatisfaction and divorce are separate concepts, for brevity we will not draw a clear distinction between them.

As we have seen above, one predictor of divorce is having experienced divorce as a child. This general finding has been referred to as the **intergenerational transmission of divorce** (Amato, 1996). There is also substantial evidence that divorce is partially caused by genetic factors. For instance, Jocklin, McGue, and Lykken (1996) found that genetically based personality factors—positive emotionality, negative emotionality, and constraint—led to a greater likelihood of divorce. They concluded that about 20% of the variability in divorce can be explained by personality factors. If so, that leaves 80% of the variability to be explained by social or situational factors.

What are the patterns of social interaction that lead to divorce? In their overview of research on divorce, Everett and Everett (1994) asserted that divorce is usually the result of years of a slowly deteriorating relationship. It is a decision that spouses rarely make at the same time—there is almost always the spouse who leaves and the one who is left. They also point out that staying together for the sake of the children rarely works.

One way of identifying factors that lead to divorce is through a *retrospective study*, in which divorced couples are asked to identify the reasons for their divorce. In a study of 160 divorcing couples, Stewart and her colleagues (1997) examined the process and effects of divorce. Families that had filed for divorce in the Greater Boston area were selected for the study if their physical separation had occurred within six months and they had at least one child between the ages of 6 and 12. Family members completed questionnaires and were interviewed twice over a two-year period. During the interview, parents were asked to describe the *main reasons* for their separation. These categorized responses are shown in Table 5–2. Specific annoying behaviors (e.g., lack of respect or support, spending too many evenings out with friends, lack of commitment to the family or to their responsibilities as husbands and wives) were listed most often, extramarital affairs were second, and serious behavioral problems (like alcoholism, gambling, or physical abuse) were listed third. Stewart et al. (1997) summarized that the high level of reported difficulties in the marriage indicates that "couples had struggled for a long time with minor and major problems and had only gradually concluded that the marriage could not be saved" (p. 54).

Stewart's data provide a glimpse into some of the variables that lead to divorce, but there are several limitations. One is the possibility that couples who remain married might also report these problems with equal frequency; without including couples who do not get divorced in the study, it is impossible to identify the factors that *caused* the divorce (White, 1990). Another is the possibility that retrospective reports may distort or overlook factors that were actually oper-

Table 5–2   Major Problems in the Marriage That Led to Separation

Problem	% Mentioning	
	Mothers	*Fathers*
Specific annoying behaviors	82%	71%
Extramarital affairs	41	41
Serious behavior problems	41	26
Developing in different directions	40	20
Money conflicts	38	38
Child-related conflicts	35	45
Lack of communication	36	32
Irritating personality characteristics	28	36
Physical violence	22	3

Source: Stewart et al. (1997, p. 54).

ating at the time of the divorce. To overcome these limitations, researchers have used longitudinal studies of couples, which measure a variety of factors at several times during the relationship.

Research using this approach has identified several demographic and social psychological variables that predict marital distress and divorce (Amato & Rogers, 1997; Gottman, 1994; Huston & Chorost, 1994). Demographic predictors include marrying at an early age (especially before the age of 20), living together prior to marriage, low income, low education, and being Black. Among possible social psychological predictors of marital satisfaction, five have received considerable research attention.

1. Equity.   Equity is the perception that one's own and one's partner's inputs and outcomes to the relationship are equal—that is, that both get out of the relationship as much as they put into it. Early theoretical work on interdependence theory suggested that equitable relationships should be more satisfying and more likely to last than inequitable relationships (Hatfield et al., 1985; Homans, 1961). However, subsequent research has shown either opposite or inconclusive results. The reason appears to be that most marriages are not based on an **exchange relationship**—the tit-for-tat repayment of benefits. Instead, marriages are **communal relationships**, where partners respond to each other's needs, and do not keep close track of "what you've done for me" (Clark & Mills, 1979, 1993). Research findings clearly show that equity is important for satisfaction with an exchange relationship, but not for communal relationships (Felmlee, Sprecher, & Bassin, 1990).

2. Positive Emotions.   Not surprisingly, marriages in which partners report being more satisfied, and in which divorce is less common, are characterized by frequent positive emotions and behaviors—like smiling, laughing, and agreement.

3. Negative Emotions.   One of the best predictors of marital satisfaction (even better than positive emotions) is a low frequency of negative emotions and behavior (sarcasm, disapproval, insults). However, negative emotions only appear to predict marital satisfaction for wives, but not for husbands (Huston & Vangelisti, 1991). Husbands' negativity toward their wives is a strong predictor of wives' dissatisfaction, but wives' negativity does not predict husbands' dissatisfaction.

4. Negative Affect Reciprocity.   As we discussed at the beginning of the chapter, intimacy can be produced through disclosure-reciprocity, and in fact satisfied couples have a slight tendency to show reciprocity of positive behaviors. In contrast, dissatisfied relationships show high levels of negative-affect reciprocity, wherein partners respond to negative behavior in kind (Levenson & Gottman, 1985; Filsinger & Thoma, 1988).

5. Demand-Withdrawal Interaction.   A final psychological variable pre-
dictive of marital distress is an interaction pattern in which one partner attempts
to discuss a problem and the other withdraws or avoids the issue. Typically, the
wife is the demander and the husband is the withdrawer (Christensen & Heavey,
1990).

An Illustrative Study

A representative study from this area of research was conducted by Amato and
Rogers (1997). Participants in the study were 2,033 married people below the
age of 55 who were initially contacted in 1980. In order to obtain a diverse and
representative sample, the researcher used a **random digit dialing procedure**.
In this procedure, telephone numbers in a targeted area are dialed at random.
The original 2,033 respondents were interviewed again in 1983 ($N = 1,592$), 1988
($N = 1,341$), and 1992 ($N = 1,189$).

Demographic measures included age at marriage, education, income, ethnicity, gender, church attendance, and employment status. Marital problems
were measured using questions dealing with relationship problems such as are
typically listed in retrospective research studies (like those reported in Table 5–2).
Respondents were asked, "Have you had a problem in your marriage because one
of you: (a) gets angry easily, (b) has feelings that are easily hurt, (c) is jealous, (d)
is domineering, (e) is critical, (f) is moody, (g) won't talk to the other, (h) has had
sex with someone else, (i) has irritating habits, (j) is not home enough, (k) spends
money foolishly, (l) drinks or uses drugs?" The study also contained a measure of
physical abuse, but it was excluded from the analysis because abuse was reported
by only a few couples. In 1983, 1988, and 1992 respondents were asked if they
had divorced or separated permanently since the previous interview. During the
12 years of the study, 231 divorces and 33 permanent separations occurred.

Data analyses were based on logistic regression, which used each of the
variables to predict whether the couple was divorced or not. The central issue was
whether a particular problem reported in 1980 increased the likelihood that a
couple would divorce in subsequent years. Combined, the results showed that for
each problem reported by husbands about their wives, the chance of divorce increased by 22%. Similarly, each problem reported by wives about their husbands
increased the chance of divorce by 30%.

A more refined analysis was also conducted based on specific problems. The
results are shown in Table 5–3. The table displays the percentage increase in the
likelihood of divorce associated with the reporting of each problem. Looking across
the rows in the table shows that the strongest predictors of divorce were infidelity,
drinking or using drugs, spending money foolishly, and jealousy. These problems
greatly increased the likelihood of divorce, regardless of which spouse was perceived as having caused the problem. For example, reported infidelity of wives increased the likelihood of divorce by 363%, and of husbands it increased it by 299%.

Table 5–3   Husbands' and Wives' Reports of Particular Marital Problems in 1980 as Predictors of Divorce Between 1980 and 1992.

Problem	Husbands' reports about wives' behavior	Wives' reports about husbands' behavior
Gets angry easily	46%	65%**
Has feelings that are easily hurt	38	7
Is jealous	101**	130***
Is domineering	63	85***
Is critical	93**	98***
Is moody	29	77**
Won't talk to the other	21	46*
Has had sex with someone else	363**	299***
Has irritating habits	127***	92
Is not home enough	−17	105***
Spends money foolishly	77*	187***
Drinks or uses drugs	216*	183***

Note: Table shows the percentage increase in chance of divorce.
* $p < .05$; ** $p < .01$; *** $p < .001$
Source: Amato & Rogers (1997).

The findings from this study are quite consistent with the results from the retrospective study by Stewart et al. (1997). In that study, irritating personal habits, extramarital affairs, serious behavioral problems, and conflicts over money were the strongest predictors of divorce. However, it is noteworthy that each of these behaviors is malleable. Most of the conflict resulting from these behaviors could be eliminated by either changing the behavior or communicating more effectively. In the next section, we examine interventions designed to prevent divorce.

PREVENTING DIVORCE

Through systematic research like that described above, researchers know quite a bit about the causes and consequences of divorce. Moreover, research evidence from several longitudinal studies suggests that the leading risk factors for divorce and marital distress can be overcome through effective communication (Gottman, 1994; Markman & Hahlweg, 1993). Over time, lack of good communication skills undermines marital happiness "through the active erosion of love, sexual attraction, friendship, trust, and commitment. These positive elements of relationships—the reasons people want to be together—do not naturally diminish over time, but are actively eroded by destructive conflict patterns" (Gottman, 1994). Happy marriages still have conflict, but a key difference between successful and unsuccessful marriages is that couples in successful marriages can resolve differences and conflicts without escalating them.

To help strengthen marriages, researchers and therapists work with couples to build positive communication skills and to reduce dysfunctional communication patterns. Using the results presented above about predicting divorce and marital distress, we can identify specific variables to change. First, we need to promote positive emotions. Second, couples need to learn how to stop the reciprocity of negative emotions. Finally, couples need to learn to recognize and avoid the demand-withdrawal interaction pattern (men, this applies especially to you). Two general approaches have been taken to produce these changes. The first is *preventative*; it involves teaching couples how to communicate before marital conflict arises. This can be done in premarital counseling or educational sessions, or early in the marriage. The second approach involves working with couples after the marriage is already in crisis. We will focus here on the preventative approach.

Several programs have been developed to help engaged couples communicate more effectively. Three such programs are Relationship Enhancement (Guerney, 1979), Couples Communication, and Prevention and Relationship Enhancing Program (PREP; Markman et al., 1993).

Prevention and Relationship Enhancing Program (PREP)

PREP is presented as an educational workshop, and not as therapy or counseling. There are different variations of the program, of which the most typical involves six 2-hour sessions. In each session, group leaders present couples with the core themes of the program through brief lectures. Some of the core themes are: recognizing the danger signs, gender differences, learning to be speakers and listeners, problem solving, handling conflict, forgiveness, commitment, and learning to preserve and enhance fun. Within each of these core themes of the program, very specific communication skills are taught.

One such technique is the Speaker/Listener Technique, where couples use an object (e.g., a stick) to designate who is the "speaker" and who is the "listener." Each role is characterized by very specific behaviors. For example, the speaker expresses himself or herself honestly. The listener then paraphrases what the speaker has said, without evaluative remarks or rebuttals. This technique is useful for preventing the demand-withdrawal interaction pattern, and also can lead to disclosure reciprocity and an increased sense of intimacy.

A second technique involves "time out" to help stop the escalation of negative emotion and to begin using more positive communication techniques (like Speaker/Listener). A third technique is *love days* in which one partner goes out of his or her way to do positive things for the other. This helps increase the frequency of positive emotions and can also lead to a reciprocation of positive affect.

In addition to the specific positive communication techniques, couples also learn to recognize certain thinking styles. One of the warning signs of a deteriorating marriage is **negative interpretations**, in which partners make internal, global, and stable attributions for their partners' irritating behaviors (note the parallels with Chapter 3's discussion of pessimistic explanatory style). For example, imagine that a couple is shopping at a mall. Because of their different interests, they separate and agree to meet at 1:00 in the food court. But one of the partners is late. At 1:15, the waiting partner gets angry. At last, at 1:20 when the other partner arrives, the waiting partner says, "You're always so inconsiderate—you never think about me." Note that the irritating behavior (being late) was attributed to the partner (inconsiderate) and not to the situation (perhaps a long line at the check-out counter). PREP helps couples to recognize this pattern of thinking and avoid it.

Evaluating PREP

Evaluation of PREP began in 1980 with 135 couples who were planning to get married for the first time, and who went through the program. For comparison, a sample of couples that were told nothing about PREP was obtained, as well as a sample of couples that declined to participate in PREP. About once every year and a half, couples from each group completed questionnaires, and were videotaped communicating about an issue. These data served as the basis for evaluation.

Results showed support for the program's effectiveness (Stanley et al., 1995). Five years after marriage, significantly fewer of the couples that had participated in PREP were divorced (8%), compared to 19% of the couples that did not participate in PREP (Markman et al., 1993). Twelve years after marriage, 19% of the PREP group were divorced, compared with 28% of the control group, but this difference was no longer statistically significant (Markman et al., 1993). Analyses of the changes in communication skills showed that PREP couples had more positive communication patterns than control couples, but that the difference between the two groups decreased over time (Markman et al., 1988; Renick et al., 1992). Analyses of self-reported marital-satisfaction data showed similar patterns. After three years, PREP couples were more satisfied with their marriage than control couples (Markman et al., 1988). In fact, PREP couples had remained high in marital satisfaction since their wedding, whereas control couples had significantly decreased in satisfaction. Five year after marriage, these results were still significant for PREP husbands, but not for PREP wives.

These findings suggest that premarital educational sessions can have a positive effect on a couple's patterns of communication, and that these changes are linked with five-year increases in marital satisfaction and decreased divorce rates. Other evaluations tend to show similar patterns. PREP has been used in many different countries (e.g., Australia, Germany, Holland), and has been sanctioned by the German archdiocese for Catholic couples seeking premarital counseling. It is also widely used by the U.S. Navy.

SUMMARY

Social psychologists have developed considerable knowledge about relationships, ranging from friendships to marriage. One approach to the study of love relationships is Sternberg's triangular theory, which conceptualizes love relationships as varying in degrees of passion, intimacy, and commitment. One of the keys to a lasting love relationship is the transition from passionate to companionate love. Foremost in this transition is the maintenance of intimacy.

Most Americans believe in the importance and permanence of marriage, and research shows that marriage has many benefits to psychological and physical health. Unfortunately, many hopeful marriages end in divorce. Currently, divorce rates are at about 4.4 per 1,000 adults—a rate that has remained at high levels since the late 1960s. Approximately 50% of all U.S. marriages end in divorce.

Despite earlier claims that children were resilient and unharmed by divorce, current evidence indicates that divorce has small, but consistent, harmful effects on a substantial proportion of children. These effects range from worse performance in school, increased behavior problems, and greater rates of depression, to long-term effects on psychological health, income, and the ability to maintain stable relationships. Fortunately, some intervention research has shown that these harmful effects can be reduced through parent-training programs.

Studies on the prediction and prevention of divorce have identified several social psychological variables that are associated with marital distress. These include less positive affect, a greater frequency of negative affect and behavior by husbands, negative affect reciprocity, and a demand-withdrawal interaction pattern.

Longitudinal intervention studies have helped couples to deal with conflict positively and avoid both negative affect reciprocity and the demand-withdrawal interaction pattern. By teaching couples effective listening techniques, how to recognize negative affect, and strategies for increasing fun and positive affect in relationships, psychologists have contributed to making marriages more satisfying and lasting.

KEY CONCEPTS

Commitment   the strength of a person's intention to continue a relationship.

Communal relationship   relationships based on meeting the perceived needs of the partner, without expectations of exact repayment.

Delayed treatment design   a study in which participants are randomly assigned to conditions, and the participants in the control condition receive the treatment at the end of the study.

Demand-withdrawal interaction   an interaction pattern in which one partner attempts to discuss a problem and the other withdraws or avoids the issue. Typically, the wife is the demander and the husband is the withdrawer.

Disclosure reciprocity   the tendency for one's level of self-disclosure to match that of one's partner.

Equity   the perception that one's own and one's partner's inputs and outcomes in the relationship are equal.

Exchange relationship   relationships based on the tit-for-tat repayment of benefits.

Intergenerational transmission of divorce   the research finding that children whose parents get divorced are more likely to have their marriages end in divorce than are children from intact families.

Intimacy   the feeling of closeness in a relationship.

Negative interpretations   attributing a partner's irritating behaviors to internal, global, and stable sources.

Passion   the physical attraction in a love relationship.

Random digit dialing   a sampling procedure in which telephone numbers in a targeted area are dialed at random.

Retrospective study   a study in which participants' recollections of past events are used to predict subsequent behaviors.

Self-disclosure   the process of revealing important aspects of oneself to others.

REVIEW QUESTIONS

1. Describe the components in Sternberg's triangular theory of love.
2. Mention four factors that are predictors of divorce. From a social psychological perspective, explain why each factor causes divorce.
3. Define and give an example of a communal and an exchange relationship.
4. The case of Mary and Michael Maxwell opened this chapter. Describe three specific behaviors that Mary and Michael could have changed in order to make their relationship more rewarding, and possibly save their marriage.
5. Mary and Michael wanted to make their separation as easy as possible for their three children. What specific behaviors could they have used to help their children adjust to divorce?

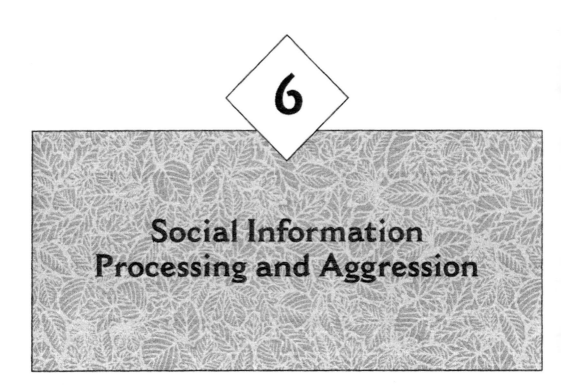

Social Information Processing and Aggression

Jonesboro is a conservative, family-oriented town about 120 miles northeast of Little Rock, Arkansas. Like residents of many small towns, parents in Jonesboro thought that their children were safe from the violence of big cities. Also like many small towns, guns and hunting are a way of life in Jonesboro, and boys are taught to shoot early in childhood.

Eleven-year-old Drew Golden was one such boy. Drew was born and raised in Jonesboro, and he was already learning to handle a gun. In a gully near his house, Drew's grandfather had built him a stand so that he could watch the deer. He had killed his first duck the year before and planned to go deer hunting in the fall. In Jonesboro, most of the boys go hunting for deer, birds, and rabbits with their fathers when they are still in elementary school. But guns fired at people are still something seen only in television and movies.

On Wednesday, March 25, 1998, 11-year-old Drew Golden and his 13-year-old friend Mitch Johnson settled into position at the edge of the woods behind the Jonesboro Westside Middle School. They were wearing full camouflage outfits and armed with semiautomatic hunting rifles that they had taken from Drew's grandfather's house. Inside the school, the sixth-grade students filed out of their classrooms for a fire drill. The children walked down a long corridor, and out the back door onto a muddy lawn. Then Drew and Mitch opened fire on the children and their teachers.

Five people were killed in the ambush, four sixth-grade girls and their teacher; nine other children and another teacher were wounded. (Adapted from Kifner, 1998.)

What do you think led these two boys to act with such violence? Are their parents to blame? Did watching television and movies give these boys ideas about violence? Do you think they were born aggressive? What role did the availability of guns in Jonesboro play?

We live in a violent society. We watch violent movies; we like violent sports; we use violence to discipline our children; as a nation, we wage war on other countries. In fact, the United States is one the most violent countries in the world. Homicide rates in the United States have risen sharply over the past 20 years, and homicide is the second leading cause of death among young people between the ages of 15 and 24. In 1994, more than 23,000 people were murdered in the United States. In that same year, an estimated 4,513,000 acts of violence occurred (Bureau of Justice Statistics, 1997).

School campuses have not been exempt from the increase in violence, and children's school experiences are increasingly becoming violent. Surveys of urban high schools have found high incidences of fighting, bullying, harassment, and the presence of weapons. In the 1996–97 school year, 10% of public schools in the United States reported at least one serious violent crime (defined as murder, rape, suicide, physical attack or fight with a weapon, or robbery; National Center for Education Statistics, 1998). In attempts to protect themselves from this violence, many students are bringing weapons to school. In a survey of students in a large urban high school in Southern California, 6% of the students reported bringing a gun to school at least once in the past year, and 33% of the students reported seeing a gun at school (Schultz & Schultz, 1996). Similar results have been found in other urban areas (Centers for Disease Control, 1991; Sheley, McGee, & Wright, 1992). Consider the following instances of violence reported during public hearings on violence and youth (Eron & Slaby, 1994):

- In Dallas, Texas, a Hispanic boy received 17 stitches at the emergency room after being beaten up because he had stepped on someone's shoe without saying "excuse me."
- A teenage boy in Brooklyn, New York, asked his mother for $150 to buy some new gym shoes. He used the money instead to buy a bulletproof vest.
- A 10-year-old Chicago boy stated, "You can't go outside. You got to duck and dive from the bullets."

These cases, like the Jonesboro case used to open this chapter, and the 1999 massacre that killed 16 students and a teacher in a Littleton, Colorado, high school illustrate the pressing need to understand and reduce violent behavior in our society. In this chapter, we will review research on the causes of violence, discuss methods of predicting who will act violently, and describe some recent interventions designed to reduce violent behavior.

UNDERSTANDING THE CAUSES OF VIOLENT BEHAVIOR

Aggression is an appropriate topic for social psychology because it always involves two persons—a victim and an aggressor. **Aggression** is defined as any behavior that is intended to hurt another living being (Baron & Richardson, 1994). **Violence** refers to extreme acts of physical aggression. Note that *intention to hurt* is a key component of aggression. By this definition, an accidental injury is not an aggressive act. It is useful to differentiate hostile aggression and instrumental aggression. *Instrumental aggression* is a behavior that is intended to hurt another living being, but where the aggression is motivated to achieve a goal. An example is a football player who intentionally hurts an opponent in order to gain an advantage on the field and win the game. By contrast, *hostile aggression* is solely intended to cause harm—for instance, a husband punching his wife during a heated argument (Baron & Richardson, 1994).

What causes aggressive behavior? Is aggression innate and unavoidable, or is it learned through experiences and therefore potentially preventable? At present, there is no unified theory of human aggression. However, over 100 years of research have produced some clear findings. At present, social psychologists have a good understanding of the many factors that contribute to aggressive behavior and can predict with considerable accuracy who is likely to act aggressively and the situations that are likely to produce these behaviors. In this section, we will briefly review some of the established research findings on the causes of aggressive behavior. We will then present a broad social psychological theory of aggression and violence.

The Biology of Aggression

One of the first explanations for human aggression was a biological one—that aggression is a biological drive, and that humans are born with aggressive tendencies. Early advocates of this perspective included William James, Sigmund Freud, and Konrad Lorenz. They argued that aggression was an innate human characteristic. Lorenz (1966), for instance, suggested that aggressive behavior is adaptive, and that aggression gives organisms an advantage in competing with others for food, territory, and mates.

There is considerable evidence that aggression is, at least partly, biologically based. Researchers in this area have focused heavily on the role of hormones in causing aggression. One hormone in particular, the male sex hormone testosterone, has been identified as an important chemical in aggressive behavior. Although both men and women have testosterone, males typically have more testosterone and less estrogen than females. Testosterone levels in males peak during puberty (at which time males also show the highest levels of aggression) and drop as men age (as does aggression; Barfield, 1984). In a convincing series of quasi-experimental studies, Dabbs and his colleagues examined prison inmates and found that prisoners incarcerated for committing violent crimes had significantly higher testosterone levels than prisoners incarcerated for nonviolent offenses. This finding held true for both male and female offenders (Dabbs et al., 1995).

This, and other data from animals and humans, suggest that testosterone plays an important role in aggressive behavior. However, it is *not* the case that high levels of testosterone compel a person to act violently. Indeed, most people, although they may feel an impulse to act aggressively, do not act on it. For instance, an anonymous survey of 312 college undergraduates asked whether they had ever seriously thought about killing someone. Overall, 68% of the students (73% of the males and 66% of the females) said that they had entertained this thought at least once in their lives. Many of the students reported having such thoughts in the past year, but none of them had acted on these thoughts (Kenrick & Sheets, 1993). This suggests that most people can control their aggressive tendencies and *not* act on them.

In summarizing the data on the biological basis of aggression, Geen (1998, p. 321) stated:

> Biological variables are best understood as moderator variables in human aggression. . . . [They] contribute to the base level of aggressiveness of the individual and thereby help to determine the type and magnitude of responses to situational provocations.

Thus, in order to understand *when* a person will act aggressively, we need to explore theories of aggression as a reaction to situational provocations; we need a more social psychological perspective.

Frustration

The frustration-aggression hypothesis was one of the first systematic theories that attempted to describe when a person would act aggressively (Dollard et al., 1939). The theory proposed that all acts of aggression are due to frustration. **Frustration** is an aversive feeling that occurs when a person is blocked from achieving a goal. A more recent version of this theory suggests that frustration will only lead to aggression if it produces a negative emotion like anger (Berkowitz, 1989).

A common belief about frustration is that it creates pent-up energy that must eventually be released. That is, even if a person does not act out the aggression immediately, the frustration will build up energy that must eventually come out. The release of unexpressed emotional energy was termed *catharsis* by Freud. The concept of catharsis suggests that it may be possible to "get out" aggressive urges in a safer, more controlled manner (like hitting a punching bag or watching a violent movie). However, the research on this topic clearly shows that this prediction (and the general notion of catharsis) is wrong. In fact, the research suggests that the opposite is true—acting aggressively (or even watching someone else act aggressively) usually leads to *more* aggression (Zillmann, 1994).

Social Learning

Another useful theory for understanding aggressive behavior is social learning theory. The social learning perspective proposes that aggression, like other social behaviors, is learned (Bandura, 1973, 1986). By watching how other people act, we learn who is an appropriate target for aggression, what actions by others should lead to an aggressive response, and in what situations aggression is appropriate.

There are "rules" or norms for acting aggressively in any society, and children learn these rules by watching other people. For instance, even if directly challenged, a grade school child knows that fighting with another student is not appropriate inside a classroom; they must "take it outside." These rules are learned by observing when an aggressive behavior is rewarded and when it is punished. Over time, children develop a set of expectations about the likely consequences of their own behavior. When they attempt to duplicate an observed behavior, they are either rewarded or punished. The social learning perspective holds that a child "who attains valuable ends through aggressing in certain situations comes to believe that further aggression will continue to deliver worthwhile rewards" (Geen, 1998).

Social Information Processing

The social learning theory described above suggests that aggressive behavior is determined largely by one's expectations about the outcome of the behavior. That is, people will act aggressively if they believe that the behavior is likely to lead to a worthwhile outcome. This assumes that social behavior requires an ability to understand one's social world. A person who is deficient in the ability to understand

and respond to social cues is likely to act in ways that are socially inappropriate. We turn now to a broad social psychological theory of aggressive behavior.

The social information processing theory is often used to explain social adjustment and maladjustment. **Social adjustment** is the degree to which children get along with their peers. Adjusted children engage in competent social behavior and inhibit behaviors that would hurt themselves or others (Crick & Dodge, 1994). According to this theory, most aggression (e.g., starting fights, hitting, or threatening) is the behavior of a maladjusted child. Hence, to understand aggression, we need to understand the factors that lead to social adjustment.

The social information processing model of social adjustment is shown in Figure 6–1. Although the focus of the research has been on children, presumably

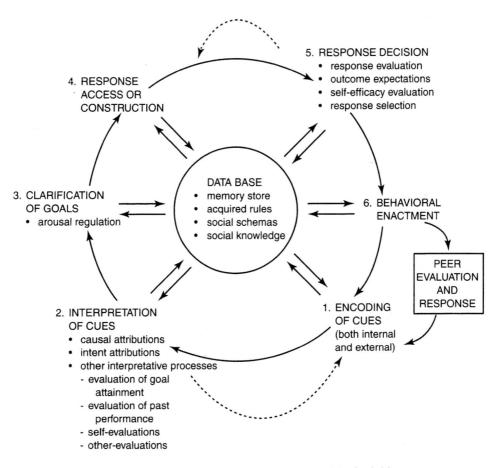

Figure 6–1   A Social Information-Processing Model of Children's Social Adjustment. *Source:* Crick & Dodge (1994, p. 76).

the same model holds for adult maladjustment as well. The basic premise of the theory is that children come to a social situation with biologically limited capabilities and a "database" of memories and past experiences (Crick & Dodge, 1994). From this database of past experiences, they attempt to interpret the behavior of others and select a course of action that, from the child's perspective, will likely lead to a desired outcome. There are six steps in this process.

1. Encoding of cues.
2. Interpretation of cues.
3. Clarification of goals.
4. Response access or construction.
5. Response decision
6. Behavioral enactment.

In steps 1 and 2, children are perceiving and making sense of their social setting. These processes are aided by schemas. A **schema** is a cognitive organization of past experiences, beliefs, and knowledge about types of persons, events, roles, or casual relationships (Fiske & Taylor, 1991). Both the encoding and interpretation of social cues are influenced by schemas (i.e., from their "database"). Past experiences and expectations guide which aspects of a social setting capture the child's attention, and also how the child interprets these cues. One important part of the interpretation stage is making attributions about the behaviors of others. As we saw in Chapter 3, **attributions** are beliefs about the causes of observed events. For instance, *why* did that person look at me that way? Do they like me? Dislike me? Do I look funny? One's past experiences and memories will help in interpreting the available social cues. Aggressive children are substantially more likely than nonaggressive children to attribute hostile intentions to other people's actions (Waas, 1988).

In step 3, the child selects a goal or outcome for social interaction. For instance, what do I expect to get out of this? Do I intend to stay out of trouble? Get even? Make a new friend? Obtain a toy? Avoid embarrassment? Oftentimes, aggressive behavior is triggered by goals that are damaging to relationships—like "winning" or "getting even." In contrast, prosocial behavior is often produced by relationship-enhancing goals—like being helpful or liked.

In step 4, children access possible responses from memory. These are ideas about how they could act in a certain situation (e.g., how can I resolve this conflict?). Children who are less well-adjusted are more likely to recall responses that are aggressive or unfriendly. Research suggests that aggressive children tend to lack schemas for achieving positive social goals. Schemas for appropriate sequences of events in well-known situations are referred to as *scripts*. For instance, an aggressive child might not have a script for making a new friend or for entering a conversation. Subsequently, when such a child is in a situation where it is necessary to approach a group of people and enter a conversation, he will do so inappropriately and may produce aggressive responses. In addition, aggressive children tend to access fewer possible behaviors than do less aggressive children.

In step 5, children evaluate the responses they accessed in Step 4 and select the one that is most likely to achieve their goal. In making this assessment, children consider the type of outcome they desire and their ability to perform the response. They consider the possible, and expected, outcomes of each recalled behavior. Aggressive children tend to expect more positive outcomes from aggressive behavior (Crick & Dodge, 1994).

Finally, in step 6, individuals act on their selected behavior.

THE STABILITY OF AGGRESSION

Aggression and violence are not mysterious behaviors that suddenly appear. Indeed, the social information processing theory described above suggests that aggression is directly linked to the ways in which people process social information, and that these *ways* of processing are learned early in life.

There is considerable evidence that a person's level of aggression is relatively stable across time (Eron & Huesmann, 1990). In an influential paper, Olweus (1979) reviewed 16 longitudinal studies in which aggression was measured at two times in the participants' lives. Measures of aggression included clinical ratings, ratings by teachers, ratings by other children, and direct observation. From each study, Olweus extracted the correlation coefficient between the two measures of aggression.

The results showed a high level of stability of aggression across time—those people who were aggressive at time 1 tended to be aggressive at time 2. The strength of the stability varied by age, with older participants showing more stability than younger ones. For instance, children as young as 3 years old showed a high level of stability over a one-year period ($r = .88$; unfortunately, no longer-term data were available for children this young. Children aged 8 showed stability 10–14 years later ($r = .48$). Children aged 12 showed stability over five years of .78, and 17-year-olds showed stability over 13 years ($r = .91$). More recently, Eron (1987) reported a stability of $r = .50$ for males and $r = .35$ for females over a 22-year period (from age 8 to age 30). Taken together, these findings show that an individual's level of aggression is very stable over time.

INTERVENTIONS TO REDUCE VIOLENCE

The research we have discussed so far clearly shows that aggression is not determined solely from biological factors, and we have introduced a social psychological theory to help understand aggressive behavior. From the social information processing theory, we learned that aggressive children (1) are more likely to interpret the behavior of others as hostile, (2) are more likely to retrieve aggressive responses from memory, and (3) are more likely to evaluate aggressive responses positively. In short, aggressive people lack the schemas necessary for positive social interaction.

This theory can be applied to help reduce aggression. The six stages in the social information processing model represent clear targets for intervention. For example, helping people to develop schemas for responding to conflict and interacting positively with others should lead to more adaptive social behavior and less aggression. We turn now to an example in which the basic findings from the social information processing theory are incorporated into a program to reduce aggression.

Social Competence Training

Social competence training is a broad term used to describe interventions aimed at providing schemas for positive social interaction. The approach is based on the assumption that violence is the response of a person who lacks the skills necessary to manage conflict with others. "Much of children's aggression with peers derives not from an excess of meanness, hostility, or aggressive energy, but rather from a lack of fundamental skills in solving problems effectively and nonviolently" (Slaby et al., 1995, p. 97). A child who learns how to assert needs, express anger without hurting others, and respond constructively to the anger of others will be less likely to respond with violence (Prothrow-Stith & Weissman, 1991). For many people, this is a novel approach to solving problems. They are raised with the belief that some situations *require* a violent response (e.g., if your mother is insulted, if you are insulted in front of others, or if you are directly challenged). Consider the following statements and decide whether you agree or disagree with each:

- A person ought to fight if challenged to fight.
- When a boy is growing up, it's important for him to have a few fist fights.
- Some people don't understand anything but force.

Survey data show that a majority of Americans agree with each of these statements (Prothrow-Stith & Weissman, 1991).

Some Components of Social Competence Interventions. Since the introduction of social competence training programs, a great many programs have been developed. Programs like Second Step, S.A.V.E. (Students Against Violence Everywhere), and the Resolving Conflict Creatively Program aim to reduce the frequency of violent behavior. Because aggressive behavioral patterns begin early in life and are relatively stable across a person's lifetime, it is important to intervene early. Most of these programs are intended for grade school children, with a few targeting junior high and high school students. Social competence training programs use a combination of the following techniques. As you read the following features of competence training programs, note that each is tied to a step in the social information processing theory.

Monitoring.   Students are taught to observe their own thoughts, feelings, and behaviors. This is often accomplished through behavior-recording exercises—for example, tallying the number of times they act in a particular way or experience a particular feeling during the day. By monitoring their feelings, children learn to identify their own strong emotions (e.g., anger, fear, sadness) and to realize that these are acceptable and normal feelings. Another aspect of monitoring is developing the ability to recognize the emotions in others—sometimes referred to as *empathy training*. Both of these techniques target step 2 in the social information processing theory.

Modeling.   Students observe a nonviolent response to a variety of provoking situations, such as failure, expressing a complaint, responding to anger, or being excluded. This process uses the concept of **role models**—individuals whose pattern of behavior is observed and then used to guide future thoughts, feelings, and behaviors. Although children's role models are often adults, the most common models are peers. A child who watches another child succeed (e.g., gaining material objects, favorable reactions from other children, or attention from teachers or adults) by acting aggressively is considerably more likely to imitate the aggressive behavior—"if it worked for you, maybe it will work for me." In social competence training, nonaggressive role models are often introduced through books, puppets, plays, or videos. These techniques target step 4 in the social information processing model.

Conflict Resolution.   Students are taught to recognize the early signs of a conflict and learn specific strategies to avoid escalation. An important aspect of conflict resolution involves generating various solutions and evaluating their consequences. Some of the early interventions in this area were intended to get children to generate as many solutions and consequences to a situation as they could. After writing their solutions down, students would share their responses with groups of peers, who then discussed likely consequences for each behavior. Such techniques target step 5 in the social information processing model.

Role-Playing.   Students in social competence training often engage in role-playing by responding to an acted-out situation. Other students watch and evaluate their responses and later practice desirable actions. These techniques target step 6 in the social information processing model.

Does social skills training work? One problem with the literature in this area is that many of the programs have not been empirically evaluated, making it difficult to know with any confidence whether the programs are producing any effects (Beelmann et al., 1994). However, there have been a few carefully conducted studies of these interventions.

An Illustrative Study

One violence prevention program that has had a considerable amount of study is Second Step. The Second Step program takes a pragmatic approach and draws on several social psychological theories—foremost of which is the social information processing theory. The program consists of curricula that target four age groups: prekindergarten, first- to third-graders, fourth- to fifth-graders, and junior high students. Our focus will be on the curriculum targeting first- to third-graders.

Each lesson lasts approximately 35 minutes and is typically taught once per week. The lessons consist of photographs accompanied by a social scenario. Each scenario describes a situation that requires problem solving and specific social skills. A sample picture and scenario are shown in Figure 6–2. After discussing the problem, the teacher models the behavior and encourages the kids to role-play. Lessons are divided into three units.

- **Empathy training**—students try to identify their own feelings and the feelings of the people shown in the picture.
- **Anger management**—students are given a specific coping strategy or social skill for tense situations and are asked to role-play how to use the skill.
- **Impulse control**—students are presented with a potential conflict and are asked to think about effective solutions.

Note that each of these units has clear connections with the social information processing theory. Empathy training targets step 2 (interpretation of cues). Anger management targets step 4 (response access). Impulse control fits with step 5 (response decision).

So the program is grounded in social psychological theory—but is it effective? Several studies have been conducted on the Second Step program. Grossman et al. (1997) reported an evaluation of the first- to third-grade Second Step curriculum. The study, funded by the Centers for Disease Control (CDC), was conducted in 12 elementary schools over a one-year period. None of the 12 schools had used the Second Step program prior to the study, and all schools agreed not to implement other violence prevention programs while the study was being conducted. Each school was paired with the most similar other school, based on the proportion of students receiving free lunch and the proportion of minority students enrolled at the school. One school from each pair was then randomly assigned to an intervention group or a control group. In each school, two second-grade and two third-grade classrooms were selected to participate in the study (49 classrooms in all). The curriculum was implemented in the intervention schools over a 16–20 week period during the spring of 1994. There were 418 children in the intervention condition and 372 in the control condition.

Outcome data were collected at three times: prior to the start of the program (during the fall of 1993), two weeks following the end of the program

Erica   Dennis

Figure 6–2 Sample Photograph and Social Scenario from the Second
Step Violence Prevention Curriculum. "In today's lesson you will learn
how to deal with wanting something that isn't yours. (*Teacher shows the
picture.*) Dennis and Erica are in an after-school play group. Dennis has
brought his new game this afternoon. Erica wants to play with it, but
Dennis says that only one person can play with the game at a time.
What is the problem? What might happen if Erica takes the game away
from Dennis? What are some other solutions to Erica's problem?"
Source: Committee for Children, 1992.

(spring, 1994), and six months after the end of the program (fall, 1994). Multiple
measures of aggressive behavior were used. First, direct observations were made
for each child in the study. Two observers used a behavior-coding system to rate
three types of social behavior: verbal aggression, physical aggression, and neu-
tral/prosocial behavior. Each child was observed for a total of 60 minutes. Observers followed the class throughout the day, so behaviors were coded in a
variety of settings, including the classroom and the playground. Observers were
blind to the study's purpose, hypotheses, or design. Other measures of student
aggression included teacher ratings and parent ratings. Teacher ratings of each
student were obtained using a standard measure (the Achenbach Teacher Report
Form). Parents used an analogous scale. The scale contained questions about a
variety of social behaviors, but for our purposes, we will focus on the aggressive
behavior subscale.

Before describing the results, it is important to consider the study's design.
Although the design was an experiment, the data analysis was not. Random assignment was based on schools ($N = 12$) and not on students ($N = 790$), but because the analyses were of individual students rather than schools, this was a

quasi-experimental study. The researchers used statistical techniques to control for many extraneous variables that might influence aggression, like gender, socioeconomic status, household size, classroom size, and quality of curriculum implementation. To simplify, we will examine the basic findings without controlling for other variables. However, the findings reported here were not changed when background variables were statistically controlled.

The results from direct observations of the intervention group showed a significant *decrease* in both physical and verbal aggression from baseline (T_0) to postintervention (T_1) and from baseline to follow-up (T_2). These results were especially strong on the playground and in the cafeteria, and less so in the classroom. Students in the control group showed significant *increases* in both verbal and physical aggression from baseline to post-intervention and from baseline to follow-up. However, the aggression ratings obtained from teachers and from parents showed no significant change in either the intervention or control conditions. Key results are illustrated in Figure 6–3.

The researchers concluded that the Second Step violence prevention curriculum "appears to lead to modest reductions in levels of aggressive behavior, and increases in neutral/prosocial behavior in schools among second and third graders. Some of these effects appear to persist at 6 months following exposure" (p. 1611). The researchers suggested that parents and teachers may not have had the opportunity to witness aggression (most of the aggression occurred on the

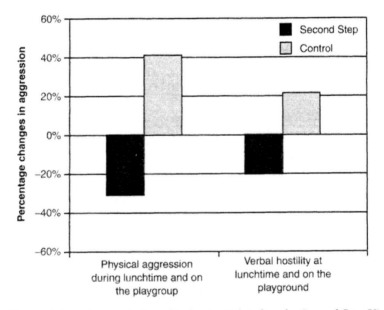

Figure 6–3 Changes in Social Behavior Related to the Second Step Violence Prevention Program: Fall to Spring. *Source:* Frey & Sylvester (1997).

playground). An alternative explanation is that both teachers and parents had clear expectations for each child, and once formed, expectations are difficult to change—even when the child's behavior changes.

VIOLENCE IN THE MEDIA

Our discussion of the social information processing theory suggests that children learn the rules for aggressiveness—who is an appropriate target, when we should be aggressive, and in what types of settings. In our society, much of this learning is apt to come from television.

The average U.S. household is exposed to approximately 55 hours of television per week (8 hours per day), with the average viewer over the age of 2 watching more than three hours per day (Andreasen, 1994). For the average American, almost from birth up through old age, television constitutes a large part of our daily activities. In fact, next to sleeping and school (or work), television is the activity that occupies the largest amount of the U.S. public's time.

So what are people watching on television? About 80% of all TV dramatic programs contain one or more violent episodes, while in some seasons 100% of network children's programs and cartoons have contained violent episodes (Liebert & Sprafkin, 1988). Prime-time TV dramas have an average of about three acts of violence during each program hour, but children's cartoons average about *32 violent acts per hour* (Gerbner, 1993).

Consider the following statement by Leonard Eron (1987, p. 440), one of the leading researchers on the effects of television:

> We consider continued television violence viewing as rehearsal of aggressive sequences. Thus, one who watches more aggressive sequences on television should have more aggressive strategies more strongly encoded and should respond more aggressively when presented with similar or relevant cues. From an information-processing perspective . . . [television] plays an important role by providing standards and values against which a child can compare his or her own behavior and the behavior of others to judge whether they are appropriate. The encoding and maintenance of appropriate standards are critical variables that distinguish aggressive from nonaggressive children.

This statement provides several theoretically based reasons for why watching television would lead to more aggression. In terms of the social information processing theory, television affects each of the six steps and provides viewers with the database with which to interpret the behavior of others and select a course of action.

Effects of Television on Violent Behavior

Research on media violence has been interpreted as providing evidence of a *cultivation effect*. That is, the violence that is so pervasive in many of the mass media is seen as having a conditioning or adaptation effect on viewers, implanting and cultivating the idea that violence in society is common, natural, and acceptable. Accordingly, research shows that heavy TV viewers (more than 30 hours per week) are more likely than light viewers to perceive high chances of encountering violence, to be afraid to walk around their neighborhood at night, to feel mistrustful of other people, and to believe that they live in a "mean world" (Gerbner et al., 1994).

Going beyond cultivation effects, much social psychological research has focused on the question of a direct causal effect of TV violence in making viewers *more violent or aggressive themselves.* This causal hypothesis was supported by the Surgeon General's Scientific Advisory Committee (1972), which concluded that television violence was probably a contributory cause of increased aggressive behavior among young viewers, and it was advanced even more strongly by the 10-year follow-up report from the National Institute of Mental Health (1982). What is the scientific evidence for this view?

Laboratory Experiments.   Some of the evidence began back around 1960 with Bandura's famous laboratory studies, in which children who had viewed filmed aggressive acts against large Bobo dolls later imitated the same actions themselves (Bandura, Ross, & Ross, 1963). Subsequent experiments showed that young boys and girls would also imitate filmed aggressive acts against live human beings. The laboratory studies since the 1960s have consistently shown that viewing violence on television can cause an increase in aggression immediately following the exposure (Hearold, 1986). Furthermore, these effects are more pronounced among people who are already predisposed to act in an aggressive manner (Josephson, 1987). Another effect of viewing media violence that has been demonstrated in laboratory experiments is *desensitization,* or lowered emotional sensitivity to violence, and this can increase children's and college students' tolerance for real-life aggression (Cline, Croft, & Courrier, 1973; Thomas et al., 1977).

A major question about all such laboratory experiments is their external validity. The studies typically take place in circumstances so different from normal TV viewing or other media use that their findings may not be applicable to real-world media issues. Therefore, many correlational studies and field experiments have been done in more realistic settings in order to investigate questions about the effects of media violence. Here the emphasis is usually not on imitation of a specific act seen in the media, but rather on the relationship between continued exposure to media violence and a pattern of heightened aggressive behavior of many sorts in everyday situations—that is, a pattern of general disinhibition of aggression (Liebert & Schwartzberg, 1977).

Correlational Research.   Studies using correlational methods have consistently found positive relationships between the amount of television a person watches and his or her levels of aggression. In a number of studies, with children ranging from third grade through high school, dependent measures which showed significant relationships to amount of violent TV viewing included deviant acts, such as:

- Petty delinquency by both boys and girls (McIntyre & Teevan, 1972)
- Having been in serious fights or hurt someone else badly (Robinson & Bachman, 1972)
- Conflict with parents, fighting, and delinquent behavior (McCarthy et al., 1975)
- Perceived effectiveness of aggression and stated willingness to use it oneself, in both American and English samples of boys and girls (McLeod, Atkin, & Chaffee, 1972)

Many of these relationships held up well even when statistical controls were introduced by holding constant the children's social class, school grades, or amount of exposure to nonviolent television.

An excellent example of the correlational data on television and aggression was reported by Eron (1987). The data were based on a 22-year longitudinal study, which began in 1960 with assessments of 870 children (average age of 8). In 1970, 427 of the original children were reassessed (average age of 19). At this time, records were also obtained from the state justice department on their criminal activities. A third wave of data was collected in 1981 from 414 of the original subjects (average age of 30), and again criminal data were obtained from the state justice department.

A sample of the results is shown in Figure 6–4. The figure shows the seriousness of criminal acts by age 30, separated by amount of television viewing at age 8 (low, medium, and high) and also by gender. Seriousness of criminal activity was based on a widely used rating system by the Criminal Justice Division for each type of offense. The results shown in the figure indicate that, overall, males committed more serious crimes than females. For our purposes, the most striking finding is for television viewing: children who watched more TV at age 8 were considerably more likely to commit serious crimes by age 30. This relationship was true for both men and women. Note that the independent variable here was TV watching in general, not watching especially violent programs. It is possible that people who watched the most violent programs might have been even more influenced toward crime and aggression.

Adding together the findings from laboratory experiments, field experiments, and correlational studies, the principle that media violence can increase viewers' interpersonal aggression seems to be thoroughly established (Friedrich-Cofer & Huston, 1986). The conclusion that media violence leads to an increase in aggression was supported in a review of 28 laboratory and field experiments on the effects of television on aggressive behavior in children and adolescents (Wood et al., 1991). The results indicated that viewing media violence significantly in-

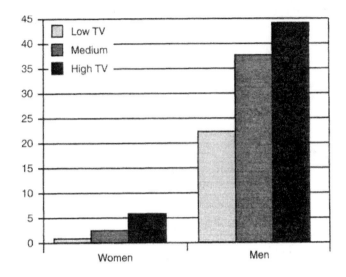

Figure 6–4 Seriousness of Criminal Acts by Age 30 as a Function of Frequency of TV Viewing at Age 8. *Source:* Adapted from Eron (1987).

creased aggressive interactions with strangers, classmates, and friends in both field and laboratory settings—although the results were stronger for laboratory studies.

The research findings on the effects of television clearly show the potential for harmful consequences. Particularly disturbing are the findings that watching violent television can *cause* an increase in aggressive behavior, that most children watch more than 30 hours of TV per week, and that children's television is particularly violent. Faced with these findings, researchers in the 1980s began to develop interventions designed to reduce or eliminate the link between watching violent television and aggressive behavior. These interventions were directed at children, and were typically implemented in school classrooms (Neuman, 1991).

Critical Television Viewing Skills

In a series of large-scale studies sponsored by the Office of Education and the National PTA, educators and social psychologists began developing a curriculum aimed at making children more critical consumers of television. These programs were designed (1) to demystify the television process by showing children how TV shows were made, and (2) to teach children to critically evaluate the messages they received from TV. It was hoped that such interventions would reduce the cultivation effects of television. Unfortunately, these early projects were not systematically evaluated (Eron, 1986; Neuman, 1991). Because the funding agencies did not require an evaluation, the funds were devoted to developing the program and not to determining whether or not it actually worked.

Fortunately, several smaller viewing-skills projects did collect evaluation data (e.g., Singer, Zuckerman, & Singer, 1980). The results from these studies showed that the critical viewing interventions did increase the *amount* of information a child could remember after watching a show. However, the interventions did not make the children more critical of the content, and more importantly, did not make them less aggressive. More recent studies have continued to show significant changes in knowledge or attitudes, but have typically not found (or not examined) changes in behavior (e.g., Vooijs & Van der Voort, 1993).

One often-cited example of effective critical viewing interventions was a longitudinal study by Huesmann et al. (1983). Participants in the study were 672 first- and third-grade children. Of these children, the 25% who watched the most television were selected for an experimental study. These 170 high-violence viewers were randomly assigned to either the experimental or a placebo condition. Unlike other critical-viewing studies, these researchers used social psychological persuasion techniques to change the children's attitudes toward television. Children were persuaded that "watching TV violence was not desirable and that they should not imitate violent television programs" (p. 904). To produce these attitudes, the researchers used *counter-attitudinal advocacy* techniques, where children wrote arguments that were opposite to their original attitude (they orginally liked violent TV shows). The results showed that the technique did in fact change attitudes. More importantly, the results showed that the children in the experimental condition were significantly less aggressive (as rated by their peers) after one year than children in the control condition ($d = -.39$).

Despite the encouraging results from this study, the amount of research devoted to the issue of critical television viewing has fallen off. As Neuman (1991, p. 116) stated:

> Curiously, the great impetus to protect children from television's excesses, as well as to enhance their selectivity and learning from the medium, quickly faded after these projects were completed. Begun in the 1980s, most did not endure past 1983. Whether it was the failure to produce demonstrable changes in children's viewing habits or whether these curricula simply demanded too much from the schools can never be determined.

In the 1990s the pendulum appears to have swung back toward regulation. Instead of relying on parents to teach or protect their children, there has been a greater emphasis on controlling the content of television shows. One notable development in the attempt to limit the amount of violence on television is the so-called violence-chip, or V-chip. This is an electronic device that will allow viewers to block programs with certain content codes. The television networks have voluntarily agreed to develop a content-rating system, much like the one used by the Motion Picture Association, and to broadcast these ratings with each program. Beginning January 1, 2000, all new television sets are required to come equipped

Box 6–1   Tools for Preventing Violence in Young Children

1. **Help children to avoid becoming victims.** Teach children to use assertiveness skills to avoid submitting to aggression, bossiness, or discriminatory acts. Children can be taught to stand up directly to an aggressive peer and only then to call for adult help if needed. Submission leads to victimization and rewards the aggressor.

2. **Reduce disciplinary violence toward children.** Hitting, spanking, paddling, or beating children will produce short-term changes in behavior, but in the long run will result in increased aggression. Other nonviolent techniques, like prohibiting desired activities, or "time-out," are equally effective at producing short-term compliance and produce substantially lower levels of aggression in the long run.

3. **Teach children safety responses to extreme violence.** Teach children *not* to intervene and when and how to seek shelter and help.

4. **Eliminate the frustration of abrupt transitions, excessive waiting, or sitting for long time periods.** Provide children with a clear set of guidelines and expectations, and give them regular feedback. For instance, "We're going to leave in five minutes, finish your game." A balanced set of activities with smooth transitions can eliminate many routine sources of frustration for children.

5. **Choose books and stories that support prosocial and nonviolent themes.**

6. **Involve children in discussions about alternative solutions to problems and their consequences.** Remind children that hitting hurts and fighting makes people unhappy. Help them discover alternative, nonviolent actions that would make them feel better.

7. **Provide children with practice in thinking of solutions, anticipating consequences, and evaluating the harmfulness of aggressive solutions.**

8. **Recognize a child's right to choose not to share.** Avoid forcing a child to give up an object in the name of sharing. Teach children that saying no is OK and how to accept no for an answer.

10. **Encourage children to label their own feelings and tell each other how they feel.** Talk about your own feelings and ask children how they feel in an atmosphere of understanding and acceptance.

11. **Reduce children's viewing of violence, and increase their viewing of prosocial television programming.**

Adapted from Slaby, Roedell, Arezzo, & Hendrix (1995).

with a V-chip. As of 1999, the television networks were working with the FCC to develop an effective rating system, but there are few efforts to reduce the amount of violence portrayed in the media.

RECOMMENDATIONS FOR REDUCING VIOLENCE

A recent book by Slaby and colleagues (1995) outlined a variety of techniques that parents, caregivers, and educators can use to prevent children from acting aggressively. Many of these techniques are consistent with the social information processing theory described in this chapter. Box 6–1 briefly summarizes some of these techniques.

SUMMARY

Aggression and violence are social problems to which social psychology can be applied. Research on the causes of aggression has identified a variety of biological and psychological factors that can lead to violent behavior. On the biological side, the data clearly show that high levels of testosterone make a person more likely to act aggressively. On the psychological side, research has demonstrated that frustration can often produce aggressive behavior, especially if the frustration leads to anger.

The social information processing theory is a broad social psychological theory that can explain social adjustment and maladjustment. The basic premise of the model is that people come to a social situation with biologically limited capabilities and a set of schemas based on past experiences. These schemas are used to interpret the behavior of others and to select a course of action that will likely lead to a desired outcome. There are six steps in this process: encoding of cues, interpretation of cues, clarification of goals, response access, response decision, and behavioral enactment. Once formed, a person's level of aggression is relatively stable across his or her lifespan.

A variety of interventions have been developed to reduce violent behavior. One of the most widely used approaches is social competence training, which is based on the assumption that aggression is largely due to a lack of skills (i.e., schemas) necessary for positive social interaction. Social competence training programs use techniques such as monitoring, modeling, conflict resolution, role-playing, and peer mediation to teach the necessary skills. Research on programs like Second Step indicates that these techniques can significantly reduce the frequency of aggressive behavior in children.

One important factor that contributes to the high level of violence in our society is television. On average, children watch more than 30 hours of television per week, and most of the television contains violent scenes. Correlational and experimental research on the effects of television converge to show that watching violence on television can cause an increase in subsequent aggressive behavior.

Given the causal connection between television and aggressive behavior, it is important to explore possible techniques that would eliminate the effects of watching violent TV. One such technique is critical television viewing—an approach which teaches children to be critical of the information shown on TV. The few evaluations that have been reported of critical viewing suggests that they do not lead to reductions in aggression, but one notable exception by Huesmann et al. (1983) showed that using counter-attitudinal persuasion techniques could change children's attitudes about violent television, and it significantly reduced their levels of aggression. A variety of other techniques to help reduce children's aggression have been proposed by Slaby et al. (1995).

KEY CONCEPTS

Aggression   any behavior that is intended to hurt another living being.

Counter-attitudinal essay   a technique used to change attitudes in which people write an argument that is opposite to their original attitude.

Critical-viewing skills   programs designed to teach children to critically evaluate messages received from television and to demystify the television process.

Cultivation effect   view that television creates in viewers the idea that violence is common, natural, and acceptable.

Frustration   an aversive feeling that occurs when a person is blocked from achieving a goal.

Monitoring   a technique used in social competence training programs where students learn to observe and recognize their own thoughts, feelings, or behaviors.

Script   schema for the appropriate sequences of events in a well-known situation.

Second Step   a violence reduction program based on social psychological theory.

Social adjustment   the degree to which children get along with their peers.

Social competence training   interventions aimed at providing schemas for positive social interaction.

Social information processing   a six-step theory for human aggression that includes encoding of cues, interpretation of cues, clarification of goals, response access, response decision, and behavioral enactment.

Social learning   theory that human behavior is learned by watching others.

Stability of aggressive behavior   evidence showing that aggressive behavior is relatively stable across time.

Testosterone   the male sex hormone.

Violence   extreme acts of aggression.

REVIEW QUESTIONS

1. Define aggression and violence. Give an example of each.
2. Describe the social information processing model of aggressive behavior.
3. For each step in the social information processing model, describe a specific technique that would help reduce the likelihood of aggressive behavior.
4. Based on the social information processing model, discuss three ways in which watching television could lead to an increase in aggressive behavior.
6. What does the research suggest about the effects of watching violence on television?
7. Briefly summarize the research on critical viewing skills. Based on the social information processing model, speculate about three ways that teaching critical viewing skills could be more effective.
8. Describe the Second Step violence prevention program and the research findings by Grossman et al. (1997).

PART FOUR

Applied
Social
Influence

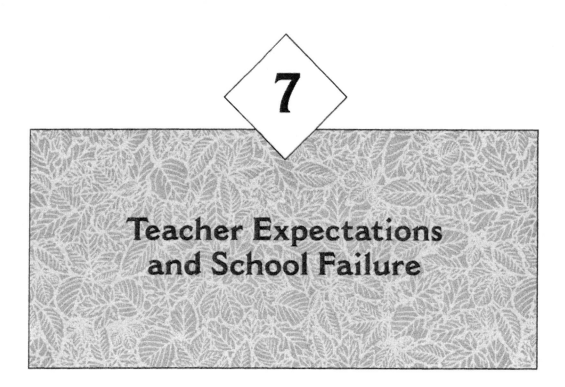

7

Teacher Expectations and School Failure

Manuel Reyes was 15 when he dropped out of school. The tatoos on his arms, long dangling earrings, and large baggy pants hint at his life experiences. At 15, he was a member of a gang; he stole cars and spent his evenings selling $20 bags of cocaine on the streets of East Dallas. "I was like crazy," he says. "When you're crazy, you're cool." He was caught selling drugs three times, was arrested for possessing a handgun, and received 15 traffic tickets by the time he was 19. His father remembers those days, "He was out of control the majority of the time."

His parents, Manuel, Sr., and Julie, were both dropouts from school. His mother was 15 when she married his father, who was 16. His mother dropped out when they got married, his father had dropped out during elementary school to help take care of his younger siblings. They divorced when Manuel was 5, and Manuel switched back and forth between his two parents. By the time he started high school, he had attended eight different schools. Neither parent was equipped to show their children how to succeed in school or how to avoid trouble. "We moved all the time," remembers Manuel's mom, "We never had any money. We got kicked out of apartments. We were irresponsible." (Adapted from Wertheimer, 1998.)

What factors do you think contributed to Manuel's dropping out of school? What could have been done to prevent it? What consequences do you think not having a high school diploma will have for Manuel's future?

What is it that leads one child to succeed in school and another child to fail? Answers that come to mind include the student's ability, parental support, self-esteem, peers, and school facilities. Of all the contemporary issues worked on by social psychologists, possibly their greatest public influence has been on the topic of education. Social psychological research evidence was used in the famous 1954 Supreme Court school desegregation case, *Brown v. Board of Education of Topeka, Kansas*, and in the years since then many researchers have done studies on the educational process and on the effects of diversity in the classroom. In recent years, social psychological research has examined issues surrounding bilingual education, teacher-student interactions, and school failure.

THE PROBLEM OF SCHOOL FAILURE

School failure is a serious social problem in the United States. Although students drop out of school for a variety of reasons, one of the most common is a sustained pattern of failure in class (Schwartz, 1995). In 1996, slightly more than 11% of students had dropped out of school. For some ethnic minorities the percentages are considerably higher. For instance, in 1996, 7.3% of White young adults between the ages of 16 and 24 were out of school without a high school diploma, while the percentage for Hispanic students was 29% and for Black students was 11%. Hispanic students born outside the United States have an even higher dropout rate of 44%. Of the foreign-born Hispanic youths who were dropouts, more than half had never enrolled in a U.S. school, and 80% of these young adults were either speaking English "not well" or "not at all." Although the percentage of students who do not complete high school has been steadily declining over the last 25 years (more so for White and Black students than for Hispanics), the dropout rate translates into more than 3 million students each year (McMillen, 1997).

The costs of failure in school are high. Compared to students who complete high school, individuals who drop out are more likely to be unemployed, more likely to be arrested for a crime, and have lower self-esteem and more mental health problems. Note that we have implied that school failure *causes* these problems. As we discussed in Chapter 2, it is important to recognize that just because two variables are correlated with each other (like school failure and unemployment) it does not mean that one caused the other. In the absence of an experiment where students are randomly assigned to either fail or succeed in school, it is impossible to know for sure whether school failure *causes* unemployment, or alternatively whether some other variable causes both unemployment and school failure.

Returning to the central question in this chapter: What leads one child to succeed in school and another to fail? From a social psychological perspective, we can ask: What aspects of a child's social environment increase his or her chances of success in school? And second, can we change some aspect of this social environment to improve the chances of success?

Two general approaches to studying this issue have been taken: student-centered and school-centered. The student-centered approach focuses on the qualities of the students and attempts to improve their likelihood of success by providing a more enriching social environment during early childhood. We will discuss this approach briefly below. The second approach to reducing school failure focuses on student-teacher interactions within the theoretical context of the self-fulfilling prophecy. We will discuss this approach later in the chapter.

A STUDENT-CENTERED APPROACH

In any classroom, students will have a variety of abilities. Their differing abilities may be cognitive, social, or physical, and can facilitate or impede their education. The greater the diversity of students, the more difficult it is to educate them all simultaneously in one classroom. American schools, and most schools around the world, attempt to reduce the heterogeneity of student ability by grouping students according to chronological age and classifying them at ability levels within each age group. Other controversial bases for reducing the heterogeneity of students in the classroom is grouping based on gender (i.e., all-female and all-male classrooms; deGroot, 1994) and grouping based on ethnicity (e.g., all-Black or all-Hispanic classes; Frieberg, 1991). However, no group of students will ever have completely equal abilities. In the section that follows, we will discuss, from a social psychological perspective, some of the issues that arise in educating students with differing abilities.

Head Start

During the 1960s, government officials became aware that half of the 30 million Americans living in poverty were children, and that a large percentage of low-income households were headed by a person who had dropped out of school (Zigler & Muenchow, 1992; Zigler, Styfco, & Gilman, 1993). Psychologists and policy-makers reasoned that part of the cause for poverty was school failure, and therefore increasing the academic achievement of low-income children would help break the cycle of poverty. It was recognized that in low-income households, many children did not receive the kind of social and educational background necessary to succeed in school, and thus they were behind from the beginning of the school process.

Through the Economic Opportunity Act of 1964, the Head Start program was established. The program was developed as a way to reach children from low-income families and provide them with the background necessary to succeed in school. The ultimate goal of the Head Start program was for all children to be "school ready" by the time they entered the public education system. In this sense it was a preventive program rather than a remedial one. It targeted children between the ages of 0 and 3 years, and it was anticipated to expand its coverage to grade-school-aged children (Kennedy, 1993). As with many large government programs, when Head Start was first established, it was not based on a solid foundation of scientific evidence. As Zigler et al. (1993) noted: "Head Start began as a hastily assembled but immense program built more on professional intuition than on scientific fact" (p. 6).

Despite this lack of an explicit initial theoretical basis, Head Start became a national laboratory, and has continued to be thoroughly studied and evaluated. Early evaluations of the Head Start program focused especially on increases in intelligence. Research showing higher IQ scores for children who graduated from Head Start than for comparable samples of non–Head Start children attracted nationwide attention. However, the enthusiasm over Head Start was dampened when a highly publicized Westinghouse research report showed that the gains in IQ and school achievement "faded out" over time. Subsequent research has confirmed the short-term gains in intelligence, and has also demonstrated a wide range of other advantages of the program, including better health, better social adjustment, improved academic performance, better high school graduation rates, greater employment rates after graduation, less juvenile delinquency and criminality, and lower teen pregnancy rates (Copple, Cline, & Smith, 1987; McKey et al., 1985).

An Illustrative Evaluation of Head Start. To help you understand the effects of Head Start, and to illustrate the type of evaluation research being done, let us consider a recent study funded by the National Science Foundation (Currie & Thomas, 1995). The purpose of this study was to compare children who had been through the Head Start program with a comparable group of children who had not been through the program. Thus, the study was quasi-experimental—existing groups of children were being compared. Almost all of the research on Head Start is quasi-experimental because of the difficulty in randomly assigning children to either a Head Start or a control condition.

All children who enter the Head Start program are assessed on a variety of measures, including a physical examination, immunization records, blood tests, and cognitive ability. For our purposes, we will examine the results for two measures: a standardized measure of academic ability (the Peabody Picture Vocabulary Test) and whether the child had to repeat a grade. Both of these variables are strongly associated with high school completion (Ensminger & Slusarcick, 1992).

Data for this study were taken from an outgrowth of the National Longitudinal Study of Youth (NLSY). The NLSY began in 1979 with a nationwide sample of 6,283 young women. These women, and the more than 8,500 children born to them, have been measured repeatedly since 1979. From this sample, approximately 4,787 children were identified who had at least one sibling. Children with siblings were needed because the siblings served as a control group in this study. Of these children, 3,285 were White and 1,502 were Black.

To test the effects of Head Start, Currie and Thomas (1995) compared children who had gone through the Head Start program with their siblings who either had attended another preschool program or had not attended any preschool program. The children who were selected varied in age, and some had attended the Head Start program up to 10 years earlier (the children were measured in 1989 and the longitudinal study began in 1979). The comparison of Head Start children to their siblings is an important aspect of this study because siblings are similar along many dimensions: they share the same parents, socioeconomic background, neighborhood, and so on. Comparisons were made separately for White and Black children.

The first set of analyses used the entire sample of children without regard to age. Thus, the researchers were testing for *general* effects of the Head Start program across all ages of children in the study. The results for White children showed that, compared to siblings who had attended another preschool, Head Start children scored 5 percentile points higher on the standardized measure of academic ability ($d = .11$; $N = 2,319$; $p < .01$). In addition, White students who attended Head Start were 40% less likely to have repeated a grade than their siblings who attended another preschool ($d = -.28$; $N = 414$; $p < .01$). The differences were even more pronounced for comparisons in which one sibling attended Head Start and the other did not attend any preschool.

The results for Black students were markedly different. For Black students, there was no difference in academic ability between students who attended Head Start and their siblings who had attended another type of preschool ($d = .01$; $N = 1,158$; $p > .05$). In addition, there was no significant Head Start advantage for having to repeat a grade ($d = .12$; $N = 314$; $p > .05$). Thus, Head Start was associated with higher achievement scores among White students but not among Black students.

Additional analyses examined the impact of the Head Start program relative to the current age of the child—that is, the number of years it had been since the child had completed the program. The results indicated that Black children showed positive effects for Head Start almost identical to those found for White children for the first few years after completing the program, but that the effects decreased over time. That is, for the first few years after completing the Head Start program, Black children showed an increase in their academic achievement scores relative to their siblings, but by age 10 the effect had disappeared. In contrast, White students showed both a short-term and a long-term gain in academic achievement from the Head Start program. As Currie and Thomas (1995, p. 358) stated:

> Our results for African-Americans are thus consistent with those of earlier studies (which tended to be dominated by African-American subjects). When we focus on only young African-American children, we find clear benefits for Head Start. However, in a sample of African-American children of all ages, there is no effect of Head Start. This is because the benefits die out very quickly. In contrast, white children experience the same initial gains from Head Start, but they retain these benefits for a much longer period.

As the research on the Head Start program continues, it is sure to bring with it changes in the program which will be aimed at reducing the rate of school failure. Research like the study by Currie and Thomas (1995) has helped increase public and governmental support for the Head Start program, and allowed the program to expand and cover a wider range of ages. The program currently extends services through age 5, and is projected to expand to cover all grade-school-aged children. In fiscal year 1994, the program received approximately $7.7 billion in federal funding, and served more than 541,000 children (Zigler et al., 1993).

Bilingual Education

Another issue that arises in diverse classroom settings is **bilingual education**. National surveys of academic achievement have consistently found that minority students, especially those with low English proficiency, are at risk for academic failure (Steinberg, Blinde, & Chan, 1984). Particularly in cities with a high immigrant population, an important question is whether students with limited English proficiency should be taught in a bilingual classroom—that is, one where teachers speak and teach in both English and the student's native language—or whether they should be immersed in an English-only instructional program. At issue are both the benefits to the child and the costs to society.

Many authors have asserted that the public school system is intended to provide similar educations to all members of our diverse populace. Therefore, classroom environments in which immigrant students do not receive an equal quality of education because of a language barrier are detrimental to this goal (DeVillar, 1994). From this perspective, students should be taught in their own language, at least until they have developed adequate English proficiency. For this reason as well as others, the multicultural movement in the American education system advocates the need for bilingual education. On the other hand, providing a similar education to all also implies that all students should eventually learn to read and speak English at an acceptable level.

From an applied perspective, the central question is whether or not students with low English proficiency are better served by special bilingual classrooms, or by **mainstreaming** them with the other children. That is, which approach produces the most beneficial results for the student? In this line of research, "beneficial" results are usually measured in terms of subsequent academic achievement and levels of English proficiency.

Costs and ideology aside, the available data indicate that low-English-proficiency students taught in a bilingual classroom require less time to master the English language and score higher on standardized math and vocabulary tests (Gonzalez, 1994; Ramirez, 1986; Willig, 1985). However, nearly all of the studies conducted in this area have been quasi-experiments in which students enrolled in different types of programs are compared, and these comparison groups are never fully equivalent. Other limitations of the research are that many studies have high attrition rates, they frequently lack complete data on many students, and usually no distinction is made between immigrant children and children who are not immigrants but whose parents do not speak English. Nevertheless, the available data do suggest that bilingual classrooms facilitate mastery of the English language, after which point their graduates can be mainstreamed with the other students.

Despite the clear evidence, several states (most recently California) have enacted "English only" policies which dictate how non-English-speaking students (most of whom speak Spanish) are taught in public schools. Such policies are based largely on ideology and not on careful empirical data, and they provide an example of what happens when social psychological research is *not* applied to a social problem.

A SCHOOL-CENTERED APPROACH

In March of 1996, President Clinton met with state governors, business leaders, and educators from all 50 U.S. states for a National Education Summit. The goal of the meeting was to develop and implement nationwide standards for school achievement. The issue of national educational standards is a controversial one because it applies the same standard across all students. This issue pits the rights of parents, communities, and states to set their own standards against the nation's need to improve the quality of public education. Consider the following quotation, taken from the summit:

As Governors and leaders of American businesses we have a stake in the quality and performance of schools in this nation. We are united by our civic responsibilities, our concerns as parents, and our common interest in securing a
prosperous future for our states and companies in the twenty-first century. We
are compelled by the urgent need for schools to improve and for student academic performance to rise. Students must be challenged to perform at higher
academic levels and be expected to demonstrate mastery of core academic
subjects. (National Education Summit, 1996)

Note that one of the key elements of this quotation involves expectations: students must be "expected to demonstrate mastery."

Calls for national standards are often made without reference to the process
by which the standards will produce increases in achievement. How is it that
changing the expectations for student performance will change actual performance? As Weinstein (1996) put it, "Attention must be paid to changing the limiting beliefs about differential ability to learn and self-defeating teaching methods
that follow from such beliefs." The point that Weinstein is making is that teachers' beliefs about student ability can influence student performance, and in order
for national standards to be effective, teachers must believe that *all* students are
able to achieve the new goals.

Self-Fulfilling Prophecies

Social psychological research on the effects of teacher expectations goes back
more than 30 years. In a classic book entitled *Pygmalion in the Classroom*, Rosenthal and Jacobson (1968) evoked much controversy in both psychology and education. In their book, Rosenthal and Jacobsen claimed that the expectations held
by a teacher had a direct causal influence on the subsequent development of students, and this claim was supported with results from an experimental study in
which students in several classes were randomly selected and identified to their
teachers as likely to "bloom" that year. This finding has been termed the **Pygmalion effect.**

The study was conducted at a public elementary school, referred to as Oak
School. The school was described as "lower-class," and the students were low
achievers. The school used a tracking system where children were sorted into one
of three tracks (fast, medium, and slow) based on reading performance. There
were approximately 600 students in the school.

In the spring of 1964, students at the school completed the "Harvard Test
of Inflection," which was purported to predict academic blooming. In reality, the
test contained a standardized measure of intelligence (IQ). All teachers at the
school were given the written description of the Harvard Test of Inflection that is
shown in Box 7–1. The flyer was distributed to all teachers three times during the
next year. The pretest data showed that the average boy at Oak School had an IQ
of 98 and the average girl had an IQ of 99.

Box 7-1   Description of "Harvard Test of Inflection"

All children show hills, plateaus, and valleys in their scholastic progress. The study being conducted at Harvard with the support of the National Science Foundation is interested in those children who show an unusual forward spurt of academic progress. These spurts can and do occur at any level of academic and intellectual functioning. When these spurts occur in children who have not been functioning too well academically, the result is familiarly referred to as "late blooming."

As part of our study we are further validating a test which predicts the likelihood that a child will show an inflection point or "spurt" within the near future. This test which will be administered in your school will allow us to predict which youngsters are most likely to show an academic spurt. The top 20 percent (approximately) of the scorers on this test will probably be found at various levels of academic functioning.

The development of the test for predicting inflections or "spurts" is not yet such that *every* one of the top 20 percent of the children *will* show the spurt or "blooming" effect. But the top 20 percent of the children will show a more significant inflection or spurt in their learning within the next year or less than will the remaining 80 percent of the children.

Because of the experimental nature of the tests, basic principles of test construction do not permit us to discuss the test or test scores either with the parents or the children themselves.

Upon completion of this study, participating districts will be advised of the results.

Source: Rosenthal & Jacobson (1968).

At the beginning of the following school year, the researchers randomly selected 20% of the student population at Oak School and assigned these students the status of being academic bloomers. Their names were included on a list which was sent to their teacher, stating that they might find it of interest to know which of their students were about to bloom. The teachers were asked not to discuss the test findings with the students or the parents. It is important to emphasize that the children were selected at random, and did not differ from the other students in any way except in the minds of the teachers.

At the end of the year, the Harvard Test of Inflection was administered again. The end-of-year IQ scores of children labeled as bloomers were compared with the IQ scores of children without the label. Results from the study are shown in Figure 7-1. As shown in the figure, the average IQ scores of the chil-

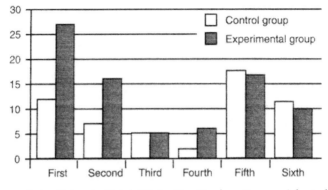

Figure 7–1 Gains in Total IQ in Six Grades. *Source:* Adapted from Rosenthal & Jacobson (1968).

dren increased across the year. However, the students in the experimental condition ($N = 65$) gained 12 IQ points over the year, while control students ($N = 255$) gained 8 points ($d = .35$; $p < .05$). As seen in the figure, the largest gains in IQ were for the first- and second-grade children, who gained 27 and 16 IQ points respectively.

The importance of these findings is not just in the positive effects of labeling children as bloomers and encouraging high expectations for them. The other side of the coin is the potential harm that teachers might do to their students through low expectations, which has been termed the **Golem effect** (Babad, Inbar, & Rosenthal, 1982). The potential for negative consequences of teacher expectations is especially problematic in ethnically diverse classrooms, where minority students may be more likely to receive expectations of lower ability. These expectations are then likely to be confirmed through student-teacher interactions.

The Pygmalion effect can be incorporated into a broader theoretical perspective. The **self-fulfilling prophecy** is a broad social psychological theory which states that a person's expectations about someone (the target) influence interactions in such a way that the target acts in a manner consistent with the expectations. Thus, the expectations become a reality. The Pygmalion effect is a specific instance of the self-fulfilling prophecy that occurs within an educational setting.

In the following sections, we will address four key issues. First, do teacher expectations influence student performance? The study by Rosenthal and Jacobson (1968) suggests that the answer is yes, but clearly we need more evidence on this issue. Second, how do the expectations become reality? Third, what are the expectations for minority students in comparison to White students? And finally, how can research knowledge be used to increase student performance on a large scale?

Do Expectations Affect Performance?

This is the most fundamental question regarding the Pygmalion effect. Although the question may appear simple, it is difficult to determine whether changes or differences in student performance are directly caused by teachers' expectations rather than by other variables. Many other potential variables (e.g., intelligence, motivation, level of aspiration, and/or parental support) could be responsible for what appears to be a teacher-expectancy effect. The original Pygmalion study produced a flurry of research, and after more than 30 years, it is possible to review and synthesize these studies into some solid conclusions.

Rosenthal and Rubin (1978) reviewed the results of 345 studies on interpersonal expectancies, and concluded that teacher expectations *do* influence student performance. This conclusion has been echoed in many subsequent studies and reviews (e.g., Harris & Rosenthal, 1985). The cumulative weight of these findings led Cooper (1993) to call the effects of interpersonal expectations a "social fact"—a strong conclusion from a science that bases findings on probabilities and statistical analyses.

How large are the effects produced by teachers? Can a teacher's expectations turn a failing student into an honor student, or vice versa? Even if the research findings support the existence of a teacher-expectancy effect, how much difference can a teacher's expectations really make in a student's performance? The research to date suggests that comparing the performance of students for whom teachers have high expectations with students for whom teachers have low expectations yields a large average effect size (d) of 1.00 (Babad, 1993; Brophy, 1983). However, it is important to note that this effect size is from experiments in which expectations regarding students are provided by the researchers. Similar effects have been found in natural contexts, although the size of the effect is typically smaller (Jussim & Eccles, 1995)

The Process of Expectancy Confirmation

Given that researchers have established that the expectations held by teachers can affect their students, the second question is how this process occurs. Methodologically, this question becomes a search for mediating variables that produce the expectation-confirmation relationship. Since the publication of the original Pygmalion research, a great many studies have investigated the self-fulfilling prophecy—many of these studies focusing on classroom settings. The cumulative results from these studies show that teachers behave in ways that lead students to act consistently with their expectations. For example, students who are perceived as low in ability tend to be called on less often in class, receive less eye contact from their teachers, and in general do not get the same amount of attention as students perceived to have high ability.

Research on the Pygmalion effect has attempted to pinpoint the types of teacher behaviors that lead students to act in ways consistent with their expectations. Some of the factors that have emerged from this research include:

1. **Climate**—teachers' affective behaviors (e.g., warmth, support, smiling, eye contact) and the socio-emotional climate they create for high- and low-expectancy students. In general, teachers tend to create a more positive learning atmosphere for the high-achieving students. For example, low-achieving students are more likely to be told about classroom or work rules, they are more likely to be punished for breaking these rules, and they are more likely to be told what to do. As one student put it, "The teacher doesn't usually work with [the smart kids] because they know how to do their stuff" (Weinstein & McKnown, in press).

2. **Feedback**—teachers' praise and criticism of students. Teachers tend to give more negative feedback, like scolding a student for not listening or not trying, to low-achieving students. Teachers also tend to give more positive feedback to high-achieving students. For example, "Like today, the teacher gave me an award saying I was the second top in the class" (Weinstein & McKnown, in press).

3. **Input**—the amount or difficulty of material presented to the student. Teachers tend to provide more opportunities, more choices, and more challenging work for higher achievers. As one student stated, "The way you know a person is smart, Miss ___ always picks on them to go different places" (Weinstein & McKnown, in press).

4. **Output**—opportunities for the student to respond. These include frequency of contact between the student and teacher, such as questions asked by the teacher (Harris, 1993; Rosenthal, 1978; Weinstein & McKnown, in press).

Through these types of behaviors, teachers influence the actions of their students. These interaction patterns "create, expand, or constrain opportunities for all children to learn and demonstrate that learning, thus resulting in comparable or differential educational experiences for different students" (Weinstein & McKnown, in press).

It is important to add that not all classrooms are characterized by such a high degree of differential treatment. In many classrooms, ability differences between students are not made salient. One fourth-grade student, who was in such a classroom, stated that "people who used to not be so smart, they're smart now" (Weinstein & McKnown, in press). Several master's theses and doctoral dissertations completed at the University of California, Berkeley, have examined the effects of low- versus high-differential treatment classrooms (e.g., Alvidrez, 1994; Brattesani, 1984; Jones, 1989; Kuklinski, 1992). These studies suggest that in classrooms characterized by high levels of differential treatment, children's expectations for themselves tend to match more closely with the teacher's expectations. That is, in high-differential-treatment classrooms, student performance is more likely to be influenced by the teacher's expectations. Later in this section, we will describe research on an intervention intended to create an equitable classroom atmosphere.

Figure 7-2 What expectations might this teacher have for her students? What strategies could she use to create an equitable classroom atmosphere?

Expectations Concerning Minority Students

One central assumption of the Pygmalion effect is that many of the expectations held by teachers are not accurate. However, because students must be randomly assigned to conditions, any experimental study of teacher expectations necessarily introduces biased information about the students. It is possible that this type of research is misleading. What if teachers usually form correct expectations for their students? In this case, the expectation process would not be changing the student in any way, but instead reaffirming student abilities (Brophy, 1985; Jussim, 1993; Madon et al., 1997).

The belief that teachers form accurate expectations about their students rests largely on the assumption that humans are rational processors of information. From this perspective, teachers are viewed as unbiased perceivers who evaluate students solely on information that is relevant to their performance. However, cognitive and social psychological research on interpersonal perception demonstrates that this is far from true. Expectations about behavior come from many sources irrelevant to the actual ability of the student, and they are subject to a multitude of cognitive biases. Particularly relevant to the issue of diversity in educational settings is the fact that expectations about a student are often based on *stereotypes* concerning categories of people that the student belongs to. These categories include gender, ethnicity, social class, and age, to name only a few. In the following brief paragraphs we will focus on ethnicity as a category.

Intuitively, it makes sense that students from minority groups, or other groups about which there are negative stereotypes, would be harmed by the Golem effect. As we saw in Chapter 4, many people are vulnerable to the stereotypes about groups to which they belong. It is probable that teachers would tend to form lower expectations for minority students based not on their ability, but on stereotypes about the group (Alexander & Entwisle, 1987; Jussim et al., 1996). Recall the story of Manuel Reyes presented at the beginning of this chapter. It seems likely that few, if any, teachers would expect Manuel to perform well in school—especially given his background. Indeed, research indicates that Black and Mexican-American students tend to receive lower teacher expectations of mental ability and academic performance than do White students (Baron, Tom, & Cooper, 1985). In addition, students from lower-income backgrounds also tend to receive lower teacher expectations for performance and ability than do students from higher-income backgrounds (Weinstein & McKnown, in press). Given the frequent relationship between ethnic minority status and lower income, this finding adds strength to the notion that teachers will hold lower expectations for minority students (Ferguson, 1998).

Though these findings indicate that teachers will tend to have lower expectations for minority children than for White children, this may not be the case for all teachers. Some teachers may be more resistant to forming lower expectations than others. Just as not all minority students are vulnerable to the negative content of the stereotype, not all teachers have low expectations for minority students. Some teachers may be less swayed by stereotypes, or some interventions may help them avoid the Golem effect.

Interventions to Raise Teacher Expectancies

Thus far, we have seen solid evidence supporting the self-fulfilling prophecy—a theory which leads to the prediction that expectations influence social interactions in such a way that the expectations become reality. We have presented considerable evidence that this theory can be used to understand the academic performance of students, and ultimately to understand school failure. A remaining question is: Can we use this social psychological theory to improve school performance? Here we have an instance where a social psychology theory (self-fulfilling prophecy) can be used as the basis for developing interventions that directly address a social problem (school failure).

To this end, many different interventions have been developed. Most of these interventions are focused either on raising the expectations of the teachers for all students or on making teachers aware of the self-fulfilling prophecy in the hope of preventing these expectations from becoming a reality (Ferguson, 1998). The research on teacher expectations has prompted a national call to raise expectations for all students, particularly those at risk for failure. If a teacher's expectations influence student performance, then raising expectations should cause an increase in student performance. These interventions are typically implemented through in-service training programs for teachers; they attempt to heighten teacher awareness of differential expectations and to change behaviors that lead to confirmation of negative expectations (Weinstein, Madison, & Kuklinski, 1995).

Project PACT.   One example of this type of intervention was reported by Weinstein et al. (1991). The purpose of the study was to increase teachers' awareness of the potential harm resulting from lower expectations for at-risk students (Weinstein, 1998), with the intended goals of (1) raising expectations for student performance, and (2) reducing the confirmation of low expectations.

The participants in the study were all incoming ninth-grade students who had been assigned to the lowest track of English classes at a high school. Over a two-year period, 158 students participated in the experimental program. These students were contrasted with 154 comparable students from the two years prior to the intervention. Thus, the study had a quasi-experimental design. The 158 selected students were 54% male, 68% Black, 7% Hispanic, 11% Asian, and 10% unknown ethnicity. Their scores were in the bottom 25 percentiles on a standardized reading test.

These students were placed in a class taught by a participating teacher. The PACT (Promoting Achievement through Cooperative Teaching) program focused on changing the classroom environment for these at-risk ninth-grade students by providing positive expectations for student achievement. Teachers, administrators, and researchers met weekly to develop, implement, and evaluate the classroom innovations. Weekly meetings focused on curriculum, discussion of individual students, and cooperative classroom strategies. Course materials were selected from the honors-level courses at the school.

The program was evaluated by comparing student records at the end of the ninth-grade and tenth-grade years with students assigned to the same track at the same school two years earlier. Initial comparisons of students in the PACT program with students from the previous two years showed no significant differences in gender, ethnicity, eighth-grade English performance, or number of absences during the eighth grade.

After one year of the intervention, students participating in the project had higher English and history grades than comparable students who did not participate in the project, as well as higher overall GPAs. At the end of the tenth grade,

19% of the students had transferred to a different school, compared to 38% in the two prior years. A year after participating in the intervention, project students were significantly less likely to drop out of high school, and less likely to attend a continuation school than were control students.

The results from this study are encouraging, and they suggest that interventions targeting teacher expectations of student performance can be an effective technique to improve the educational experiences of at-risk students. The findings illustrate how social psychological theories can be applied to practical situations to help solve social problems. Rather than speculating about what will and won't be effective, this case illustrates how theory can provide the basis for intervention, and then scientific methods can be used to evaluate its effectiveness.

Concluding Comments

Throughout the chapter, we have suggested that dropping out of school has negative consequences. However, many dropouts eventually return to school and earn a high school diploma. For instance, Manual Reyes, the Hispanic gang member described at the beginning of the chapter, who dropped out of high school at the age of 15, returned to school four years later to pursue his diploma. In returning to school, he faced very low expectations for his performance. "He looked to me like a hardened criminal," said the assistant principal of the high school. Nevertheless, Manuel graduated from high school in 1998 at the age of 22. He now rents a house with his sister and her two children. He is a full-time maintenance worker at an apartment complex in northeast Dallas. Manuel's story shows that it is possible to succeed even when low expectations and negative past experiences might present difficult obstacles to overcome (Wertheimer, 1998).

SUMMARY

Much social psychological research has focused on the issue of school failure. National studies show that around 11% of students drop out of school, and school failure has negative long-term consequences for children.

There are two general approaches to addressing the issue of school failure. A student-centered approach to understanding and preventing school failure focuses on meeting the needs, or deficiencies, of the student. A pioneering social program for teaching students with differing abilities is the Head Start program, which helps preschool students from a poor socioeconomic background to acquire the skills necessary to succeed in school. Evaluations of the program have demonstrated short-term increases in IQ scores, as well as more long-term improvements in social adjustment, high school graduation rates, less teen pregnancy, and less juvenile delinquency. Research by Currie and Thomas (1995) indicated that Head Start causes both short- and long-term gains in academic performance for White students, but only short-term gains in academic performance for Black students.

Other student-centered educational programs, such as bilingual education, have evoked much controversy. However, empirical data indicate that educating students in their native language has beneficial consequences, with few drawbacks, though policy-makers are often unaware of these social psychological research findings.

A school-centered approach to understanding and preventing school failure focuses not on the students, but on the school system—for example, the teachers and the interpersonal dynamics in the classroom. The Pygmalion effect occurs when teachers act in ways that cause students to fulfill the teachers' expectations. Initial research by Rosenthal and Jacobson (1968) showed that teachers who had expectations that certain children would bloom led these children to perform better than students without this label. More recent research has demonstrated how teachers create self-fulfilling prophecies for their students—through the classroom climate, feedback to students about their performance and abilities, and the opportunities they provide for input to and output from students.

These research findings indicate the likelihood of problems for students who come from a minority group about which teachers may have negative stereotypes and lower expectations. However, research by Weinstein et al. (1991) has demonstrated that interventions with teachers can succeed in reducing the negative consequences of low teacher expectations.

KEY CONCEPTS

Bilingual education   classrooms in which teachers speak and teach in English and in the student's native language.

Golem effect   the potential harm that teachers might have on their students through low expectations.

Head Start   a national program designed to provide children who are at risk for school failure the skills necessary to succeed in school.

Mainstreaming   educational setting in which students with differing abilities are taught in the same classroom.

National Education Summit   a national meeting in which policy-makers, business leaders, and educators met to discuss the development and implementation of national standards for school achievement.

National Longitudinal Study of Youth   an ongoing longitudinal study of more than 6,000 women and their children.

Project PACT   a program developed to reduce the harm caused to students by low teacher expectations, by increasing teachers' standards and making them aware of the Pygmalion effect.

Pygmalion effect   the finding that the expectations held by teachers about their students influence student-teacher interactions in such a way that students often perform in ways consistent with the expectation. It is a specific instance of the self-fulfilling prophecy.

School-centered   an approach for reducing school failure by changing the patterns of student-teacher interactions.

Self-fulfilling prophecy   theory that expectations influence behavior such that the expectations become reality.

Stereotypes   overgeneralized sets of beliefs about members of a particular social group.

Student-centered   an approach to reducing school failure by providing a more enriching social environment during early childhood.

REVIEW QUESTIONS

1. Compare and contrast the school-centered and student-centered approaches to reducing school failure.
2. What are the short-term and long-term effects of Head Start?
3. What is the Pygmalion effect?
4. What are the processes by which teachers' expectations influence student performance?
5. If you were a school administrator, how would you increase the success of the students who are at risk of academic failure in your school?
6. What are the arguments for and against mainstreaming students with low English proficiency? What does the research show?

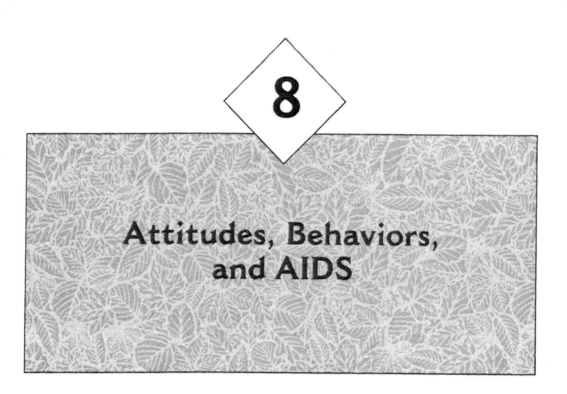

8

Attitudes, Behaviors, and AIDS

George Gannett was a full-time architecture student at the Rhode Island School of Design in Providence. While he studied the nuts and bolts of building codes and regulations, George also restored several of Providence's beautiful but neglected old houses.

George's long-time friend and lover, Peter, had died of AIDS in 1985. "When Peter was sick, attitudes were very different. There was more the feeling, 'we can't discuss this in public.' I think I was as supportive as I could be, for him, but there are times when I think I could have done better."

Two years later, during the summer of 1987, George became constantly tired. He lost 20 pounds. He developed several dark lesions. That fall, at the age of 34, George was diagnosed with AIDS. At that time, he reported, "So far, I haven't felt very sick from AIDS. I have a serious love relationship now. Ron and I met at the march in Washington; we had heard a lot about each other for years, had a lot of friends in common, but had never really connected until then. I'd just been diag-

Figure 8–1   Ron McClelland (left) and George Gannett (right), Boston, August 1988.

nosed, and we were talking about how to proceed with this relationship. I said, 'I hope AIDS doesn't keep us apart.' And he said, 'I really hope AIDS doesn't pull us together.'"

By January 1989, George was in the hospital. AIDS was affecting his vision, his muscle control, his digestion, and his concentration. Friends and family came from California, from Boston, and from Providence, and set up a shifting cordon of support and assistance. After several weeks George decided to stop treatment altogether, and return home. He arranged for a hospital bed to be moved into his living room, and there he stayed. Too weak to walk, eat, or talk, he withdrew from most of his family and ceased taking most of his medicines. Ron spent every weekend, and many evenings, with George. George Gannett died at home on February 27, 1989. (Adapted from Nixon & Nixon, 1991.)

Could George's infection with HIV have been prevented? If so, how? What do you think George's attitudes were toward safe sex in his first relationship with Peter? Do you think that his attitudes and behavior were different during his relationship with Ron?

THE AIDS EPIDEMIC

The AIDS epidemic continues to grow. Acquired Immune Deficiency Syndrome is a disease that results from an infection with the HIV retrovirus—an infection which reduces the body's natural ability to fight off disease. As of 1999, there is no cure or vaccine for AIDS, and once it is contracted AIDS is terminal. Fortunately, unlike colds and other viral infections, HIV can only be transmitted through the exchange of body fluids. Until a vaccine can be discovered to prevent HIV infection, the best strategy for stopping the spread of AIDS is to reduce risky behaviors that could lead to HIV infection.

In this chapter, we will examine how social psychological theory can be used to predict why people engage in risky sexual behavior, and to change these behaviors. We will begin by examining the prevalence of HIV infection and AIDS, and the behaviors that are likely to lead to infection. Then we will discuss the concept of attitudes and the relationship between attitudes and behaviors. Finally, we will describe a large-scale social psychological program designed to reduce behaviors that put a person at risk for HIV infection.

How Widespread Are HIV and AIDS?

Consider the following problem: There is a large pond, and on this pond grow lilypads. The lilypads spread so rapidly that their number doubles every day. On the first day there is one lilypad, on the second day, two, and so on. On what day will the pond be half-covered with lilypads?

Clearly a numerical answer cannot be given to this problem without more information. However, we can say that the pond will be half-covered on the day before the last day. What if instead of a pond and lilypads, we were describing a disease and the human population? On what day would half of the population be infected? On what day should public health protective measures start? Would the day before the last day be too late to intervene?

The first case of AIDS was detected in 1981, and since then the prevalence of AIDS has grown dramatically. As of 1998, an estimated 30 million people worldwide had contracted HIV, and 11.7 million people had died of AIDS. Even more alarming, the number of HIV-infected people worldwide continues to increase. "These deaths will not be the last; there is worse to come. . . . Today, although one in every 100 adults in the most sexually-active age bracket (15–49) is living with HIV, only a tiny fraction know about their infection" (WHO, 1998, p. 7). The World Health Organization estimated a 19% increase in the number of people worldwide infected with HIV during 1997.

As of 1999, there had been approximately 650,000 cases AIDS in the United States, and more than 400,000 of these people had died (250,000 were living with AIDS). As recently as 1996, AIDS was the leading cause of death for people aged 25–35 (CDC, 1998). However, between 1996 and 1997 the number of AIDS deaths in the United States and the number of new AIDS cases decreased. This reduction was attributed to more effective treatment for AIDS patients, leading them to live longer with AIDS, and also to new medications that help delay the progression from HIV to AIDS (CDC, 1998). However, these numbers can be misleading—although the number of new AIDS cases and AIDS-related deaths decreased, the number of HIV-positive people in the United States continued to *increase*.

AIDS-Risky Behaviors

HIV is a viral infection transmitted through the exchange of body fluids. Examining the behaviors that lead to HIV infection reveals that sexual contact and using intravenous drugs account for most of the cases. Table 8–1 shows a breakdown of where people with AIDS contracted HIV. As seen in the table, for men, homosexual sex (57%) and injecting drug use (22%) are the two primary modes of transmission. For women, heterosexual contact (39%) and injecting drug use (43%) account for most of the cases.

From the data shown in Table 8–1, it is clear that the best way to avoid HIV infection is to abstain from sexual relationships or injecting drug use. However, it is often difficult to convince drug users or sexually active people to abstain. Fortunately, there are techniques for reducing HIV transmission that do not require abstinence. For sexual activity, limiting the number of sexual partners and using latex condoms are the primary safe-sex methods. For injecting drug use, bleaching equipment to sterilize needles or using clean needles are the primary means of protection.

Let's focus on sexual behavior. The first question we need to ask is, Are people engaging in risky sexual behavior? When people think of research on sexual behavior, they probably think of the work of Alfred Kinsey and his colleagues (1948, 1953) or of Masters and Johnson (1966). Yet, famous as these studies are,

Table 8–1   AIDS Percentage by Exposure Category (for Adult/Adolescent AIDS Cases Classified Through June, 1998 in the United States)

Behavior	Males (N = 553,048)	Females (N = 104,028)
Men who have sex with men (MSM)	57%	—
Injecting drug use (IDU)	22	43%
MSM and IDU	8	
Heterosexual contact	4	39
Blood/blood products	2	3
Other	7	14

Source: CDC, 1998b.

none of them was even close to obtaining a representative sample. A **representative sample** is one in which the characteristics of the participants in the study accurately reflect the characteristics of the population. The most straightforward way to obtain a representative sample is to select people randomly from the population. However, most studies do not use random samples, and instead obtain data from people who are easy to find and who are willing to participate in the study. Such samples are called **convenience samples**, and findings based on these samples often do not reflect the general population. For instance, Kinsey and his colleagues conducted face-to-face interviews with nearly 18,000 people. They approached groups such as fraternities, PTAs, even hitchhikers going through town, and asked them questions about their sexual experiences. Thus, their respondents were a convenience sample, and probably do not reflect the general experiences of people in the United States.

A much closer approximation to a representative sample was obtained in the National Health and Social Life Survey (Laumann et al., 1994; Michael et al., 1994). Data for the study were obtained through interviews with 3,432 randomly selected households. The interviews were conducted in the respondents' homes and lasted nearly one and one-half hours. The 3,432 completed interviews comprised 79% of the total number of randomly selected households. A brief summary of relevant findings is shown in Table 8–2. The table shows the percentage of respondents who reported various frequencies of sexual contact and various numbers of sexual partners. As seen in the table, 37% of the single, noncohabiting respondents reported having more than one sexual partner in the past year.

Similar data are available for adolescents. The Youth Risk Behavior Surveillance System is a survey of various risk behaviors of high school students (CDC, 1998a). This data source, which we used in Chapter 2 to identify the frequency of teenage pregnancy, includes a representative sample of students in grades 9–12 in the 50 states; the 1997 data set contained 16,262 responses. Data pertinent to our discussion of sexuality are summarized in Table 8–3. As shown in the

Table 8–2   Selected Results from the National Health and Social Life Survey

Group	Not at all	A few times per year	A few times per month	2 or 3 times a week	4 or more times a week
		Frequency of Sex in Past 12 Months (%)			
Men	14%	16%	37%	26%	8%
Noncohabiting	23	25	26	19	7
Cohabiting	0	8	36	40	16
Married	1	13	43	36	7
Women	10	18	36	30	7
Noncohabiting	32	23	24	15	5
Cohabiting	1	8	35	42	14
Married	3	12	47	32	7

Group	0	1	2 to 4	5 or more
	Number of Sex Partners in the Past 12 Months			
Men	10%	67%	18%	5%
Women	14	75	10	2
Never married, noncohabiting	25	38	28	9
Never married, cohabiting	1	75	20	5
Married	2	94	4	1

Source: Michael et al. (1994, pp. 16 and 102).

table, in 1997, 48% of all female high school students reported ever having sexual intercourse (down from 51% in 1991), and 49% of all male high school students reported ever having sexual intercourse (down from 57% in 1991). When currently sexually active students were asked about condom use during their last sexual intercourse, 51% of females reported condom use (up from 38% in 1991) and 62% of males reported condom use (up from 54% in 1991). These trends toward more condom use are encouraging, and may reflect some of the intervention work done by social psychologists.

Early social psychological interventions were aimed at teaching people about AIDS and the modes of transmission. These interventions were based on the assumption that people who were engaging in AIDS-risky behaviors simply did not know any better. However, evaluations of these programs found that

Table 8–3   Selected Results from the Youth Risk Behavior Survey

Gender	Year of survey	Ever had sexual intercourse	Four or more sex partners during lifetime	Condom use during last sexual intercourse[a]
Male				
	1991	57%	23%	54%
	1993	56	22	59
	1995	54	21	60
	1997	49	18	62
Female				
	1991	51	14	38
	1993	50	15	46
	1995	52	14	49
	1997	48	14	51

[a]Calculated only for sexually active students.
Source: CDC, 1998*a*.

knowledge about AIDS did not predict avoidance of risky behaviors (Fisher & Fisher, 1992, 1996). More recent research has focused instead on attitudes and other psychological factors that can lead people to cope directly with the threat of HIV. We turn now to a discussion of attitudes and the relationship between attitudes and behaviors.

ATTITUDES

The concept of attitudes is one of the oldest and most important in the field of social psychology. **Attitudes** are favorable or unfavorable evaluations of an attitude object; they are predispositions to respond in a particular way toward the attitude object (Oskamp, 1991). An attitude object can be a person, a group, an object, an event, or an abstract concept, such as capital punishment. One common view of attitudes is that they have a cognitive, an affective, and a behavioral component. The *affective dimension* of an attitude refers to the feelings and emotions evoked by the attitude object. The *behavioral component* consists of readiness to respond in specific ways to the object. Finally, the *cognitive dimension* of an attitude involves ideas and beliefs about the attitude object. Think of these dimensions as the ABC's of attitudes.

Do Attitudes Predict Behavior?

One of the central issues for attitude researchers is the relationship between attitudes and behaviors. The relationship between attitudes and behavior is not always straightforward. In a classic study, LaPiere (1934) traveled through the United States with a Chinese couple in the early 1930s—a time when prejudice against the Chinese was still running high in the United States. He found that they were refused service at only one of the 250 motels and restaurants they visited. Six months later, LaPiere sent a questionnaire to each of these establishments and asked if they would serve Chinese people. An overwhelming majority said they would not. LaPiere therefore concluded that attitudes are not reliable predictors of actual behavior.

Despite this early conclusion, most subsequent research indicates that attitudes *can* predict behavior, and that they are strongly related in some situations (Eagly, 1992; Kraus, 1995). A variety of situational and personal factors help to determine whether the relationship will be strong or weak (e.g., Schultz & Oskamp, 1996). Variables like the strength of the attitude, how easily it can be remembered, how salient a particular attitude is in a given situation, and how relevant the attitude is to the particular behavior being measured help determine whether people will act in accordance with their attitudes (Eagly & Chaiken, 1993). For example, LaPiere measured attitudes toward Chinese people in general and then used that to predict a more specific behavior toward an attractive and personable Chinese couple. If LaPiere had asked about attitudes toward the particular Chinese people who traveled with him, rather than about Chinese people in general, the correlation between attitudes and behavior probably would have been higher.

Personality traits are also important. Some people consistently match their actions to their attitudes (Norman, 1975). Others have a tendency to override their own attitudes in order to behave "properly" in a given situation. As a result, attitudes do not predict behavior as well for some people as for others (Snyder & Tanke, 1976). In particular, people who are high on **self-monitoring** are especially likely to override their attitudes to behave in accordance with others' expectations. Before speaking or acting, high self-monitors observe the situation for cues about how they should react. Then they try to meet those situational "demands" rather than behave according to their own beliefs or sentiments. In contrast, low self-monitors express and act on their attitudes with great consistency, showing little regard for situational clues or constraints. For example, a high self-monitor who disagrees with the politics of a respected dinner guest may keep her thoughts to herself in an effort to be polite and agreeable, while a low self-monitor who disagrees might dispute the speaker openly, even though doing so might disrupt the social occasion (Snyder, 1987).

THE THEORY OF REASONED ACTION

For over 20 years, the most widely cited and studied theory of attitudes and behavior has been the **theory of reasoned action**, originally formulated by Fishbein and Ajzen (1975). As its name implies, the theory proposes that people

generally act in ways that are reasoned—in the sense of being based on their beliefs and attitudes and understanding of social norms—though it does not claim
that their reasoning is strictly logical.

According to the theory, the best predictor of a person's behavior is his or
her **intentions** to act (Fishbein, Middlestadt, & Hitchock, 1994; Fishbein &
Rhodes, 1997). For instance, whether or not a person uses a condom during sexual intercourse is best predicted by his or her intention to do so. These intentions
in turn are determined by a person's attitudes and normative beliefs. Attitudes reflect a person's positive or negative evaluation of performing the behavior based
on the consequences that he or she expects. For example, a woman may evaluate
using condoms positively due to their protective benefits, or she may have negative attitudes toward condom use because of the potential embarrassment of asking her partner to use a condom. **Subjective norms** are a person's perceptions
of the social pressures to perform the behavior. For instance, what do other people think about using condoms? More recently, Ajzen has added a third variable
to the prediction of intention—**perceived control** is a person's beliefs about his
or her ability to perform the behavior. For example, do I know where to buy condoms and how to use them? The theory that includes perceived control as a predictor of behavioral intentions has been referred to as the *theory of planned
behavior*. A graphical representation of this theory is shown in Figure 8–2.

Of course, people often act in a flash. They don't usually stop to think about
each element; they don't score their beliefs, attitudes, and subjective norms
mathematically and compute their behavioral intention before taking action.
However, the theory of reasoned action posits that their actions are normally

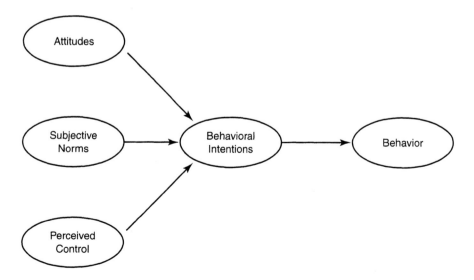

Figure 8–2   Theory of Planned Behavior.

based on just such an implicit process of reasoning. The proof of the theory's value is in its ability to predict behaviors correctly, and on this score it has generally been very successful. It has been used effectively to predict behaviors ranging from engaging in premarital intercourse, to using birth control pills, to attending church regularly, to buying many types of consumer products. In these studies the average correlation coefficients for predicting intentions were as high as +.7 or +.8, and the correlation between intentions and overt behaviors ranged from +.4 to as high as +.9 (Ajzen, 1988, pp. 114, 119; Fishbein & Ajzen, 1975, pp. 310–311, 373–374). But how well does the theory predict risky sexual behavior?

Predicting Sexual Behavior

A great many studies have applied the theory of planned behavior to understanding HIV-risky behavior (Cochran et al., 1992; Terry, Gallois, & McCamish, 1993). In general, these studies have found that the theory can predict safe-sex practices—particularly condom use—among a variety of populations (e.g., gay men, male and female heterosexual college students, prostitutes). As an illustration, let us consider a study by Jamner et al. (1998).

Data for this study were obtained as part of the AIDS Community Demonstration Project—a five-city community intervention program that targeted people at risk for contracting HIV (e.g., injecting drug users and their female sex partners, female commercial sex workers—i.e., prostitutes—and men who have sex with men). For now, let us focus on the results for female commercial sex workers. We will return to this project later in the chapter when we discuss applying social psychology to change sexual attitudes and behavior.

Interviews were conducted with 634 women between October, 1992 and June, 1994. Participants were recruited individually on the streets in neighborhoods having a high prevalence of drug use and/or prostitution. Participants were initially offered a $2 fast-food coupon to complete a short anonymous questionnaire. Based on responses to the short questionnaire, participants who were classified as high-risk were offered $5 cash if they provided additional information about their sexual practices. On average, the 634 female sex workers were 34 years old, 66% were African American, 84% reported smoking crack cocaine within the past month, 25% were married, and 51% reported having a "main partner." Only 6% of the women reported using a condom every time with their husbands or main partners, and 27% reported using condoms every time with their paying partners.

Items in the questionnaire were designed to measure each aspect of the theory of planned behavior. The female respondents were told, "When I ask if you used a condom, I mean did your partner use a condom?" *Intentions* to use a condom for vaginal sex with main and paying partners were measured using a seven-point scale. A sample item is, "How likely do you think it is that from now on you will use a condom every time you have vaginal sex with your main partner?" Responses were on a scale from –3 ("extremely sure I won't") to +3 ("extremely sure I will"). A similar seven-point scale was used to assess *attitudes* toward condom use—i.e., was it good-bad, wise-foolish, pleasant-unpleasant, like-dislike, easy-difficult? *Subjective norms* were measured with questions like, "Do most of the people who are important to you think that you should or should not use a condom for vaginal sex with your paying partners?" Finally, *perceived behavioral control* was assessed with questions like, "If you wanted to use a condom every time you have vaginal sex with your paying partner, how sure are you that you could?"

Analyses tested the ability of attitudes, subjective norms, and perceived control to predict respondents' intentions to use condoms with their paying partners. Results showed that 47% of the variability in intentions could be explained using the three predictor variables. The relationship between attitudes and intentions to use condoms was $r = .37$ ($p < .001$), the relationship between subjective norms and intentions to use condoms was $r = .01$ (not significant), and the relationship between perceived control and intentions to use condoms was $r = .40$ ($p < .001$). Based on these and other findings, the authors concluded that "the results from this study provide support for the utility of the Theory of Planned Behavior as a framework for investigating the factors that influence female sex workers to form intentions to ensure that their main and paying male partners use condoms" (Jamner et al., 1998, p. 200).

APPLYING SOCIAL PSYCHOLOGY TO PREVENT THE SPREAD OF AIDS

Our discussion above indicates that the theory of planned behavior can be used to understand safe-sex practices. A remaining question is: Can we use this knowledge to decrease HIV-risky behaviors? The research project described below was a large-scale intervention based primarily on the theory of planned behavior.

The AIDS Community Demonstration Project (ACDP) was a four-year five-city program "using community volunteers to deliver a theory-based intervention designed to increase consistent condom use or consistent bleach use in a number of ethnically diverse, traditionally hard-to-reach, high-risk populations" (Fishbein et al., 1996, p. 178). These populations included men who had sex with men, injecting drug users and their female partners, and female prostitutes, in sections of Dallas, Denver, Long Beach, New York City, and Seattle (Krauss et al., 1999; Wolitski et al. 1999).

One of the goals of the project was to increase the use of condoms for high-HIV-risk groups. Intentions and behaviors were measured using a five-point classification scale adopted from earlier research (Prochaska, DiClemente, & Norcross, 1992). The stages on this scale were classified as:

1. **Precontemplation**—never or almost never uses condoms and has little or no intention to use condoms every time in the future.

2. **Contemplation**—never or almost never uses a condom but has some intention to use condoms every time in the future.
3. **Preparation**—Sometimes uses condoms and intends to use condoms every time in the future.
4. **Action**—has used condoms every time for less than six months.
5. **Maintenance**—has used condoms every time for six months or more. (Wolitski et al., 1999)

Six months of research in each city determined, through wide-ranging interviews and observations, the geographic areas where high-HIV-risk individuals gathered, what specific risk behaviors were most common, and which local people were "gatekeepers" who were trusted by the high-risk individuals and could provide access to them. In addition, in each city, the project outreach workers recruited peer group members and other community people, who would later deliver the intervention. These network members were kept involved by the provision of small incentives, recognition for their activities, and frequent meetings and parties at the project's storefront headquarters.

During this period, the intervention materials were developed to address the specific attitudes and circumstances of the target populations. The materials used a variety of social modeling stimuli to increase positive attitudes toward condoms, increase social norms, and promote perceived control—each of which is a core component of the theory of planned behavior. Pamphlets and other "small-media" materials provided HIV-prevention messages in the form of role-model stories. Each story described a role-model's progress toward the consistent practice of risk-reduction behaviors (condom use with main partners, condom use with nonmain partners, or use of bleach to clean injecting drug equipment). A sample pamphlet is shown in Figure 8–3. These materials were distributed to at-risk members of the community through identified gatekeepers. In addition, condoms and bleach kits were made more readily available.

With these materials developed, a research design was implemented in which one area of each city was randomly chosen as an intervention area, and a comparable area was designated as an untreated control area. Of course, individuals could not be assigned to be in one area or another (as in a randomized experimental design), so it was possible that some individuals might move from the intervention area to the comparison area, or vice versa—thus causing some diffusion of the treatment. The intervention materials were delivered by the recruited network members, who had been carefully trained to encourage acceptance of and attention to the distributed materials and to reinforce community members' attempts to change their target high-risk behaviors.

Before implementing the intervention, *baseline surveys* of eligible community individuals were conducted from February through June 1991. Then, from July 1991 through August 1993, a total of 15,205 interviews were conducted. To collect data, trained interviewers went, at times when community residents were

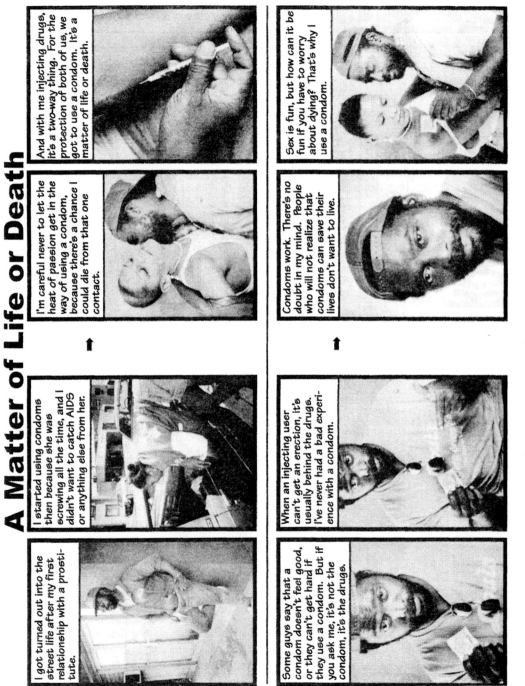

Figure 8–3 Sample pamphlet from the AIDS Community Demonstration Project.

159

normally present, to a randomly determined location in the treatment or the comparison area, and randomly selected respondents there to be interviewed with a standard protocol. This brief street interview (BSI) determined respondents' eligibility (based on their having had sexual intercourse and/or shared drug injection equipment in the last 30 days), and asked them about their consistency of using condoms and/or using bleach on needles. Other questions determined their relevant attitudes, perceptions of local norms, feelings of efficacy, exposure to AIDS information, exposure to the project intervention materials or network members during the last three months, and so on. The interviews were entirely anonymous. A total of 10 waves of data were collected and were segmented into four phases of the project, from baseline to full implementation.

From this description, you can see that the interviews obtained a cross-sectional sample of eligible people who happened to be in that location on the interview occasions. To avoid counting the same individuals more than once within a phase, respondents were eliminated if they matched a previous interview on gender, ethnicity, and place and date of birth. The data were averaged within a phase and plotted to compare changes across phases of the project. The key dependent variables were respondents' stages of change on consistent condom use for vaginal intercourse with (1) main partner, (2) other partners, and on (3) condom carrying. Data were also collected on the sterilization of injecting-drug-use equipment.

The first set of results showed that people in the intervention communities were exposed to the materials. Data indicated that 54% of the people from the intervention areas interviewed during the last wave of data collection reported seeing some of the materials. In contrast, only 5% of the people interviewed in the comparison areas reported seeing the materials (Wolitski, 1999). These findings show that there was some cross-diffusion of the treatment, but not much.

Condom Use with Main Partners.   A total of 9,457 individual responses were obtained regarding condom use with main partners (these data are based on all of the people interviewed, and not just the female sex workers whose findings were summarized above). Results showed that intentions to use condoms increased from 1.66 during the baseline, to 2.07 during the final wave of interviews ($p < .0001$) for people in the intervention areas. However, intentions to use condoms also increased for respondents in the comparison areas as well—a change from 1.60 during baseline to 1.82 during the last wave of interviews ($p < .05$).

Condom Use with Nonmain Partners.   A total of 7,760 responses were obtained for condom use with nonmain partners. In the intervention condition, intentions to use a condom increased from 2.76 during baseline to 3.18 during the final wave of data collection ($p < .0001$). No change was observed in the comparison aeas—average scores were 2.82 during baseline and 2.90 during the last wave of data collection. On average, people in both areas were still in the preparation stage of regular condom use.

Condom Carrying.   A final measure obtained in the study was condom carrying. A total of 13,958 respondents were asked if they were carrying a condom. If they stated that they were, they were asked to show it. During baseline, 17.4% of intervention, and 18.5% of comparison respondents, were carrying condoms. By the end of the intervention, 30.2% of the intervention group, but only 18.9% of those in the comparison areas, were carrying a condom ($p < .0001$). The percentage of respondents carrying condoms at each month of the intervention is shown in Figure 8–4.

Thus, these research findings are hopeful in showing that hard-to-reach, high-risk community populations *can* be contacted and interviewed through sustained and intensive efforts, and their risk behaviors can be modified. The stages-of-change model is helpful in showing that behavioral changes take time and often occur in small steps, and the research demonstrates that community-level interventions can be mounted successfully. But the findings are challenging in showing how much more attitude and behavioral change will be needed to move people fully into safe health practices.

DO BEHAVIORS PREDICT ATTITUDES?

In the preceding section, we saw that attitudes can predict behavior. A final question that we need to address in this chapter is whether behaviors predict attitudes. Perhaps people act first, and then form or change their attitude after a behavior occurs. For example, suppose that a female you know (Becky) is attracted to a male friend of yours (Alex), but decides not to ask him out on a date.

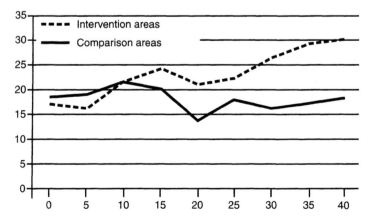

Figure 8–4   Percentage of Respondents Observed to be Carrying a Condom over Time. *Source:* Wolitski et al. (1999).

Becky has a favorable attitude toward dating Alex, but has not acted in a way consistent with the attitude. Would her attitude then change to reflect this decision? Becky may think to herself, "Perhaps he's not such a great person after all."

Cognitive Dissonance Theory

Cognitive dissonance theory proposes that people are motivated to think and act in a consistent manner. That is, our attitudes and behaviors *should* be similar. Inconsistency between our thoughts and behaviors leads to a state of **dissonance**—an aversive state that people are motivated to reduce. For example, the cognition "I would like to go out with him" and the behavior "I didn't ask him out" are inconsistent and might result in dissonance. It is important to note that dissonance results from a psychological inconsistency (i.e., a perceived inconsistency) and not necessarily a logical inconsistency (Festinger, 1957, 1964). Recently, researchers have found that dissonance is more likely to occur when people act in a way that is discrepant from their notions of themselves as competent individuals. That is, dissonance most often occurs when we do something that makes us feel absurd, stupid, or immoral (Aronson, 1997, 1998).

Once dissonance is produced, the individual is motivated to get rid of it. There are a number of ways to reduce dissonance. One way is to change the behavior to be consistent with the dissonant cognition. For example, Becky can call Alex and ask him out. A second way to reduce dissonance is to change the thought (e.g., the attitude) to be consistent with the behavior. For instance, "I don't want to go out with him anyway" or "He's really not that attractive." A third reduction strategy is to create new cognitions that justify the inconsistency. For instance, "I'm a very choosy person" or "First, he should ask me out." Let us now look at an application of cognitive dissonance theory to safe-sex behaviors.

Dissonance and Condom Use

Can we use dissonance theory to promote safe sex? Several studies by Stone and his colleagues suggest that we can (Aronson, Fried, & Stone, 1991; Stone et al., 1994; Stone et al., 1997). Let us consider the methods and results from one of these studies. Stone et al. (1994) examined the effect of hypocrisy—one form of cognitive dissonance—on condom use among college students. Participants in the study were 72 sexually-active, heterosexual undergraduates. Each participant was given $4 to participate in the study.

Cognitive dissonance was induced by obtaining a public statement regarding favorable attitudes toward condom use, and then making participants aware that their behaviors were inconsistent with this statement. For the commitment manipulation, participants were asked to develop a persuasive speech about AIDS and safe sex, and then to deliver this speech in front of a video camera. They were told that the researcher was trying to find the best communicator to get the safe-sex message out to high school students, and that their tape might be used in a high school safe-sex program. Participants who were not in the commitment condition prepared the speech, but were not asked to deliver it in front of a video camera. A second independent variable involved making the participants aware that they did not always practice safe sex. Participants in the "mindful" condition were asked to make a list of the circumstances surrounding their own failure to use condoms in the past. The researcher said that these were needed to "help high school students deal more effectively with these situations" (p. 119). Participants who were not in the mindful condition were merely given information about AIDS and safe sex.

Thus, the study had four conditions: commitment plus mindful (the dissonance condition), commitment only, mindful only, and a control group that received information about AIDS and prepared a speech but did not give it. Participants in the dissonance condition had the following cognitions: "Safe sex is important—I just told high school students that I think so—and I have not always practiced safe sex."

Several dependent measures were obtained—we will focus on two. The first was a measure of condom buying. At the end of the study, participants were given a participation credit slip, handed four $1 bills, and asked to fill out a receipt. The experimenter then said:

> Before you start that, let me tell you that the AIDS educators from the Health Center sent over some condoms and pamphlets on AIDS when they heard about our prevention program. They wanted us to give our subjects an opportunity to buy condoms for the same price they are sold at the health center—10 cents—and this way you don't have to go across campus and stand in a long line. I need to go next door and prepare for the next subject, so go ahead and finish this receipt; you can leave it here on the table. And if you want to buy some condoms or take some pamphlets, just help yourself to anything on the desk; that dish has some spare coins so you can make change. OK? Thanks again for coming in today.

The experimenter then left the room. After the participant left, the researcher returned and determined whether the person had purchased any condoms or taken any of the pamphlets. A second dependent measure was self-reported condom use after participating in the study. Ninety days after the experiment, participants were interviewed over the telephone and asked about their sexual behavior since the study.

Results from the experiment showed that people in the dissonance condition changed their behavior to be consistent with their publicly stated attitude. In the hypocrisy condition, 85% purchased a condom, compared with 33% in the commitment-only condition, 50% in the mindful-only condition, and 44% in the control condition. Participants in the hypocrisy condition also purchased more condoms (mean = 4.95), than those in the commitment-only (mean = 3.50), mindful-only (mean = 2.40), or the control condition (mean = 3.50).

Follow-up data were obtained from 64 of the original 72 participants. Of these, 52 reported having sex at least once in the 90 days since the study. There were three participants who reported having extreme levels of sexual activity—sexual intercourse 90 or more times since the study—and were excluded from the analysis as outliers. When the remaining 49 were asked about condom use, 92% of the participants from the dissonance condition reported using a condom, a figure which was significantly higher than for participants in the commitment-only condition (55%), mindful-only condition (71%), and control condition (75%).

These results suggest that inducing cognitive dissonance can be an effective technique for increasing condom use among sexually active college students. Participants in the study who performed the behavior of publicly stating that safe sex was important, and who were made mindful of the fact that they did not always use a condom, were more likely to purchase a condom, purchased more condoms, and reported more condom use 90 days later, than did subjects in the commitment-only, mindful-only, or control conditions.

SUMMARY

The research findings presented in this chapter illustrate the application of social psychological theory to both understanding and solving a social problem. Using social psychological theories of attitudes, such as the theory of planned behavior, and cognitive dissonance, we can predict with considerable accuracy who will engage in AIDS-risky behaviors, and we can also develop theoretically based interventions to change these behaviors. A fundamental question for attitudinal researchers is whether attitudes can predict a person's behavior. In general, the research suggests that attitudes are a moderate predictor of behaviors, and that the strength of the relationship depends on variables like the accessibility of the attitude, salience of the attitude, and relevance of the attitude to the behavior.

The theory of planned behavior (building on the earlier theory of reasoned action) posits that attitudes, subjective norms, and perceived control lead to an intention to act, and that the intention then leads to a behavior. Research has generally supported this theory. We examined a recent study by Jamner et al. (1998) that used the theory of planned behavior to predict condom use among female sex workers. Results showed that attitudes and perceived control were positively related to intentions to use condoms, but that subjective norms were not.

Extending these findings, the AIDS Community Demonstration Project attempted to change HIV-risky behaviors among people classified as at-risk for infection. Results from five cities and more than 15,000 interviews showed that providing information aimed at changing attitudes, subjective norms, and perceived control was associated with changes in condom use with nonmain partners, and with condom carrying. Condom use with main partners also showed a significant increase over time, but these results did not differ from those in the comparison communities, which also increased.

Finally, we examined the reverse relationship—that behaviors can change attitudes. Cognitive dissonance is an aversive state that results when a person's attitudes and behaviors are inconsistent. Research by Stone and colleagues indicated that making people mindful of hypocrisy—by getting them to publicly state that people should practice safe sex, and making them aware that they themselves do not always do so—produced significant increases in condom buying and also increases in condom use over a three-month period.

KEY CONCEPTS

ACDP (AIDS Community Demonstration Project)   a five-city intervention program that attempted to change the behaviors of people at risk for contracting HIV.

AIDS (Acquired Immune Deficiency Syndrome)   a disease that results from infection with the HIV virus. Worldwide, an estimated 1.7 million people have died from AIDS, and more than 650,000 AIDS cases have been diagnosed in the United States.

Attitudes   favorable or unfavorable evaluations of a person, object, concept, or event.

Cognitive dissonance   an aversive state that results when a person's thoughts and/or behaviors are inconsistent.

Convenience sample   a selected subset of the population who are not randomly chosen and whose characteristics do not represent the larger population.

Intention   a person's plan or intent to perform a particular behavior.

Perceived control   a person's beliefs about his or her ability to perform a behavior.

Reasoned action   a theory that proposes that behavior is determined by intentions, and that intentions are determined by attitudes and subjective norms. The revised version of this theory, known as the theory of planned behavior, adds perceived control as a third determinant of intentions.

Representative sample   a selected subset of a population whose characteristics accurately reflect the characteristics of the population.

Self-monitoring   a personality characteristic in which the person is likely to override his or her attitudes in order to fit the situation and to behave in accordance with others' expectations.

Subjective norms   a person's perceptions of the social pressures to perform a behavior.

REVIEW QUESTIONS

1. What is an attitude? Give an example of the affective, behavioral, and cognitive components of a person's unfavorable attitude toward condom use.

2. Summarize the theory of planned behavior. Using the sample pamphlet shown in Figure 8–3, select one sentence that is focused on changing each aspect of the theoretical model.

3. The message conveyed in the ACDP materials shows images and describes people using drugs and/or engaging in prostitution. Is this kind of behavior appropriate for applied social psychological work? What effect do you think this message has on drug users and prostitutes?

4. George Gannett, whose story you read at the beginning of the chapter, was infected with HIV during a stable homosexual relationship. How could the materials used in the ACDP be adapted to this population? Give specific examples.

5. Your friend Jeff is a sexually active college student who refuses to use condoms when he has sex. He says, "Safe sex is important, but AIDS is a gay disease. And besides, I don't think that the women I am with would let me use a condom." Based on your knowledge of attitudes, what could you say to change his behavior? Make sure to base your answer on specific social psychological theories.

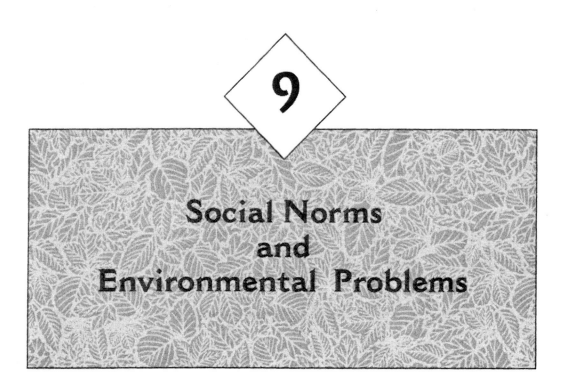

Social Norms
and
Environmental Problems

Joyce Brooks walks through the aisles of her local supermarket on her weekly trip to buy the family food. She buys groceries and products that her family of five will use on a daily basis: meat, milk, eggs, bread, crackers, cookies, paper towels, toilet paper, and so on. Returning home, she is greeted by her three kids, who reluctantly help put the groceries away in the refrigerator and cupboard.

During the week, as they use the products, the plastic, paper, aluminum, tin, and cardboard are thrown in the trash, and then on Monday morning, the trash cans are dragged to the curb and collected by the local trash company—out of sight, out of mind. But what happens to this trash? If Joyce's family is like the average U.S. household, in one month she will throw away:

- *28 pounds of newspaper*
- *7 pounds of tin cans*
- *2 pounds of aluminum*
- *4 pounds of plastic soda and milk containers*
- *17 pounds of glass*

Across the United States, a large percentage of this material (more than 70%) is buried in landfills. But so what? Why not use up and trash these products? It's convenient. It's easy. It's economical—at least in the short run. But will Joyce's children or her grandchildren be able to live this same throw-it-away lifestyle? And what would happen if everyone on the planet lived this lifestyle?

How long can this pattern of consumption continue? How much trash can be buried before we run out of space in which to bury it or run out of the natural resources needed to make the products?

Recycling is one way to reduce the amount of trash, but how can we get people to recycle consistently? And what other ways can we find to cut down on the amount of resources we use and throw away, in order to lessen the impact we have on the planet?

Human beings and the natural world are on a collision course. . . . We the undersigned, senior members of the world's scientific community, hereby warn all humanity of what lies ahead. A great change in our stewardship of the earth and the life on it is required, if vast human misery is to be avoided and our global home on this planet is not to be irretrievably mutilated. (World Scientists' Warning to Humanity, 1992. Document signed by more than 1,500 scientists from 69 countries, including 100 Nobel Prize laureates.)

As indicated by this quotation from the World Scientists' Warning, human actions are destroying the natural environment. This may be viewed as a shocking statement. Though most people in the United States today, and many people worldwide, are concerned about the widespread environmental destruction, the severity of environmental problems, the causes of these problems, and beliefs about how to solve them are heatedly disputed (Dunlap, Gallup, & Gallup, 1993; Schultz & Zelezny, 1999). In this chapter, we will highlight some of the environmental problems that face the world today. We will then focus on one proenvironmental behavior—recycling—and discuss the application of social psychological theories of normative influence to promote recycling.

Figure 9-1   More than 70% of the 220 million tons of trash generated in the United States each year is buried in landfills. The Miramar landfill, shown above, covers 802 acres.

SOME ENVIRONMENTAL PROBLEMS

Population

A central underlying cause of many environmental problems is the number of humans living on the planet. More people means more pollution, less space, and a greater demand for natural resources. At the time of this writing, there were approximately 6 billion people living on the earth, and the number is increasing exponentially by nearly 100 million every year.

> The time needed to add a billion people to the world's population has become ever shorter. It took nearly one century (1830–1930) to advance from 1 billion to 2 billion people, 30 years (1930–1960) to advance to 3 billion people, 15 years (1960–1975) to attain a fourth billion, and 12 years (1975–1987) to grow from four billion to 5 billion people. (David, 1994, p. 334)

According to the United Nations, if we make very strong assumptions that fertility rates will soon be reduced to, and stay at, replacement levels (about two children per woman), then the world's population should level off by 2150 at around 11 billion. If instead, fertility rates remain at 1990–95 levels, the world will have to support approximately 96 billion people by 2150 (United Nations, 1998).

It is unclear how many humans the earth can support, but it is clear that there is an upper limit. The **carrying capacity** of the planet for human life depends largely on the amount of food that can be produced and on the quality of life that is desired for each person (Brown, 1998). As the number of people living on the planet increases, the resources available to each individual decrease. Some responsible environmental scientists have estimated that we have already overshot the *long-term* carrying capacity of the earth, which may be *less than half* of the number of humans who are alive today (Meadows, Meadows, & Randers, 1992; Pimentel et al., 1994). Clearly the United Nation's forecast of 96 billion is not sustainable.

Pollution

In 1969, the Cuyahoga River in Cleveland, Ohio, actually caught on fire because its water was so heavily polluted with petroleum chemicals. At that time, industrial smokestacks around the country billowed toxic smoke into the air freely, and there were few regulations to prevent toxic pollution of water and land. In the United States today, many of these blatantly harmful actions have been stopped through environmental legislation. However, many developing countries around the world, in their quest for an industrial society, have been increasing their polluting actions (Gore, 1992).

Air Pollution. Air pollution is caused by the release of chemical by-products into the atmosphere. These chemicals come primarily from the generation of the energy that powers our automobiles, heats our houses, and produces electricity. Other extremely serious air pollutants are compounds of chlorine, such as the chlorofluorocarbons (CFCs) that are used as refrigerants. These pollutants have been linked to many environmental problems, such as acid rain, holes in the ozone layer, and the greenhouse effect.

Acid rain is produced when sulfur from burning coal, and nitrogen from burning gasoline, combine with oxygen in the atmosphere to form acids. These acids are then returned to the earth in the form of rain and snow, damaging plants and trees, and killing all the life in many rivers and lakes.

Air pollution is also seriously damaging the **ozone layer**. Ozone is a relatively rare gas that forms a protective layer in the earth's upper atmosphere, blocking much of the ultraviolet rays coming from the sun. Reductions in the amount of atmospheric ozone mean that more ultraviolet radiation will hit the earth, producing increases in human skin cancer and cataracts, and reductions in agricultural yields due to damage to many animals and plants (including plankton in the oceans; Brown, 1998).

In the 1980s, scientists first discovered reductions in the amount of ozone in a large region over the Antarctic. Today, it is clear that there is a similar "ozone hole" over the northern Arctic region as well, and an 8% reduction in the amount

Figure 9–2   One of the primary causes of air pollution is automobile exhaust. Conservative estimates suggest that by the year 2010, demand for oil will far exceed supply.

of ozone in the Northern Hemisphere was documented between 1979 and 1990 (Gribbon & Gribbon, 1993). This ozone depletion is caused by chlorine atoms chemically reacting with many ozone ions, producing a new compound and eliminating the free ozone ions. The primary source of chlorine in the upper atmosphere is the escape of CFCs, such as Freon, a chemical manufactured for use as a coolant in air-conditioners and refrigerators, and formerly as a propellant in spray cans. Almost all of the world's nations have signed a treaty, the Montreal Convention, agreeing to phase out the production of CFCs, but unfortunately the treaty has been attacked as unnecessary by ill-advised politicians in the United States and other countries (Wager, 1995–96).

   Global warming is another result of gases in the upper atmosphere. The term refers to an increase in the earth's average temperature, which occurs through a process rather similar to the way that glass panes in a greenhouse let in warming sunlight but prevent warm air from escaping. Energy from the sun constantly heats the earth's surface, but much of this energy is reflected back into space either as visible light or as infrared radiation. In the upper atmosphere, several types of gases allow visible light to penetrate, but reflect the earth's infrared radiation back to earth, thus heating it further. The primary one of these "greenhouse gases" is carbon dioxide (CO_2), which is produced by the burning of fossil fuels, such as natural gas or petroleum, in industries, homes, and automobile engines (Walsh, 1993). The amount of CO_2 in the upper atmosphere has been steadily increasing for decades, and its damaging effects are now becoming clear in floods, tornadoes, and other signs of large-scale climate change.

The result of the greenhouse effect is that the earth's temperature will gradually increase. Global warming is already occurring and is predicted to drastically change life as we know it (Martens, 1998). As President Clinton stated in his 1998 State of the Union Address: "The vast majority of scientists have concluded unequivocally that if we don't reduce the emission of greenhouse gases at some point in the next century, we'll disrupt our climate and put our children and grandchildren at risk."

A 1–2 degree Fahrenheit change in the earth's temperature would change rainfall patterns, flooding some areas while creating deserts elsewhere in place of current agricultural lands, disrupting food production, and causing the extinction of many species. A 2–3 degree Fahrenheit increase would eventually melt the polar icecaps and raise the level of the oceans, flooding many low-lying seacoast areas. Research data on the average temperature of the earth's surface show a steady rise over the last 100 years—about 1 degree Fahrenheit since 1850. Figure 9-3 shows this general trend. The most frightening aspect of these data is that such changes, once underway, may be irreversible. As Stern (1992, p. 271) stated:

> Global changes may be impossible to control once they get started; by the time a catastrophe is foreseen, it may already be too late to prevent it. Humanity is conducting a grand experiment on its natural environment, and cannot afford to fail. We have only one earth on which to experiment.

Natural Resources

The earth's resources are finite. Many of the materials that are used in manufacturing processes are not from renewable sources (e.g., oil, minerals, underground water supplies). However, industries and consumers act as if there were an unlimited supply. Estimates of natural resource supplies remaining are typically calculated as the number of years the resources will last at the present annual consumption rate. For example, there is an estimated 14-year supply of lead, 65 years of nickel, 179 years of iron ore, and 25 years of zinc (Simmons, 1991). These estimates are based on average annual consumption figures, and do not include undiscovered deposits, but there is also a limit on the number of undiscov-

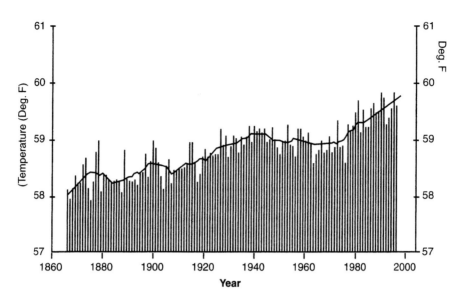

Figure 9-3 This graph shows changes in global temperature since 1880, when reliable temperature records became available worldwide. Each vertical bar represents the global average temperature for that year. The curved line shows the overall trend. The global average temperature has risen nearly 1°F (0.5°C) since 1880. *Source:* Environmental Defense Fund (http://www.edf.org).

ered deposits that can feasibly be exploited. Estimates for oil suggest that by the year 2010, demand will far exceed supply (Ivanhoe, 1996, 1997).

The United States is by far the largest consumer of the world's production of raw materials (Brown, 1994). Nevertheless, we continue to discard about 73% of all materials after using them only once, rather than reuse or recycle them into new products (Hurley, 1998). Figure 9-4 shows the total amount of trash generated by year for the past 40 years, and the amount of the trash that is deposited in landfills. The difference between the total and net amounts of trash is due to recycling (27% for 1995). Though we can postpone the final depletion of resource supplies by digging deeper, using less-concentrated mineral bodies, and finding substitutes for depleted raw materials, our practice of using up the earth's resources must eventually stop. Instead, we must adopt a new lifestyle of reducing our consumption, reusing products that still have a useful life, and recycling the materials in products that are no longer serviceable (U.S. Environmental Protection Agency, 1992).

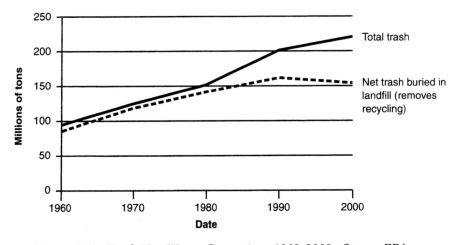

Figure 9–4   Total Net Waste Generation, 1960–2000. *Source:* EPA (1998a). Note: The difference between the total amount of trash generated and the net trash buried in landfills equals the percentage of material recycled in a given year.

Social Psychology Can Help.   Psychologists can make important contributions to preserving the earth's resources and the natural environment. All of the problems listed in the preceding section (population growth, pollution, depletion of natural resources) are *caused* by human behavior. Consequently, any solution to these problems will require behavior change. As the World Scientists' Warning stated, "a great change in our stewardship of the earth is required." There are many ways in which behaviors can change to lessen the impact of human activity on the natural environment. People could drive less, purchase environmentally friendly products (especially large products like cars, refrigerators, washing machines and dryers), or recycle the material in used products.

RECYCLING

What is the single largest monument to human activity on earth? The pyramids of Egypt? The Great Wall of China? The World Trade Center in New York? In fact, the answer is the Fresh Kills Landfill in Staten Island, New York, which contains more material than any other single human-made object (Steger & Bowermaster, 1990). Each day, 13,000 tons of garbage are dumped at the Fresh Kills Landfill. When it reaches its final height and closes on December 31, 2001, it will contain more than 200 million tons of garbage (Department of Sanitation, 1998).

The disposal of solid waste is becoming both an environmental and an economic burden. In 1972 there were approximately 20,000 landfills operating in the United States. In the years since, many of these have been filled to capacity and closed, leaving 2,100 operating landfills in 2000 (Lacerta Group, 1998). For many of us, throwing something into the trash requires little thought. Rarely do we stop to consider what will happen to the waste we throw in the trash can. In fact, most of the solid waste that is generated worldwide is buried in landfills.

In 1989, the EPA announced a national goal of reducing landfill use. In the years since this announcement, all 50 U.S. states have passed legislation requiring cities to reduce the amount of trash buried in landfills. Curbside recycling programs are the most commonly implemented strategy in this quest. **Recycling** refers to the collection, processing, and use of old products to make new products. Nationally, there are more than 8,000 curbside recycling programs that serve more than 134 million people, and both numbers are growing rapidly (Environmental Protection Agency, 1998b).

Recycling has the potential to divert thousands of tons of reusable materials away from landfills. However, many people are unwilling to recycle, citing such reasons as lack of knowledge, the extra time required, lack of space for recycling bins, and lack of interest (Oskamp et al., 1998). For the past 20 years, applied social psychologists have been developing various behavioral interventions to increase recycling rates. Some of these techniques include information campaigns, prompts, and reinforcements, each of which is briefly discussed below (Schultz et al., 1995).

Interventions Used to Promote Recycling

Information campaigns are a favorite influence technique of government agencies and private organizations (e.g., public utilities, waste disposal companies, energy producers). Information strategies are intended to make people more knowledgeable—about recycling, for instance—which in turn is often expected to lead to a change in behavior. However, findings on the effectiveness of information interventions in increasing proenvironmental behaviors are mixed and typically show only weak effects (Gardner & Stern, 1996; Leeming et al., 1993). Nevertheless, information campaigns are often used in attempts to change behavior—in part because they are relatively inexpensive and easy to implement.

In many ways, information campaigns ignore the fact that people are social animals. Information campaigns assume that *if* people only knew how, when, what, and where to recycle, they would. However, from social psychology we know that even when people have favorable attitudes toward an action, they often do not act in a consistent manner. As we saw with the research on attitudes and safe sex behavior (Chapter 8), although attitudes can predict behavior, other motivational variables like perceived control and subjective norms need to be considered. In general, information campaigns tend to increase knowledge about the behavior and also to foster positive attitudes toward the behavior, but they produce only small changes in actual behavior.

Prompts are brief signals about what actions to take. They can vary from general ("Please recycle") to specific ("Place all aluminum cans in this bin"). There is good research evidence that more specific prompts—ones that indicate who, what, where, and when—are more successful than vague prompts. Also, prompts tend to be more successful if they are polite rather than demanding, request a response that is easy to perform (such as turning off a light switch, as contrasted with taking materials to a drop-off recycling center), and are administered close to the point of response (e.g., a sign near the light switch and room exit, or above a recycling bin; Geller, 1981). In general, prompts are more effective when combined with reinforcing consequences (Austin et al., 1993).

Monetary incentives are programs that offer money in an attempt to increase the frequency of a behavior. As learning theory predicts, these types of program have been found to be effective in increasing a wide range of proenvironmental behaviors, including energy conservation, recycling, using public transportation, and ride sharing (Everett & Watson, 1987). An excellent example of research on monetary incentives was Deslauriers and Everett's (1977) study, which attempted to increase the number of people who rode a university campus bus system. The authors rewarded the behavior with either a continuous reinforcement or a variable-ratio reinforcement schedule, by giving riders tokens that could be exchanged for discounts at many local stores. In the continuous condition, riders received one token for each trip, whereas in the variable-ratio condition every third rider received a token. Results for a control condition showed no change in ridership from the baseline level. In contrast, there was a 27% ridership increase in the continuous-reinforcement condition, and a 30% increase in the variable-ratio condition. The findings from this study have been applied by transportation systems in Spokane and Seattle, Washington, Portland, Oregon, and Bridgeport, Connecticut. However, the results across these cities have been mixed (Everett & Watson, 1987).

Although the research on monetary incentives indicates that they can be an effective tool for increasing proenvironmental behaviors, there is an important social psychological consideration—the **overjustification effect**. Social psychological research has clearly shown that receiving an external reward for an activity, even an activity we originally enjoy, can reduce the intrinsic motivation for the behavior (Amabile et al., 1994; Deci & Ryan, 1985). For instance, consider a teenager who works hard to get good grades in school because her parents have offered to give her a reward (like a car) for a specified performance. What happens once she reaches the goal and there is no longer an external incentive for working hard? Chances are, she will not work as hard—her motivation for doing well in school was mostly external (i.e., she did it for the car) and not internal, and the external incentive has been removed.

If we look at changes in behavior produced by reward programs that have been used to encourage proenvironmental behaviors, we find evidence of the overjustification effect. The change in behavior produced by reward programs tends to be short-lived, and once the intervention is terminated, behaviors typically return to their original levels (or in some cases, to lower levels). Rewarding people for actions that they already want to do might lead them to make an *external attribution* for the behavior. For instance, they may come to believe that they are recycling because of the reward rather than because they want to help solve environmental problems (Boggiano et al., 1987). In such cases, when the reward stops, the justification for the behavior no longer exists, and the frequency of the behavior decreases.

A contrast to this finding is seen in the "bottle bills" that have been passed by ten states (Environmental Protection Agency, 1998a). These laws specify a monetary payment for returning beverage containers for recycling, and they are the only large-scale positive-reinforcement procedures adopted by governments in the United States. They have been outstandingly successful in increasing the percentage of returned containers, to levels as high as 90%, and thus have dramatically reduced the amount of roadside litter (Shireman, 1993). A key reason that bottle bills are so successful is because the external incentive is never removed—people always get the reward (e.g., the 5 cents per bottle or can). But what would happen to recycling if the bottle bills were revoked? Would people continue to return the cans and bottles? Probably not nearly as much. Also, bottle bills may lead people to expect rewards for other proenvironmental behaviors, making it difficult to produce long-term changes in behaviors like water conservation or using public transportation.

Monetary disincentives are programs that attempt to reduce the frequency of a behavior by imposing monetary costs on the behavior. For example, increasing the cost of gasoline and electricity and higher energy taxes are expected to decrease consumptive behaviors (O'Brien & Zoumbaris, 1993). Evidence from other countries suggests that disincentives can be very effective; countries with high energy taxes provide a strong disincentive to use or waste energy. In most Western European countries gasoline costs from $4 to $5 per gallon, and consequently consumers there use it much more sparingly than in the United States and Canada. Cheap energy in the United States is undoubtedly one of the major reasons for our overconsumption of oil—we use it at more than twice the per capita rate of Western European countries and Japan ("Wasting Opportunities," 1990).

An example of monetary disincentives from the recycling area is a per-bag waste disposal fee. In these types of programs, householders are required to purchase stickers that must be placed on all garbage at the curbside for pickup, whereas recyclables are collected free of charge. The Environmental Protection Agency (EPA) conservatively estimates that this simple approach can reduce the amount of trash by at least 10% (Cohn, 1992). In fact, in Seattle, research has shown that the number of bins of trash set out per week declined by as much as 60% after a pay-per-bag system was inaugurated (Shireman, 1993).

Information, prompts, and monetary incentives, although occasionally effective in the short term, have difficulty in producing long-term behavioral change (Schultz et al., 1995). Monetary incentives and disincentives also are costly to maintain and can produce an overjustification effect. Would it be possible to find a social psychological theory that will lead to long-term behavioral changes without being costly or producing overjustification effects? One useful set of theories for behavior change—theories of social influence—may provide an answer to this question.

SOCIAL INFLUENCE

Social influence refers to the use of social power to change the thoughts, feelings, or behaviors of another person in a specified direction. Social influence is any attempt to get another person to think, feel, or act in a certain way. Influencing other people is a daily occurrence. Advertisers and marketers want to influence you so that you will buy their product. Law enforcement agents want to influence you so that you won't break the law. A friend may try to influence you to give her a ride to work. And so on.

Since the earliest days of social psychology over 100 years ago, researchers have studied tactics of social influence. Some of the more widely studied tactics include reciprocation, social validation, consistency, liking, scarcity, and authority (Cialdini, 1993).

Reciprocation refers to feelings of obligation to return a favor. We are generally more likely to comply with a request from someone who has done something for us, or made a concession to us. In general, we feel obligated to pay people back when they do something for us. For example, if we receive a "free gift" from a company (like envelope labels with our address on them), we are more likely to purchase a product or donate money to the organization.

Social validation refers to our tendency to act in ways resembling the behavior of people around us, particularly those who we believe are similar to ourselves. Ad slogans like "best selling" or "market leader" rely on this strategy.

Consistency refers to our desire to think and act in a consistent manner. Once we have committed ourselves to a position or action, we are likely to accept or find evidence to support the position and to comply with requests that preserve our consistency. For example, we are more likely to endorse a politician or a political issue after we sign a petition in favor of it, than if we had not signed the petition. Likewise, we are more likely to listen to a radio station if we put a station bumper sticker on our car.

Liking refers to our tendency to comply with requests made by friends or by people we like or admire. Advertisements with well-known actors or athletes (like Michael Jordan or Tiger Woods) use this technique.

Scarcity refers to our tendency to value things that are hard to get. We will try harder to obtain, pay more for, and value more those things that are scarce or limited in quantity or availability. The following statements made in advertisements illustrate this technique: "supplies are limited," "for a limited time only," "12-hour sale," "while supplies last."

Authority refers to our tendency to trust and comply with requests made by someone who is perceived to be an authority figure. Advertisements with dentists or doctors (even if not a real doctor, as in "I'm not a doctor, but I play one on TV") use this tactic.

Social Norms

Recently, psychologists have begun to study the role of social norms in determining behavior, and also the possibility of using social norms to change a person's actions. Social norms are standards and rules, shared by members of a group, that guide and/or constrain behavior (Cialdini & Trost, 1998). Stated differently, social norms are beliefs about the ways in which other people within our perceived group are, or should be, acting. Social norms are learned through interaction with other people, and are used to determine appropriate ways of acting.

It is useful to distinguish between descriptive and injunctive social norms. *Descriptive* norms are beliefs about what other people are doing. By watching the behavior of others, it is possible to learn what is normative in a given situation— information that is especially important if we are in an ambiguous situation or are unclear about how to act. A sizable amount of research indicates that people use descriptive norms to determine how to act (Sherif, 1935; Cialdini et al., 1990). In Chapter 6 we saw that watching violence on television creates a descriptive norm about the prevalence of aggressive behavior.

Because descriptive norms are used by individuals to determine their behavior, changing them should change behavior. Imagine that you are walking to your car after a trip to the library. When you reach your car, you find a brightly colored flier on your windshield. You look around and find that you are alone in a highly littered parking lot. The question is: What do you do with the flier? Do you take it with you to discard later, or do you throw it on the ground? Research by Cialdini et al. (1990) suggests that the littered parking lot conveys a descriptive norm— other people have thrown things on the ground. Research has shown that people in a littered parking lot are considerably more likely to throw the flier on the ground than are people in a clean parking lot.

Injunctive norms are beliefs about what other people think *should* be done— that is, injunctive norms prescribe "proper" behavior (Cialdini et al., 1990). Acting in a manner consistent with an injunctive norm is likely to lead to rewards, while deviating from an injunctive norm is likely to lead to disapproval or punishments. Imagine again that you are in the littered parking lot and that there is a flier on your windshield. However, as you were walking to your car, you witnessed a person picking up a piece of litter from the ground and putting it in a trash can. Now, would you litter? The research evidence indicates that you would be considerably less likely to litter after witnessing such an act, because the person's actions activated an injunctive norm. That is, seeing another person pick up a piece of litter makes it clear that that person (and presumably other people) think littering is wrong (Cialdini, Kallgren, & Reno, 1991; Reno, Cialdini, & Kallgren, 1993).

Normative Social Influence

As we have seen, people often use normative beliefs to determine how to act. A related question is: If these normative beliefs are changed, will it produce a change in behavior? Research indicates that the answer to this question is yes.

Let us consider a recent example from research on drug-prevention programs. Donaldson et al. (1994, 1995) examined the effects of resistance training (like that provided by the D.A.R.E. program) as compared with normative education. **Normative education** focuses on students' beliefs about the prevalence and acceptability of substance use among their peers. That is, normative education attempts to change descriptive norms (i.e., their beliefs about the prevalence of substance use) and injunctive norms (i.e., their beliefs about the acceptability of substance use). Donaldson et al. developed a normative education program consisting of five lessons that "corrected erroneous perceptions of prevalence and acceptability of alcohol and drug use among peers and established a conservative normative school climate regarding substance use" (1994, p. 201). This intervention was based on prior research which had demonstrated that adolescents who believed that alcohol and drug use was accepted and commonly practiced by their peers had a substantially higher risk of early use of drugs and alcohol. The intervention program, called the Adolescent Alcohol Prevention Trial, involved nearly 12,000 students in 130 school units (both public schools and private Catholic schools) in Los Angeles and San Diego counties.

Results from Donaldson et al.'s (1994) research indicated that resistance-skills training (the D.A.R.E. approach to learning to "just say no") did improve adolescents' refusal skills, but that their refusal skills did *not* predict their subsequent amount of alcohol, tobacco, or marijuana use. In contrast, normative education, as predicted, reduced students' estimates of the prevalence of substance use and their beliefs that such use was acceptable. Most importantly, these two belief changes, in turn, were associated with lower alcohol, tobacco, and marijuana use in eighth and ninth grades, one and two years after the intervention

To probe why resistance training was not effective in reducing substance use, further studies were conducted, comparing it with normative education and with an intervention combining normative education and resistance training (Donaldson et al., 1995). Two important findings resulted. First, refusal skills did predict subsequent lower alcohol use for those students who believed it was not acceptable for adolescents to drink alcohol, but *not* for those who believed it was acceptable to drink. Second, a harmful effect of resistance-skills training (like D.A.R.E.) was found among the students attending public schools—it increased their beliefs that a high level of substance use was prevalent in their schools. It is as if teaching kids how to say "no" subtly conveyed that many kids are already drinking, smoking, or using drugs. In contrast, normative education did not lead to an increase in those beliefs. Even better results were obtained by combining the two approaches, which led to the lowest level of prevalence estimates.

Changing Normative Beliefs to Promote Recycling: An Illustrative Study

The data described above indicate that changing normative beliefs can produce a corresponding change in behavior. Could these findings be used to change recycling behavior? A recent field experiment indicates that they can (Schultz, 1999).

Participants.   Participants in the study were 605 single-family homes in a residential suburb of Los Angeles. Approximately 120 houses were systematically assigned to each of five experimental conditions: individual normative feedback (targeting injunctive social norms), group normative feedback (targeting descriptive social norms), information, plea-only, and control. For convenience in data gathering, households were grouped by small contiguous geographic areas, ranging in size from 5 to 16 houses, and these small areas were randomly assigned to experimental conditions. In assigning the housing groups to conditions, the conditions were equated on their members' past recycling participation, as measured during previous baseline observations. The assignment to conditions produced five groups of approximately 120 households, with each group possessing an average baseline rate of recycling participation within 1% of each other.

Materials and Procedure.   Households had been observed for eight weeks in order to establish this recycling baseline. Observations were made weekly by a team of observers. Each week, shortly before the arrival of the recycling truck, observers recorded whether or not the recycling bins were placed at the curb, and if they were, how much material was in the bins.

When the interventions began, all households except for those assigned to the control condition received a plea to recycle. The plea stated: "In order for [the city] to achieve the benefits of recycling, please try to recycle as much as possible." This information was printed on one side of a green door hanger and placed on the doorknob of each household in the four experimental conditions. The plea served two purposes. First, it signaled to these four groups that a study was being conducted. Second, its effects as a manipulation were tested by having it as the only intervention for the plea-only group.

Beginning in the second week of the experimental period, houses in the other three experimental conditions (injunctive normative feedback, descriptive normative feedback, and information) received materials for four weeks on green door hangers on their front doorknob. The door hangers were delivered later on the morning of the trash pickup day, after the observers had completed observations of recycling for all households in the area.

Households in the injunctive norms condition received feedback about their specific recycling behaviors, and *not* about the behavior of other people. The feedback informed each household about the amount of each type of recyclable material collected the previous week, the amount of each type of material collected the current week, and the total amount of each material collected for the duration of the study. This information was handwritten on preprinted door hangers. It conveyed to residents that they *should* be recycling, and not that other people were recycling.

Households in the descriptive norm condition received a handwritten door hanger similar to the individual feedback form, for the same four-week period, but with feedback information about the recycling amounts for their residential area (i.e., approximately 200 contiguous houses of their SES level—relatively high, medium, or low). This material conveyed to residents that other people in their community were recycling.

Households assigned to the information condition received four green door hangers during the four-week intervention, each with a different type of information. The first door hanger reminded householders which materials were recyclable in the recycling program, and the second gave a list of nonrecyclable materials and frequent contaminants. The third door hanger described important features of the recycling process, from collection to reuse of recycled materials. The final door hanger gave information about the conservation of energy, landfill space, and natural resources that results from recycling.

After the four-week interventions, the recycling of all households was observed for an additional four weeks in follow-up observations.

Results.   The data analysis was based on three time periods: baseline (8 weeks), intervention (4 weeks), and follow-up (4 weeks). Analyses showed a significant increase in the frequency of participation and the amount of material recycled for the injunctive and descriptive norm conditions, but not for the information, plea-only, nor control conditions. The results for weekly participation are shown in Figure 9–5. On the average, households in the injunctive norm condition recycled significantly more often and more material per week during the four-week follow-up period than during the baseline period. For the descriptive norm condition, results showed a similar significant increase in the frequency of participation and in the amount of material recycled.

Additional analyses examined changes in recycling separately for residents who were high and low in recycling before the interventions began. Results showed that residents low in recycling increased from a 5% participation rate dur-

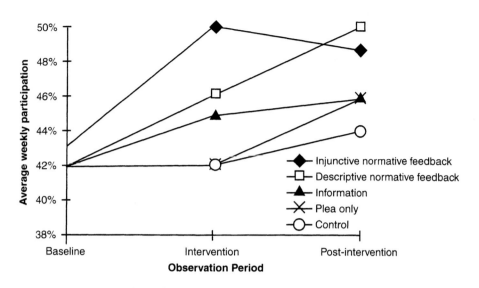

Figure 9–5 The Effects of Normative Information on Recycling Behavior. *Source:* Schultz (1999).

ing the baseline period to a 25% recycling rate during the follow-up period in the injunctive condition, and from 5% at baseline to 13% at follow-up in the descriptive norm condition. In contrast, residents who were initially high in recycling decreased somewhat from 85% at baseline to 79% at follow-up in the injunctive condition and from 86% at baseline to 84% at follow-up in the descriptive norm condition. No substantial changes were found for residents in the control condition. These analyses suggest that residents were using the normative feedback to guide their behavior—those residents who were below the norm increased, and those residents who were above the norm decreased.

These data could also be interpreted as **regression to the mean**—a term used to refer to the tendency of extremely low or extremely high scores to become more moderate over time. That is, perhaps the norms were not changing behavior, but instead residents who were low tended to become more average over time. However, if this were true, then we would expect to find the same trend for the high and low groups in the control condition. Analyses revealed that the high-recycling control group did not change substantially from baseline to follow-up (83% to 83%), nor did the low-recycling control group (5% to 6%). These findings show that the results were not due to regression to the mean and support the conclusion that people used the provided norms to change their behavior.

Thus, the theoretically predicted effect of targeting injunctive and descriptive norms was found to occur at a substantial level in this experiment, demonstrating a relatively easy way to encourage people to recycle more often and greater amounts of material.

I'M JUST ONE PERSON—WHAT CAN *I* DO?

The quotation on page 168 from the World Scientists' Warning to Humanity stated that "*a great change in our stewardship of the earth and the life on it is required, if vast human misery is to be avoided and our global home on this planet is not to be irretrievably mutilated.*" Throughout this chapter, we have seen several applications of social psychology to change human behavior toward more sustainable lifestyles—ways of living that could be supported indefinitely, given the earth's finite resources of food, water, and minerals. Indeed, we all need to change our lifestyles.

Unfortunately, there is a tendency when faced with the large-scale nature of many environmental problems to believe that our behavior is only a drop in the ocean. We are part of the problem, but we often think, "What can I do?" In many instances, living a more sustainable lifestyle means making sacrifices, and if everyone isn't making equivalent sacrifices, it isn't fair. For example, taking long, hot showers is not sustainable. The energy required to heat the water and the total volume of water consumed are substantial. But why should *I* give this up if my neighbor does not? Problems like this are often referred to as a **commons dilemma**—a situation in which acting in one's self-interest is detrimental to the group. Taking a shower is beneficial to you, but harmful to the group.

Box 9–1 lists 10 things that you can do to live a more sustainable lifestyle. We encourage you to seriously consider incorporating some of these actions into your daily life, and to be aware of the long-term consequences that your behavior has on the natural environment. You *can* make a difference.

Box 9–1   Ten Simple Things You Can Do to Live a More Sustainable Lifestyle

1. **Drive less.** Nearly half of all the energy consumed by individuals in the United States is for automobile transportation. Consider walking or riding a bike to work or school. Take this issue into serious consideration when you decide where to live. If you only change one behavior, let this be it.
2. **Consider the environmental impact when making large purchases.** More efficient refrigerators, water heaters, and cars can substantially reduce the amount of energy consumed each year.
3. **Recycle.** Separate and recycle your aluminum, tin, glass, plastic, and paper products. Recycling materials saves both natural resources and also the energy costs needed to process new materials. Making aluminum from recycled cans requires 95% less energy and generates 95% less pollution.
4. **Turn off the water when it's not in use.** When brushing your teeth, showering, or washing your dishes, don't let the water run continuously. It takes 5 gallons of water to fill the sink for washing dishes, but letting the water run continuously can use 30 gallons of water.

5. **Vote environmental.** Nearly 80% of U.S. voters consider themselves to be environmentalists, yet few vote that way. Consider the environmental impact of policies, platforms, and actions of politicians, and use that information to guide your vote.

6. **Be a green shopper.** On a daily basis, buy products that can be recycled, products that are concentrated or that use less packaging, and products made from recycled material.

7. **Reset your thermostats.** Space heat uses nearly 30% of the total amount of energy consumed by an individual. Set your thermostat back from 72 degrees F to 68 degrees during the day and 60 degrees at night. Also, lower your water heater thermostat by 20 degrees.

8. **Dispose of hazardous waste properly.** Oil, paint, car batteries, antifreeze, and many household cleaning products are extremely toxic and harmful to the environment. Paint accounts for 60% of the hazardous waste dumped by individuals. Try using latex paint instead of oil-based paint, and make sure that you dispose of paint properly with your local hazardous waste program. If you don't know whom to contact, call the EPA hotline at (800) 424-9346. *Don't pour these dangerous chemicals down the drain!*

9. **Upgrade your insulation.** Nearly half of all energy consumed in our homes is wasted. Many utility companies offer free energy audits to find the leaks in your house or apartment.

10. **Join an environmental organization.** Environmental groups provide an important link between individuals and public policy. By joining an environmental group, you can keep current on important national and local issues. Some of the larger organizations are Sierra Club (*www.sierraclub.org*), Greenpeace (*www.greenpeace.org*), and the Environmental Defense Fund (*www.edf.org*). Learn more about these groups and consider becoming an activist for environmental issues.

SUMMARY

Unless we change our behavior, environmental problems threaten to destroy life on our planet. Environmental problems of population growth, pollution of air, water, and land, and crises in the use of energy and other natural resources provide critical challenges for applied social psychologists. In this chapter, we summarized several environmental problems, examined recycling and some of the techniques that have been used to promote recycling, discussed social influence,

and summarized several applied studies that used normative beliefs to change behavior in the areas of littering, drug and alcohol use, and recycling.

Americans generate approximately 200 million tons of trash per year—
that's nearly 1 ton per person. Most of this trash (73%) is buried in landfills.
Recycling has the potential to divert millions of tons of solid waste from landfills and to conserve our remaining natural resources. Psychologists have examined a variety of techniques to help promote recycling. Information campaigns are often ineffective at producing any sizable change in recycling
behaviors. Prompts, on the other hand, have been found to be effective at producing small, short-term changes in behavior, especially if the prompt is specific. Monetary incentives and disincentives can also be effective at promoting
recycling. However, incentives and disincentives can backfire because they
tend to produce overjustification effects and lead people to be motivated by
the promise of reward. As long as the incentive remains in place, the behavior
may follow. However, if the incentive is removed, behavior typically returns to
original levels.

An alternative approach is to use social psychological theories of normative
influence to change recycling behavior. Social norms are beliefs about the ways in
which other people are, or should be, acting. Research by Schultz (1999) has
shown that providing normative feedback (both individual norms and group
norms) about curbside recycling increased recycling rates. Results from a study of
more than 600 households showed significant increases in both the frequency of
participation and the amount of material recycled for households that received
injunctive or descriptive feedback.

KEY CONCEPTS

Acid rain   damaging acids formed through chemical reactions in the atmosphere that fall to the earth in snow and rain. The principal chemicals involved in
acid rain are nitrogen and sulfur from burning coal and gasoline.

Carrying capacity   the number of people the earth can sustain.

Commons dilemma   a situation in which acting in one's self interest is detrimental to the group.

Descriptive social norms   beliefs about the behavior of other people.

Global warming   an increase in the earth's average temperature due to trapped
energy from the sun. The primary chemical responsible for global warming is carbon dioxide produced from burning fossil fuels like natural gas and petroleum.

Information campaigns   interventions intended to make people more knowledgeable about an issue, which in turn is expected to lead to a change in behavior.

Injunctive social norms   beliefs about what other people think is appropriate behavior.

Monetary disincentives   attempts to decrease the frequency of a behavior by imposing financial costs.

Monetary incentives   attempts to increase the frequency of a behavior by offering money as a reward.

Normative education   interventions that attempt to change children's beliefs about the prevalence and acceptability of substance use among their peers.

Overjustification effect   the reduction in intrinsic motivation produced when a person receives a reward for a behavior.

Ozone hole   localized reductions in atmospheric ozone caused by air pollution. The main chemical that causes ozone depletion is chlorine from CFC's like Freon and other chemicals used in refrigerants.

Prompts   brief signals about what actions to take.

Recycling   the collection, processing, and use of old products to make new products.

Regression to the mean   the tendency for extremely low or extremely high scorers to become more moderate over time.

Social influence   the use of social power to change the thoughts, feelings, or behaviors of another person in a specified direction.

Social norms   standards and rules, shared by members of a group, that guide and/or constrain behavior.

Sustainable lifestyle   ways of living which, if adopted by all people on the planet, could be supported indefinitely given the earth's finite resources.

REVIEW QUESTIONS

1. Describe three ways in which human behavior is harming the natural environment. For each environmental problem, identify a specific behavior that could be changed to help lessen the impact.

2. Are information campaigns effective at changing behavior? Why or why not?

3. If you were a state legislator, would you support or oppose a new bottle bill in which there was a 25-cent deposit on every beverage container? Why or why not?

4. Describe injunctive and descriptive social norms, and give an example of each.

5. Does changing a social norm lead to changes in behavior? Provide evidence to support your position.

6. Bill Spreewell is the recycling coordinator for a large waste-disposal company. If Bill can increase the amount of recyclables collected in the company's curbside recycling program, it will mean that less trash is put in the landfill and more revenue is generated from the sale of recyclable materials (it will also probably mean a promotion for Bill). Using what you have learned about social influence, how would you go about making this change? Be as specific as possible.

Activism For Social Change

As a boy, Cesar Chavez and his family were among 300,000 migrant workers who followed the crops in California. They traveled all over the state, picking whatever was in season for the farm owners. The migrant workers had no permanent homes. They lived in dingy overcrowded shacks, without bathrooms, electricity, or running water. Sometimes, they lived in the pickup trucks in which they traveled. Like the Chavez family, most of them were of Mexican descent.

Chavez worked part-time in the fields while he was in school. After graduation he began to work full-time. He kept noticing that the labor contractors and the land owners exploited the workers. He tried reasoning with the farm owners about higher pay and better working conditions, but most of his fellow workers would not support him for fear of losing their jobs. As a solitary voice, Chavez had no power.

To help inform the migrant workers of their rights, Chavez became a part-time organizer for the Community Service Organization. During the day, he picked apricots. In the evening, he organized farm workers to register to vote. By 1962, he became unwilling to see the workers being taken advantage of, working long hours for low pay. At the age of 35, he left his own well-paid job to devote all his time to organizing the farm workers into a union. His wife had to become a fruit picker in the fields to feed their children. Chavez traveled from camp to camp organizing the workers. In each camp, he recruited a few followers. At the end of six months, 300 members of the first farm workers union met in Fresno, California.

With a strong leader to represent them, the workers began to demand fair pay and better working conditions. A major confrontation occurred in 1965, when the

Figure 10–1   Cesar Chavez worked to promote change for migrant farm workers in California.

grape growers ignored union demands, and the farmhands wanted a strike. At first, Chavez wanted to avoid a strike, but he was finally convinced that there was no other way. The workers left the fields, and the unharvested grapes began to rot on the vines. The growers hired illegal workers and brought in strikebreakers and thugs to beat up the strikers.

The dispute was bitter. Union members—Chavez included—were jailed repeatedly. But public officials, religious leaders, and ordinary citizens from all across the United States flocked to California to march in support of the farm workers. Finally, in 1970, some grape growers signed agreements with the union. The union lifted the grape boycott, and its members began to pick grapes again. That same year, Chavez organized a nationwide boycott of lettuce.

By 1973, relations between the United Farm Workers of America and the grape growers had once again deteriorated, so a grape boycott was added to the boycott of lettuce. On several occasions, Chavez fasted nearly to death to protest the violence that arose. The union is still struggling to end inhuman conditions in the fields and win a fair day's pay. (Adapted Cesar Chavez Institute for Public Policy, 1999)

The preceding chapters of this book examined social psychological theories and the applications of these theories toward understanding and solving social problems—problems such as depression, divorce, environmental degradation, prejudice, teenage pregnancy, and violence. We hope that as you read about some of these issues, you were inspired to want to do something—to make a change—to use your knowledge to address a social issue. In this chapter, we examine some large-scale change programs that have utilized social psychological knowledge, as well as some of the roles for psychologists (from students to professionals) interested in making a change.

SOCIAL EXPERIMENTS

The activities of psychologists have customarily been confined to research, evaluation, dissemination of knowledge, and utilization of knowledge. Previous chapters of this book have presented many examples of the *research* projects and the *evaluation* activities of social psychologists. **Dissemination of knowledge** includes teaching, scholarly writing, and the less common activity of popularizing psychological knowledge to the general public. The **utilization of knowledge** role includes the typical nonactivist work of clinical and counseling psychologists, as well as a trend toward using social science findings to attack many kinds of social problems (Levine, Toro, & Perkins, 1993).

Rigorous research methods can provide useful information in the development of social programs. Campbell (1969, 1988) advocated just such an approach in order to create an "experimenting society." In such a society, experimental methods would be used (rather than guesswork, intuition, superstition, popular stereotypes, or "common sense") in deciding important issues of public policy. For instance, research could be applied to such questions as:

- Do stiffer punishments reduce the amount of crime?
- Are single-parent families less successful than two-parent families in raising children to be responsible adults?
- Would a guaranteed annual income reduce people's incentive to work?
- Does job-training reduce the amount of time a person spends on welfare?

Often the results of such research have provided surprising new insights about our society.

Fortunately, a wide range of innovative social research projects and even some large-scale true experiments have been conducted in areas such as education, housing, welfare, criminal justice, and energy use (Friedlander & Burtless, 1995; Hausman & Wise, 1985). Some of these studies have been truly monumental and long-term in scope. For instance, the Experimental Housing Allowance Program, sponsored by the U.S. Department of Housing and Urban Development, included three subsidiary experiments that lasted seven years and cost about $350 million to conduct (Friedman & Weinberg, 1983).

What is the value of these huge experiments? The most persuasive answer is that every dollar spent on research is returned later in greater savings. For example, a cost-benefit analysis of the Perry School Project—a predecessor of the Head Start program—found that for every dollar spent on the preschool intervention program, a $7 savings to society was seen after 20 years, due to less welfare use, less crime, lower expenditures on education, and increased employment rates (Schweinhart, Barnes, & Weikart, 1993). In general, social programs that spend more money on applied research produce more beneficial effects.

Social Experimentation on Welfare Programs

Nowhere has social experimentation been more prominent than in the area of welfare reform. Beginning in the late 19th century, programs of charity for the poor were implemented at the state and local levels, and in 1935 such support was federally funded through the Social Security Act (Schram, 1995). Since 1935, the purpose of welfare has changed. Early programs were intended to allow single mothers to focus on child care, and to keep women from competing with men in the labor force. More recent programs have been designed to encourage welfare recipients to work and become financially independent (Norris & Thompson, 1995). Early welfare programs were based solely on the hunches of policy-makers, and were not driven by social science evidence. However, social science data have played an increasingly important role in redesigning and improving the programs.

Welfare in the United States is largely administered through a federal program that provides cash allowances for children who have lost the support of a

parent who is absent, deceased, incapacitated, or unemployed. States have flexibility in determining the monthly level of support, and the amounts vary widely
from state to state (Norris & Thompson, 1995). Families in this program auto-
matically qualify for other entitlements, like food stamps and Medicaid. In 1992,
13.6 million Americans received money from this program at a cost of $22.2
billion.

Experiments with Welfare Reform.   In 1981 the Omnibus Budgeting
Reconciliation Act (OBRA) provided states increased flexibility in developing
welfare programs. This produced a proliferation of state programs and several
large-scale social experiments. These state-level programs were designed to accomplish two related goals. First, the reform programs attempted to increase the
earnings of people who received support, and subsequently to reduce the amount
of cash each participant received. With this in mind, many states implemented
so-called workfare programs to help people get off welfare and return to work.
We will briefly review the results from four such experimental programs implemented in Virginia, Arkansas, Maryland, and California, and reported by Friedlander and Burtless (1995).
    Participants in the experiments were applicants for the federal Aid to Fami-
lies with Dependent Children (AFDC) program. The applicants were randomly
assigned to either an experimental or a control condition. Control participants received the AFDC benefits normally provided in their area. Experimental recipients were required to participate in an additional program or risk reductions in
their AFDC benefits. The experimental interventions in the workfare programs
were:

- Virginia. Help in conducting a job search, and three months of unpaid work
  assignments intended to provide the recipient with work experience.
- Arkansas. Job search help, with some three-month unpaid work assignments.
- Baltimore, Maryland. Initial skills assessment with some choice in the job
  search process, along with either unpaid work assignments or education/
  training.
- San Diego, California. Assisted job search, three months of unpaid work assignments, followed by some education/training.

Sample sizes were 3,150 for Virginia, 1,127 for Arkansas, 2,757 for Baltimore,
and 3,211 for San Diego. Data were obtained from each participant quarterly for
two years, at which time the experimental intervention was discontinued. However, data were still collected for three years after the intervention was discontinued.
    Results from the five years of data are summarized in Figure 10–2. The fig-
ure shows the program's impact in terms of increased earnings, reduced AFDC
payments, and the net program cost for each of the four welfare experiments.

The dollar figures for earnings impact are the average difference between the experimental and control groups over the five-year period. Thus, the average experimental participant in Virginia earned $1,179 more than the average control participant over the five-year period. The earnings impacts for the four studies ranged from about $1,100 to about $2,100. A similar procedure was used to calculate the AFDC payments impact, where the average amount of AFDC received by the control group was subtracted from the average amount for the experimental group. Thus, participants in the Virginia experiment received $323 less over the five-year period than control participants. These savings ranged from about $60 to about $1,900. Figure 10–2 also shows the net cost (i.e., cost of the

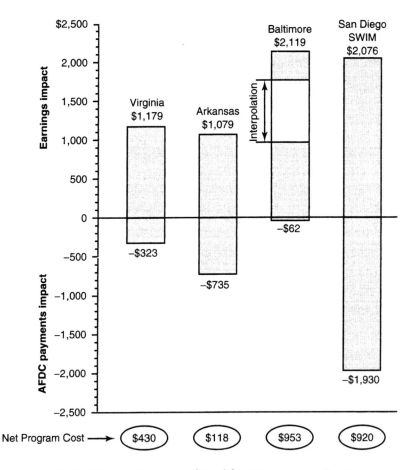

Figure 10–2   Observed Impacts of Workfare Programs on Participants'
Earnings and AFDC Payments in Four Experimental Programs. *Source:*
Friedlander & Burtless (1995, p. 11).

services provided per individual) for each program participant over the two-year experimental period. (The interpolation shown for the Baltimore program was due to a period when no data were collected, so that the impact assessment was based on estimates from the previous year.)

By the late 1980s the early results from these experiments were available, and in 1988 the Family Support Act was passed, providing support for the Job Opportunity and Basic Skills Training program (JOBS). The JOBS program was patterned after the earlier workfare programs and provided federal funding for education, training, and assisted job searches for AFDC applicants whose youngest child was at least 3 years old. In addition, the JOBS program provided payments for child care—a much-needed addition (Phillips, 1991).

1996 Welfare Reform. The largest recent change in U.S. welfare policy was signed into law by President Clinton in 1996 (Katz, 1996; Stanfield, 1996). This reform ended a guarantee of federal money to all eligible mothers and children, and it is estimated to save $54 billion by 2002. Some of the core elements of the program include:

- Welfare is funded through block grants to states, which allows for greater flexibility in administering the program at the state level.
- Adults who receive welfare benefits are required to begin work within two years, with some exceptions (e.g., single mothers with children under the age of one year).
- There is a maximum lifetime eligibility of five years for all welfare benefits.
- Only U.S. citizens are eligible for welfare benefits.

This legislation represents the largest overhaul of the welfare system in 61 years— but will it work? Clearly the intent of these changes is to motivate people to return to work. However, the changes were not based on the findings of empirical research, and predicting their exact effects is hazardous. Future research is needed to assess their impact.

Failures of Social Research to Influence Policy

Despite the success of numerous social experiments, many cases can be found where relevant social research has not been used to influence public policy (Pallak, 1990). Since the late 1960s several blue-ribbon scientific commissions have been assembled to report on the relationship of public policy to knowledge from the behavioral and social sciences, and all have agreed that the amount and quality of research utilization has been disappointing. Two prominent cases where research has failed to produce commensurate public policy concern the effects of pornography and gun control.

Public Policy and Pornography.   The 1970 Presidential Commission on Obscenity and Pornography provided social scientists an opportunity to summarize the research evidence for policy-makers. With a $2 million budget and two years to summarize the available social science evidence, the commission concluded that exposure to most forms of pornography did not cause changes in attitudes toward women or increase sexually violent tendencies. However, the commission was sharply criticized by knowledgeable inside observers for completely ignoring available research findings, citing inadequate and unconvincing research, selectively mentioning research that fit its viewpoint, and disregarding inconsistent data (Reuter, 1979; Zillman, 1992).

Another chance to summarize research on the effects of pornography came with the 1986 Attorney General's Commission on Pornography, which assembled evidence over the course of one year at a cost of $400,000 (Zillman, 1992). This commission concluded that sexually violent (as opposed to only violent or only sexual) pornography causes negative changes in attitudes, perceptions, and in some cases an increase in aggression toward women. However, the policy recommendations made by the commission were to strengthen *local* obscenity laws—laws allowed by a 1973 ruling of the Supreme Court, which stated that each community has the right to establish its own standard of obscenity, and that communities can use this standard to regulate the distribution of sexually explicit material (Linz, Malamuth, & Beckett, 1992). Thus, although certain types of pornography have clearly harmful effects, nothing was done federally to address it (see Linz et al., 1992, for several instances of local policy regarding pornography).

Public Policy and Gun Control.   The final report from the National Commission on the Causes and Prevention of Violence (1964) summarized research evidence on the effects of guns in the United States. The commission concluded (pp. 169–188):

> After extensive study we find that the availability of guns contributes substantially to violence in American society. . . . Our studies have convinced us that the heart of any effective national firearm policy for the United States must be to reduce the availability of the firearm that contributes to the most violence. This means restricting licensing of the handgun. . . . Reducing the availability of the handgun will reduce firearm violence.

The report went on to outline explicit strategies to reduce the availability of handguns, including strict licensing procedures and a prohibition against selling "junk guns." Despite the research evidence and the strong conclusions reached by the commission, the President and Congress did little to reduce the availability of handguns (Toch & Lizotte, 1992). As described in Chapter 1, the major reason for this inaction was the extensive lobbying and congressional campaign contributions of the National Rifle Association and other organizations opposed to any form of gun registration or control. These organizations prevailed despite the longtime favorability of a large majority of the U.S. population toward restrictive gun control laws (Moore & Newport, 1994).

ACTIVIST ROLES FOR SOCIAL PSYCHOLOGISTS

Clearly there are many public policies to which social psychological theory and research are relevant. The use, or misuse, of findings is a particularly crucial question for applied social psychologists. Because they are *applied* scientists, they are even more eager than other researchers to see their work used for the benefit of humanity, not just for the advancement of scientific knowledge.

Social activism is an unfamiliar role for most psychologists. Yet it is a vital role in accomplishing important social goals, and it is one that applied psychologists need to know about, whether or not they choose to adopt it themselves. We will define **activism** as *behaviors directed at accomplishing social change or attacking social problems.* Most psychologists and other social scientists have not concentrated their efforts in the fields of social change or social problems, although there are some outstanding exceptions.

One of these exceptions was Kurt Lewin. Lewin pioneered the concept of **action research**, in which research to advance knowledge is integrated into social action projects in a mutually beneficial merger. He was also instrumental in founding the *group dynamics* approach, which has subsequently expanded into a broad movement stressing personal growth and organizational development (including such techniques as T-groups, sensitivity training, encounter groups, etc.). Many of the people working within that movement are still faithfully pursuing Lewin's concept of applying scientific knowledge to create beneficial changes in interacting individuals, groups, and organizations (Wheelan, Pepitone, & Abt, 1990). In his *field theory*, Lewin presented theoretical ideas about how planned social change could be accomplished—for instance, through "unfreezing," moving, and "refreezing" group norms and standards (Lewin, 1951).

Followers of Lewin have systematically expanded on his theories and procedures for encouraging social change (Alderfer, 1993). One of the foremost of those disciples was Ronald Lippitt, who coined the term **change-agent** to describe an activist who tries to apply scientific principles and knowledge to produce desirable planned changes in society. The work of a change agent can include several different forms: expert consultation, collaboration, advocacy, and coercion (Ottaway, 1983). In the sections that follow, we will elaborate on each of these roles.

Expert Consultation

In the **expert role**, the change-agent uses his or her knowledge of research methodology and psychological theory to foster social change. An outstanding example is the work of Kelman and his colleagues to resolve international conflict

(Kelman, 1995). Through the use of **international problem-solving workshops**, Kelman has brought together unofficial representatives of contending factions in international and inter-ethnic disputes. These participants spend several intensive days examining one another's perspectives through informal but analytical discussion. These discussions are facilitated by social scientists knowledgeable about group dynamics and about the history of the conflict, and their procedures are informed by a large body of social psychological research on negotiation and third-party mediation (Lumsden & Wolfe, 1996). Such workshops have been employed effectively for over 20 years in the Israeli-Palestinian dispute by Kelman and his colleagues, and recently also in the Northern Ireland conflict and the Greek-Turkish dispute on Cyprus (Fisher, 1993). These workshops have been credited with contributing importantly to ongoing, official-level peace discussions, particularly since a number of their past participants have later held important policy-making positions (Kelman, 1995; Lumsden & Wolfe, 1996).

An even more ambitious research program is a huge social psychology project designed to change the quality of life of Thailand's 62 million people. Duangduen Bhanthumnavin directs an interdisciplinary action research team of 120 psychologists and behavioral scientists, health workers, teachers, and health service professionals. A variety of controlled experiments and correlational studies have been conducted as part of the project. Current projects include studies with police officers, parents, teachers, and various student groups. They focus on seven important behavioral areas: work, morality, health, family, democratic beliefs, natural resource conservation, and good citizenship (Fiedler, 1999; Bhanthumnavin, 1996, 1998).

Collaboration

The social psychologist can also take a **collaborative role**, maintaining a continuing relationship with the organization and sharing the responsibility for designing the research and implementing the changes that evolve from the research findings. In this **action research**, the research is an integral part of a program of social action, and the results of the action program contribute to new theoretical and empirical knowledge. Because Kurt Lewin originated this concept, many of his students and followers have done outstanding action-research studies. One classic example was the study conducted by Coch and French (1948) in a garment factory. There they used group-discussion and group-decision methods to decrease workers' resistance to the frequent necessary changes in work activities as different types of garments were produced. Some of the results of this approach included better worker morale, less disruption of production, increased productivity, and reduced employee turnover.

A more recent industrial example was a project at a Xerox plant in New York (Whyte, Greenwood, & Lazes, 1991). There, management had proposed the necessity of closing a major department and laying off its 180 workers in order to save over $3 million per year. Instead, for an interim period, a cooperative labor-management "cost-study team" was formed. This newly formed team of two managers and six union members worked full-time for six months, and was given full access to management financial information and an adequate budget, as well as the right to propose changes in work rules and labor contracts. Creatively addressing formerly out-of-bounds areas, the team found that huge savings could be made in training costs for new personnel by stabilizing the workforce and avoiding the former high rates of employee transfers; similarly, previous high overhead charges could be cut by having the necessary services performed within the department. These and other projected savings added up to more than $3.5 million, and consequently the recommended changes were made and the department was not closed. Management was so happy with the results that it extended the cost-study team mechanism to other departments, with annual savings that reached 40% for some departments.

Advocacy

Social psychologists can also produce social change by influencing public policy—typically using an **advocacy role**. Advocates trying to change a social condition often aim their efforts, not at the problem itself, but at mobilizing legislators, courts, or disadvantaged groups to take action directed toward reform. A common way to influence public policy is to consult with legislators as they develop proposed laws and programs (Lee et al., 1994). One view of the policy advocate's task is to "speak truth to power"—the description originally given by Rexford Tugwell of his role in President Franklin D. Roosevelt's circle of advisors (Wildavsky, 1979). Of course, the classic way of influencing prospective legislation is by lobbying, as has been done with increasing effectiveness in recent years by the American Psychological Association and the American Psychological Society (cf. Melton, 1995; Vincent, 1990).

An important question for advocates is: To what extent do government officials listen? One way to answer this question is to see the extent to which mass public opinion (a particular type of research evidence) is incorporated into public policy. A later section of this chapter will examine the research on this topic.

Organizing and Agitating

We come now to the final form of activism for social psychologists, the **coercive role**. In contrast to the previous approaches, which made use of *consensus* tactics, organizing and agitating frequently rely on *conflict* as a tactic. The conflict-arousing activities of **agitators** often diverge sharply from those of **reformers**—individuals who generally try to work within the norms of the system in their efforts to change it. Community organization as a professional area had its heyday in the 1960s and declined somewhat during the subsequent decades (Reisch & Wenocur, 1986). However, recent years have seen the emergence of many diverse examples of **grassroots organizing**—a form of advocacy which originates with local community members and aims to empower them toward achieving locally determined collective goals (Wittig & Bettencourt, 1996).

Though conflict and agitation have a negative public image, it is nevertheless important to be familiar with these tactics and to understand their strengths and limitations in achieving social change.

SAUL ALINSKY: A RENOWNED COMMUNITY ORGANIZER

Since there is little research evidence on conflict and coercive tactics for social change, we will rely here primarily on experiential reports from those who have used these tactics and written about their experiences. Among these, one of the most colorful and influential figures was Saul Alinsky. Drawing on more than 30 years of personal involvement as a community organizer, he wrote a book titled *Rules for Radicals: A Practical Primer for Realistic Radicals* (Alinsky, 1971), which he characterized as follows: "*The Prince* was written by Machiavelli for the Haves on how to hold power. *Rules for Radicals* is written for the Have-Nots on how to take it away" (p. 3).

Alinsky had graduate training in sociology, but his tactics were largely self-taught and innovative ways of applying social psychological principles of social influence. He believed in appealing to the self-interest of all parties in a conflict, and his tactics were designed to convince the opposition that it was in their best interest to grant the demands of his community groups. Alinsky wrote about revolution and often appeared eager to shock his readers and listeners as a way of getting them to think more deeply about the nature of our social system. However, by revolution he did not mean armed insurrection or the use of violence. He was a radical in the sense that the word means "attacking the *root* of a problem." And he was committed to working within the system even while he was challenging the power and perquisites of the establishment.

Alinsky's first major community-organization project was behind the stockyards in Chicago, a vicious slum area about which Upton Sinclair had written in his book, *The Jungle*. In 1940 Alinsky founded the Industrial Areas Foundation, through which he and his staff members took on organizing jobs in many cities across the country. His famous organizing efforts included the Woodlawn Organization in the Black ghetto near the University of Chicago; FIGHT (Freedom, Integration, God, Honor, Today) in the Black area of Rochester, New York; BUILD in Buffalo, New York; the Chelsea Community Council in a multi-ethnic area of New York City; and organizations in White, Puerto Rican, and Hispanic areas of several other cities. During breaks in his organizing efforts, some of them spent in jail for his activities, Alinsky wrote several books about community organizing that became highly influential texts for other organizers, and later Alinsky set up a training institute for community action workers.

Alinsky stressed that conflict and coercive tactics are used only after consensus and collaborative approaches have been thoroughly tried and have failed.

Even then, conflict tactics should be used in combination with other, milder advocacy strategies, to provide variety and impact, and to emphasize the seriousness of one's cause. Alinsky and his organizing team were usually called into community-problem areas only when all customary avenues of redress were blocked or fruitless. An extensive study of eight of Alinsky's most representative community-organizing campaigns has corroborated Alinsky's typical use of less-conflictive techniques before resorting to more extreme tactics (Lancourt, 1979).

Alinsky's Conflict Tactics

Though Alinsky often used cooperative or advocacy tactics, we will concentrate here on his conflict tactics because they are more colorful and less known to conventional psychologists. Box 10–1 presents some of Alinsky's rules for winning conflicts.

A particularly poignant example of how to apply these rules was suggested by Alinsky when he was helping African-Americans in the Woodlawn Organization negotiate with Chicago authorities. Some commitments by city hall were not being honored, and the frequently effective threat to vote for someone else was not effective at this time because it was in the middle of the 1964 Johnson-Goldwater presidential campaign, and Blacks saw no alternative to supporting Johnson. Consequently, organizers needed some other way to keep the pressure on city hall. The target chosen was Chicago's O'Hare Airport, the world's busiest airport. The method proposed was to tie up all of O'Hare's toilet facilities by busing loads of Woodlawn residents to the airport and having them occupy every stall, remaining there reading a magazine or newspaper, and thus preventing travelers from satisfying their bodily needs—what Alinsky called a "shit-in." Scouts were sent to the airport to count the number of toilets and urinals, and Woodlawn Organization leaders began fantasizing how this strategy would get worldwide publicity and mortify the Chicago city authorities. Alinsky (1971, pp. 143–144) reports that the plans for this tactic were leaked to informers, who quickly told city hall, and the simple threat was all that was necessary.

> Within forty-eight hours the Woodlawn Organization found itself in conference with the authorities who said that they were certainly going to live up to their commitments and they could never understand where anyone got the idea that a promise made by Chicago's City Hall would not be observed. At no point, then or since, has there ever been any open mention of the threat of the O'Hare tactic. Very few of the members of the Woodlawn Organization knew how close they were to writing history.

This example clearly illustrates many of Alinsky's principles. Using toilets in public facilities was a familiar experience to Alinsky's followers, but having all the toilets in a whole airport permanently occupied was far beyond the experience of the authorities, and they had no procedures for handling such a situation. The Woodlawn residents would have enjoyed creating such a spectacle, and the result would have held the Chicago authorities up to international ridicule. This contin-

Box 10–1   Alinsky's Conflict Tactics

1. "Power is not only what you have but what the enemy thinks you have." Alinsky suggested that if you have developed a large mass-organization in your community, you can parade it visibly to impress the opposition; if your organization is small, you can still make a lot of noise; and "if your organization is too tiny even for noise, stink up the place." You have to start from where you are and use whatever you've got.

2. "Never go outside the experience of your people." By this, Alinsky meant that tactics should always be something your members are familiar and comfortable with.

3. "Wherever possible go outside of the experience of the enemy." By doing something unexpected and foreign to their experience, you can produce confusion, fear, and retreat. An example from the Civil War is Sherman's marching through Georgia instead of fighting a conventional battle against the Confederate armies.

4. "Make the enemy live up to their own book of rules. You can kill them with this, for they can no more obey their own rules than the Christian church can live up to Christianity."

5. "Ridicule is man's most potent weapon. It is almost impossible to counter-attack ridicule. Also it infuriates the opposition, who then react to your advantage."

6. "A good tactic is one that your people enjoy. If your people are not having a ball doing it, there is something very wrong with the tactic."

7. "The threat is usually more terrifying than the thing itself."

8. "The major premise for tactics is the development of operations that will maintain a constant pressure upon the opposition. It is this unceasing pressure that results in the reactions from the opposition that are essential for the success of the campaign." And your side's actions are in turn responses to the opposition's reactions.

9. "The price of a successful attack is a constructive alternative." You have to know what you want and be ready with a proposal or a plan whenever the opposition gives in to your pressure.

10. "Pick the target, freeze it, personalize it, and polarize it." Freezing the target means singling out whoever is to blame for a given problem and not letting them get off the hook. Personalizing means picking out a particular person or persons who are responsible (such as the mayor, or the officers of a corporation), not an anonymous organization. Polarizing it means to get people to line up strongly against your target, acting as if it were 100% bad.

Source: Excerpts from Alinsky (1971, pp. 126–130).

ued pressure was necessary to ensure the city's living up to commitments previously won by other pressure tactics. City hall knew that Alinsky's group had the power to carry out this tactic, and consequently only the hint of a threat to do it was enough to gain the authorities' renewed cooperation.

Outcomes of Alinsky's Organizing

How successful are such tactics? It is difficult to give a single answer because the results have varied so much in different campaigns with differing external conditions. In more than 30 years of organizing, Alinsky either founded or consulted on a regular basis with 14 major community organizations in many cities. Each had its own grievances, goals, and priorities, around which Alinsky and his staff built the organization. In a general sense all the goals involved reducing neighborhood deterioration through a process of citizen participation and community control. The most frequent target areas for improvements were the quality of housing, schools, and prospects for employment. Other goals of some of the organizations included improvement of welfare services, city services, police and fire protection, consumer problems, small business opportunities, and various neighborhood service programs (Finks, 1984; Lancourt, 1979).

These community campaigns achieved many of their specific goals, though it was often necessary to refight the same or similar battles to maintain the gains over time. Some of the success stories included the Woodlawn Organization's planning and building a 500-apartment development of low-income housing, complete operation of a ghetto-area grade school in Buffalo, and a campaign against the Kodak Company in Rochester, New York, that won commitments for over 1,000 new jobs for minorities in one year. Other goals were never reached or abandoned as too difficult, but since each organization had a series of goals, there were usually enough successes to keep the group functioning. Indeed, a setback often led to more cohesion and dedication from the members. Even where there seem to have been few objective achievements, it is quite possible that the neighborhoods would be even worse off now if Alinsky and the organization had never been there. Some of Alinsky's organizations continued as active forces in their communities in Chicago, Rochester, Buffalo, and other cities for as long as 40 years.

Probably the most important national impact of Alinsky's organizations was in providing an influential model for other citizen-action programs and a training ground for scores of community organizers who went on to work in other action programs—individuals like Cesar Chavez, who later founded the United Farm Workers union (Lancourt, 1979). Many current community organizers draw heavily on Alinsky's methods, and there are many testimonials to their success, though there is little direct research evidence on the subject (Horwitt, 1989; Reitzes & Reitzes, 1986).

Many current activist groups have adopted some of Alinsky's confrontational and polarizing tactics. One of the most successful of these is Greenpeace, which specializes in direct-action campaigns on environmental and health issues. For example, publicity generated by Greenpeace prevented the Shell Oil Company from dumping an abandoned North Sea oil platform holding 130 tons of toxic waste into the deep ocean. Techniques used included nonviolent occupation of the abandoned platform, bringing journalists to observe and photograph the tugs pulling the platform, and mobilizing political and diplomatic support in eight other nations to boycott Shell products and pressure the British government to revoke the permit it had granted for dumping the platform. After several days of this confrontation, Shell admitted that its revenues were being decimated, and it agreed not to dump the rig in the ocean (*Greenpeace*, 1995).

EFFECTS OF PRESSURE GROUPS

All of our discussion of activism has implicitly or explicitly assumed that it can be an effective technique, and there is much evidence to support this view. Many analysts stress that our political system is heavily influenced by the actions of pressure groups (Knoke, 1990). Some even claim that groups are so dominant in our system that the political and social views of any individual are irrelevant unless they are registered through group pressures. Though this is probably an overstatement, it emphasizes how important group pressures are in our system because of their potential political effects.

People often ask what they, as single individuals, can do to encourage social change. The answer is simple—*join an organization!* Better still, you can join several organizations that take public stands on social issues and work to support their positions (e.g., a political party, a civil-rights group, an environmental organization, or a single-issue organization working on a topic like smoking or handgun control). It is true that individuals may occasionally influence their representatives through a friendly contact or a thoughtful letter, but the real political power in our pluralistic system lies in groups that are willing to organize and work to reach their goals (Zigler & Muenchow, 1984). As an experienced change agent wrote, "Whatever your role—company manager . . . college dean, missionary or society hostess—if you need more power to act, your aim must be to build (or change) an appropriate organization to provide it for you" (Peabody, 1971, p. 523).

Citizens who do not register their opinions through an organized pressure group will have little influence on political or social events. By contrast, taking part in group plans and activities can increase one's sense of personal efficacy and reduce feelings of social alienation. To further your sense of self-efficacy, Table 10–1 provides names, brief descriptions, and contact information for several different activist organizations. However, there are thousands of local, national, and international organizations devoted to many different causes. We encourage you to join one.

Table 10–1 Activist Organizations

Organization	Description	Cost	Website	Address
Action on Smoking and Health (ASH)	Educational organization fighting for the rights of nonsmokers and against public health risks from tobacco.	$25	http://ash.org	2013 H Street, NW; Washington, DC, 20006. (202) 659-4310
American Civil Liberties Union (ACLU)	Ensures that the Bill of Rights—amendments to the Constitution that guard unwarranted governmental control—are preserved for each new generation.	Donation	www.aclu.org	125 Broad Street, 18th Floor; New York, NY 10004-2400
American Psychological Association (APA)	Works to advance psychology as a science, as a profession, and as a means of promoting students human welfare.	$27 for students	www.apa.org	750 First Street, NE; Washington, DC 20002. (202) 336-5500
American Psychological Society (APS)	Promotes, protects, and advances the interests of scientifically oriented psychology in research, application, and the improvement of human welfare.	$48 for students	www.psychological-science.org	1010 Vermont Avenue NW, Suite 1100; Washington, DC 20005-4907. (202) 783-2077
Amnesty International	Seeks to free all prisoners of conscience, ensure fair and prompt trials for political prisoners, abolish the death penalty, torture, and cruel treatment of prisoners, and end political killings	Donation	www.amnesty.org	1 Easton Street; London WC1X 8DJ; United Kingdom
Children's Defense Fund	Seeks to ensure every child a Healthy Start, a Head Start, a Fair Start, a Safe Start, and a Moral Start in life, and successful passage to adulthood with the help of caring families and communities.	Donation	www.childrensdefense.org	25 E Street NW; Washington, DC 20001. 202-628-8787
Coalition to Stop Gun Violence	Seeks the orderly elimination of the private sale of handguns and assault weapons in the United States and the reduction of gun violence.	$15 for students	www.gunfree.org	1000 16th Street, NW, Suite 603; Washington, DC 20036
Common Cause	Fights for open, honest, and accountable government at the national, state, and local levels.	$10 for students	www.projectindependence.org	1250 Connecticut Avenue, NW; Washington, DC 20036

Table 10–1 Activist Organizations (cont.)

Organization	Description	Cost	Website	Address
Greenpeace	Protects the environment by peaceful means.	$30	*www.greenpeace.org*	1436 U Street, NW; Washington, DC 20009. 1-800-326-0959
National Association for the Advancement of Colored People (NAACP)	Seeks to ensure the political, educational, social, and economic equality of minority-group citizens of the United States.	$10	*www.naacp.org*	4805 Mt. Hope Drive; Baltimore, MD 21215
National Peace Foundation	Mission: to abolish nuclear weapons, to create an International Criminal Court, and to use science and technology for constructive purposes.	$15 for students	*www.wagingpeace.org*	1187 Coast Village Road, Suite 123; Santa Barbara, CA; 93108. (805) 965-3443
Natural Resources Defense Council	Fosters the fundamental right of all people to have a voice in decisions that affect their environment. Seeks to reduce environmental burdens borne by people of color and others who face social or economic inequities.	$10	*www.open.igc.org/nrdc/*	40 West 20th Street; New York, NY 10011 (212) 727-2700
Society for the Psychological Study of Social Issues (SPSSI)	Brings psychological theory and practice into focus on social problems of the group, the community, and the nation.	$10 for students	*www.spssi.org*	PO Box 1248; Ann Arbor, MI, 48106-1248.
Student Conservation Association	Fosters lifelong stewardship of the environment by offering people the opportunity to serve and protect our nation's valuable national parks, forests, and urban communities.	Donation	*www.sca-inc.org*	689 River Road; PO Box 550; Charlestown, NH 03603-0550. (603) 543-1700
Union of Concerned Scientists	Promotes stewardship of the global environment; promotes energy technologies that are renewable, safe, and cost effective; seeks to transform the nation's transportation system away from use of polluting fuels and to curtail weapons proliferation.	Free	*www.ucsusa.org*	2 Brattle Square; Cambridge, MA 02238-9105. (617) 547-5552

DOES PUBLIC POLICY FOLLOW PUBLIC OPINION?

A central principle of democracy is that government derives its legitimacy from the consent of the governed, and therefore that public policy should generally follow the will of the people. Even politicians who view their role as leading the public usually realize that they can't get too far out in front of the people and still retain a following. Today, leaders use polls to determine the views of the total public, or any relevant subgroup, on any particular issue. In election campaigns, many politicians now use opinion polls to position themselves on major current issues—for instance, by adopting campaign stands, or arguments for their stands, that the polls show will receive a favorable public response.

An Illustrative Study

How well do government actions actually follow public opinion? Some important evidence on this question was provided by research that examined the relationship between liberal-conservative ideology and liberal-conservative policies at the state level (Erikson, Wright, & McIver, 1993). An index of liberal state policies was created by examining state policies on a variety of issues. Public opinion in each state was assessed by combining the results from 122 CBS surveys. Both indices were found to be extremely stable between 1976 and 1988. The resulting relationship between public opinion and public policy across the 50 states is shown in Figure 10–3. The statistical correlation between these two measures was $r = .82$.

These results show a strong relationship between public opinion and public policy. However, the conclusion that public opinion *causes* public policy, and not the reverse, is debatable. Although several authors have made a strong case for such a causal connection, there are some instances where public opinion can be changed by public policy. For instance, the change in U.S. racial attitudes and reductions in prejudice since 1950 would probably not have occurred without the 1954 ruling of the Supreme Court requiring integrated public schools.

ETHICAL ISSUES

The topic of influencing public policy inevitably raises questions of values and ethics. What goals will applied social scientists try to accomplish, and in whose interests will they work? In the past, when psychologists did applied work, it was most often in the service of the status quo and the establishment, rather than aimed at social change (Prilleltensky, 1990). As a result, many individually-oriented psychologists unfortunately tended to "blame the victims" of social ills by studying their "deficits," rather than attack the underlying social problems, such as poverty, poor health care, and inadequate educational systems (Caplan &

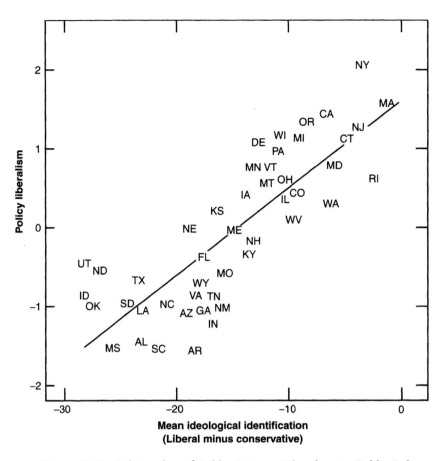

Figure 10-3   Relationship of Public Opinion Liberalism to Public Policy Liberalism Across 50 States. *Source:* Erickson, Wright, & McIver (1993).

Nelson, 1973). Consultation to the poor and weak is an unusual role for most psychologists, as Morton Deutsch (1969, p. 33) pointed out:

> If we have given any advice at all, it has been to those in high power. The unwitting consequence of this one-sided consultant role has been that we have too often assumed that the social pathology has been in the ghetto rather than in those who have built the walls to surround it, that the "disadvantaged" are the ones who need to be changed rather than the people and the institutions who have kept the disadvantaged in a submerged position.

Even where social scientists avoid these problems, in trying to influence public policy they need to carry out evaluation research to study the effects of policy changes. It is important to note that even well-intentioned social reforms and interventions can often produce unexpected harmful effects, such as welfare programs that leave their clients more disadvantaged and dependent than before (Lindblom, 1990; Sieber, 1981).

There are no simple answers to these questions, but an important starting place is for applied social psychologists to be aware of them. The ethical code of the American Psychological Association (1992) stresses the importance of serving the public interest above the interests of other individuals or groups. The most important guideline in trying to influence public policy is that social scientists must be constantly vigilant to ensure that their efforts genuinely do "promote the general welfare."

SUMMARY

This book has examined some of the ways in which social psychological theory can be used to help understand and solve social problems. Our focus has been on interventions conducted at the individual or community level. In this chapter, we examined social activism and the application of psychological theory at higher levels of government. In an *experimenting society*, public policy would be informed by research. For example, U.S. welfare reform has been shaped, to some extent, by research on workfare and job-training additions to traditional welfare assistance. Unfortunately, this sort of research influence is the exception more than the rule, and applied social psychologists need to be familiar with the roles of activists.

Social activism is an unfamiliar role for psychologists. Kurt Lewin was one of its first proponents within social psychology, and his followers in the group dynamics movement are still among the most dedicated change-agents. One classification of change-agent behaviors lists four kinds of activist roles: expert, collaborative, advocacy, and coercive.

In the expert role, psychologists may conduct research for social change, as illustrated by Kelman's international problem-solving workshops. Collaboration involves maintaining a continuing relationship with an organization in order to help implement changes based on research findings. In the advocacy role, social psychologists work toward reform by influencing decision-makers. Organizing and agitating, the most intense form of activism, often involve a coercive role in which social conflict is encouraged in order to reach certain valued ends. This strategy is illustrated by Saul Alinsky's colorful confrontation tactics and his community organizations, which have provided influential models for citizen-action programs and training grounds for community organizers.

Our political system is heavily influenced by the actions of pressure groups, whereas individuals acting alone can rarely exert any influence. Therefore, it is important that you join an activist organization and work for the general welfare of our society.

KEY CONCEPTS

Action research   type of research advocated by Kurt Lewin in which research to advance knowledge is integrated into social action projects in a mutually beneficial merger.

Activism   behaviors directed at accomplishing social change or attacking social problems.

Advocacy role   mobilizing legislators, courts, or disadvantaged groups to take action directed toward reform.

Agitators   change-agents who rely on conflict as a tactic to produce change.

Change-agent   an activist who tries to apply social psychological principles and knowledge to produce desirable planned changes in society.

Coercive role   making use of conflict, threats, or violence to produce social change.

Collaborative role   maintaining a continuing relationship with an organization and sharing the responsibility for designing research and implementing the changes that evolve from the research findings.

Dissemination of knowledge   teaching, scholarly writing, and popularizing of psychological knowledge to the general public.

Experimenting society   a society in which experimental methods are used in deciding important issues of public policy.

Expert role   using professional knowledge of research methodology and psychological theory to foster social change.

Grassroots organizing   a form of advocacy which originates in mobilizing local community members and aims to empower them toward achieving locally determined collective goals.

International problem-solving workshops   an approach to resolving international conflicts in which unofficial representatives of contending factions in international or inter-ethnic disputes are brought together for several intensive days to examine one another's perspectives through informal but analytical discussion.

Reformers   individuals who generally try to work within the norms of the system in their efforts to change it.

Utilization of knowledge   includes the nonactivist work of clinical and counseling psychologists, as well as activist efforts to use social science findings to attack many kinds of social problems.

REVIEW QUESTIONS

1. Describe three benefits of conducting social experiments. For each benefit, give a specific example.
2. Summarize the changes that were made to U.S. welfare policy in 1996. Based on your knowledge of social psychological theory, what effects do you think these changes will have? Is there any research evidence to support your answer?
3. Does public opinion influence public policy? Support your answer.
4. Your friend Aaron is concerned about violence and wants to reduce handgun-related shootings. Describe four tactics or activist roles that Aaron could use to influence local policies on handguns. For each, give a specific example.

Photo Credits

Chapter 1. 01-01., *Clash between Pro-choice and Pro-life Advocates outside Supreme Court.*, Photographer: Reuter. Source: Corbis. **01-02.**, *Social Activities.*, Source: Schultz.
Chapter 2. 02-01., *Wylita, age 17, and her two daughters Do'Nissa and Monica.*, Source: Schultz.
Chapter 4. 04-04., *Students in class.*, Source: Schultz.
Chapter 5. 05-02., *Couple in love.*, Source: Schultz
Chapter 6. 06-02., *Sample photograph and social scenario from the Second Step Violence Prevention Curriculum.*, Source: Committee for Children.
Chapter 7. 07-02., *Teacher with students.*, Source: Schultz.
Chapter 8. 08-01., *Ron McClelland and George Gannett.*, Source: Nicholas Nixon. **08-03.**, *Centers for Disease Control and Prevention Pamplet.*, Source: Centers for Disease Control and Prevention (CDC)
Chapter 9. 09-01., *Landfill.*, Source: Schultz. **09-02.**, *Cars on the freeway.*, Source: Schultz.
Chapter 10., 10-01., *Cesar Chavez.*, Source: Cesar E. Chavez Institute for Public Library.

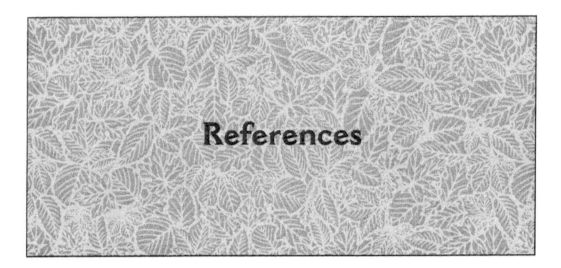

References

Abramson, L. Y., Seligman, M. E. P., & Teasdale, J. D. (1978). Learned helplessness in people: Critique and reformulation. *Journal of Abnormal Psychology, 87,* 49–74.

Ackerman, P. L., & Humphreys, L. G. (1990). Individual differences theory in industrial and organizational psychology. In M. D. Dunnette & L. M. Hough (Eds.), *Handbook of industrial & organizational psychology* (2nd ed., Vol. 1, pp. 223–282). Palo Alto, CA: Consulting Psychologists Press.

Ajzen, I. (1988). *Attitudes, personality, and behavior.* Chicago: Dorsey.

Ajzen, I. (1991). The theory of planned behavior. *Organizational Behavior and Human Decision Processes, 50,* 179–211.

Ajzen, I., & Fishbein, M. (1980). *Understanding attitudes and predicting social behavior.* Englewood Cliffs, NJ: Prentice-Hall.

Alderfer, C. P. (Ed.). (1993). Emerging developments in action research [Special Issue]. *Journal of Applied Behavioral Science, 29,* 389–492.

Alexander, K. L., & Entwisle, D. R. (1988). Achievement in the first 2 years of school: Patterns and processes. *Monographs of the Society for Research in Child Development, 53,* 1–157.

Alinsky, S. D. (1971). *Rules for radicals: A practical primer for realistic radicals.* New York: Random House.

Allport, G. W. (1954). *The nature of prejudice.* Reading, MA: Addison-Wesley.

Altemeyer, B. (1994). Reducing prejudice in right-wing authoritarians. In M. P. Zanna & J. M. Olson (Eds.), *The psychology of prejudice: The Ontario Symposium* (Vol. 7, pp. 131–148). Hillsdale, NJ: Erlbaum.

Alvidrez, J. (1994). Early teacher expectations and later student achievement. Unpublished master's thesis. University of California, Berkeley.

Amabile, T. M., Hill, K. G., Hennessey, B. A., & Tighe, E. M. (1994). The work preference inventory: Assessing intrinsic and extrinsic motivational orientations. *Journal of Personality and Social Psychology, 66,* 950–967.

Amato, P. R. (1996). Explaining the intergenerational transmission of divorce. *Journal of Marriage and the Family, 58,* 628–640.

Amato, P. R., & Keith, B. (1991a). Parental divorce and adult well-being: A meta-analysis. *Journal of Marriage and the Family, 53,* 43–59.

Amato, P. R., & Keith, B. (1991b). Parental divorce and the well-being of children: A meta-analysis. *Psychological Bulletin, 110,* 26–46.

Amato, P. R., & Rogers, S. J. (1997). A longitudinal study of marital problems and subsequent divorce. *Journal of Marriage and the Family, 59,* 612–625.

American Council on Education. (1990). *Minorities in higher education.* Washington, DC: Office of Minority Concerns.

American Psychological Association. (1982). *Ethical principles in the conduct of research with human participants* (rev. ed.). Washington, DC: APA.

American Psychological Association. (1992). Ethical principles of psychologists and code of conduct. *American Psychologist, 47,* 1597–1611.

Anderson, C. A., Horowitz, L. M., & French, R. D. (1983). Attributional style of lonely and depressed people. *Journal of Personality and Social Psychology, 45,* 127–136.

Andreasen, M. (1994). Patterns of family life and television consumption from 1945 to the 1990s. In D. Zillman, J. Bryant, & A. Huston (Eds.), *Media, children, and the family: Social scientific, psychodynamic, and clinical perspectives* (pp. 19–36). Hillsdale, NJ: Erlbaum.

Aron, A., & Aron, E. N. (1999). *Statistics for psychology.* Upper Saddle River, NJ: Prentice-Hall.

Aron, A., Melinat, E., Aron, E. N., Vallone, R. D., & Bator, R. J. (1997). The experimental generation of interpersonal closeness: A procedure and some preliminary findings. *Personality and Social Psychology Bulletin, 23,* 363–377.

Aronson, E. (1997). The theory of cognitive dissonance: The evaluation and vicissitudes of an idea. In C. McGarty & S. Haslam (Eds.), *The message of social psychology: Perspective on mind and society* (pp. 20–35). Oxford, England: Blackwell.

Aronson, E. (1998). Dissonance, hypocrisy, and the self-concept. In E. Harmon-Jones & J. S. Mills (Eds.), *Cognitive dissonance theory: Revival with revisions and controversies.* Washington, DC: American Psychological Association.

Aronson, E., Blaney, N., Stephan, C., Sikes, J., & Snapp, M. (1978). *The jigsaw classroom.* Beverly Hills, CA: Sage.

Aronson, E., Fried, C., & Stone, J. (1991). Overcoming denial and increasing the intention to use condoms through the induction of hypocrisy. *American Journal of Public Health, 81,* 1636–1638.

Aronson, E., Wilson, T. D., & Brewer, M. B. (1998). Experimentation in social psychology. In D. T. Gilbert, S. T. Fiske, & G. Lindzey (Eds.), *The handbook of social psychology* (4th ed., Vol. 1, pp. 99–142). New York: Oxford University Press.

Austin, J., Hatfield, D., Grindle, A., & Bailey, J. (1993). Increasing recycling in office environments: The effects of specific informative cues. *Journal of Applied Behavioral Analysis, 26,* 247–253.

Babad, E. (1993). Pygmalion—25 years after interpersonal expectations in the classroom. In P. Blanck (Ed.), *Interpersonal expectations: Theory, research, and application* (pp. 125–153). Paris, France: Cambridge University Press.

Babad, E., Inbar, J., & Rosenthal, R. (1982). Pygmalion, Galatea, and the Golem: Investigators of biased and unbiased teachers. *Journal of Educational Psychology, 74,* 459–474.

Ball-Rokeach, S. J., Rokeach, M., & Grube, J. W. (1984). *The great American values test: Influencing behavior and belief through television.* New York: Free Press.

Bandura, A. (1973). *Aggression: A social learning analysis.* Englewood Cliffs, NJ: Prentice-Hall.

Bandura, A. (1986). *Social foundations of thought and action: A social cognitive theory.* Englewood Cliffs, NJ: Prentice-Hall.

Bandura, A. (1997). *Self-efficacy: The exercise of control.* New York: Freeman.

Bandura, A., Ross, D., & Ross, S. A. (1963). Imitation of film-mediated aggressive models. *Journal of Abnormal and Social Psychology, 66,* 3–11.

Barfield, R. J. (1984). Reproductive hormones and aggressive behavior. In K. J. Flannelly, R. J., Blanchard, & D. C., Blanchard (Eds.), *Biological perspectives on aggression* (pp. 105–134). New York: Alan Liss.

Barnett, W. S. (1992). Benefits of compensatory preschool education. *Journal of Human Resources, 27,* 279–312.

Baron, R. A., & Richardson, D. (1994). *Human aggression.* New York: Plenum.

Baron, R. H., Tom, D. Y., & Cooper, H. M. (1985). Social class, race and teacher expectations. In J. Dusek (Ed.), *Teacher expectations* (pp. 251–270). Hillsdale, NJ: Erlbaum.

Beelmann, A., Pfingsten, U., & Losel, F. (1994). Effects of training social competence in children: A meta-analysis of recent evaluation studies. *Journal of Clinical Child Psychology, 23,* 260–271.

Berkowitz, L. (1989). Frustration-aggression hypothesis: Examination and reformulation. *Psychological Bulletin, 106,* 59–73.

Berkun, M. M., Bialek, H. M., Kern, R. P., & Yagi, K. (1962). Experimental studies of psychological stress in man. *Psychological Monographs, 76* (15, Whole No. 534).

Berscheid, E. (1992). A glance back at a quarter century of social psychology. *Journal of Personality and Social Psychology, 65,* 525–533.

Berscheid, E. (1998). A social psychological view of marital disfunction and sta-
    bility. In T. Bradbury (Ed.), *The developmental course of marital disfunction*
    (pp. 441–459). New York: Cambridge University Press.
Berscheid, E., & Lopes, J. (1997). A temporal model of relationship satisfaction
    and stability. In R. J. Sternberg & M. Hojjat (Eds.), *Satisfaction in close rela-
    tionships* (pp. 129–159). New York: Guilford.
Berscheid, E., & Reis, H. (1998). Attraction and close relationships. In D. T.
    Gilbert, S. T. Fiske, & G. Lindzey (Eds.), *Handbook of social psychology* (4th
    ed., Vol. 2, pp. 193–281). Boston, MA: McGraw-Hill.
Bersoff, D. N. (Ed.). (1995). *Ethical conflicts in psychology*. Washington, DC:
    American Psychological Association.
Bhanthumnavin, D. (1996). The applications of research findings from psycho-
    behavioral science for the development of Thai individuals. *Thai Journal of
    Psychology, 3*, 46–60.
Bhanthumnavin, D. (1998, August). A new model of socialization for improving
    work performance and quality of life in Thailand. Invited paper presented at
    the International Congress of Applied Psychology, San Francisco.
Blankenhorn, D., Bayme, S., & Bethke, E. J. (Eds.). (1990). *Rebuilding the nest: A
    new commitment to the American family*. Milwaukee: Family Service America.
Blanton, H., VandenEijnden, R. J. J. M., Buunk, B. P., Gibbons, F. X., Gerrard,
    M., & Bakker, A. (1998). Accentuate the negative: Social images in the pre-
    diction and prevention of unsafe sex. Unpublished manuscript.
Boggiano, A. K., Barrett, M., Weiher, A. W., McClelland, G. H., & Lusk, C. M.
    (1987). Use of the maximal-operant principle to motivate children's intrin-
    sic interest. *Journal of Personality and Social Psychology, 53*, 866–879.
Bold, K. (1998, August 18). Voice of reason. *Los Angeles Times*, E1.
Brattesani, K. A. (1984). The role of initial self-evaluation in student susceptibil-
    ity to teacher expectations. Unpublished doctoral dissertation. University of
    California, Berkeley.
Brehm, S. S. (1992). *Intimate relationships* (2nd Ed.). New York: McGraw-Hill.
Brewer, M. B., & Miller, N. (1984). Beyond the contact hypothesis: Theoretical
    perspectives on desegregation. In N. Miller & M. B. Brewer (Eds.), *Groups
    in contact: The psychology of desegregation* (pp. 281–302). Orlando, FL: Acad-
    emic Press.
Briggs, H. E., & Paulson, R. I. (1996). Racism. In M. A. Mattaini & B. A. Thyer
    (Eds.), *Finding solutions to social problems: Behavioral strategies for change*.
    Washington, DC: American Psychological Association.
Brophy, J. (1985). Teacher-student interactions. In J. Dusek (Ed.), *Teacher expec-
    tations* (pp. 303–328). Hillsdale, NJ: Erlbaum.
Brown v. Board of Education of Topeka, Kansas, 347 U.S. 483 (1954).
Brown, L. R., et al. (1994). *State of the world 1994*. New York: Norton.
Brown, L. R., et al. (1995). *State of the world 1995*. New York: Norton.
Brown, L. R., et al. (1998). *State of the world 1998*. New York: Norton.
Bureau of Justice Statistics. (1994). *Criminal victimization in the United States,
    1992*. Washington, DC: Department of Justice.

Bureau of Justice Statistics. (1997). *Criminal victimization in the United States, 1994* (NJS-162126). Washington, DC: Department of Justice.

Campbell, C. P. (1995). *Race, myth and the news*. Thousand Oaks, CA: Sage.

Campbell, D. T. (1969). Reforms as experiments. *American Psychologist, 24*, 409–429.

Campbell, D. T. (1988). The experimenting society. In D. Campbell & S. Overman (Eds.), *Methodology and epistemology for social science: Selected papers* (pp. 290–314). Chicago: University of Chicago Press.

Caplan, N., & Nelson, S. D. (1973). On being useful: The nature and consequences of psychological research on social problems. *American Psychologist, 28*, 199–211.

Carver, C. S., Pozo, C., Harris, S. D., Noriega, V., Scheier, M. F., Robinson, D. S., Ketcham, A. S., Moffat, F. L., & Clark, K. C. (1993). How coping mediates the effects of optimism on distress: A study of women with early stage breast cancer. *Journal of Personality and Social Psychology, 65*, 375–390.

Center for Population Options. (1992). *Teenage pregnancy and too-early childbearing: Public costs, personal consequences* (6th ed.). Washington, DC: Center for Population Options.

Centers for Disease Control. (1991). Weapon carrying among high school students. *Journal of the American Medical Association, 266*, 2342.

Centers for Disease Control. (1997). *HIV/AIDS surveillance report*. Atlanta: Department of Health and Human Services.

Centers for Disease Control. (1998). *HIV/AIDS surveillance report*. Atlanta: Department of Health and Human Services.

Centers for Disease Control and Prevention. (1998a, Sept. 18). Trends in sexual risk behaviors among high school students—United States, 1991–1997. *Morbidity and Mortality Weekly Report, 47*, 749–751.

Centers for Disease Control and Prevention. (1998b). *National HIV Prevalence Surveys, 1997 Summary*. Atlanta: Centers for Disease Control and Prevention.

Cesar Chavez Institute for Public Policy. (1999). *Cesar E. Chavez biography*. San Francisco: Author. (Available online at *http://thecity.sfsu.edu/nccipp/cesarbio5-12.html*)

Chemers, M. M., Oskamp, S., & Costanzo, M. A. (1995). *Diversity in organizations: New perspectives for a changing workplace*. Thousand Oaks, CA: Sage.

Christensen, A., & Heavey, C. L. (1990). Gender and social structure in the demand/withdraw pattern of marital conflict. *Journal of Personality and Social Psychology, 59*, 73–81.

Cialdini, R. B. (1993). *Influence: Science and practice* (3rd. ed.). New York: HarperCollins.

Cialdini, R. B., Kallgren, C. A., & Reno, R. R. (1991). A focus theory of normative conduct: A theroetical refinement and reevaluation of the role of norms in human behavior. *Advances in Experimental Social Psychology, 21*, 201–234.

Cialdini, R. B., Reno, R. R., & Kallgren, C. A. (1990). A focus theory of normative conduct: Recycling the concept of norms to reduce littering in public places. *Journal of Personality and Social Psychology, 58*, 1015–1026.

Cialdini, R. B., & Trost, M. R. (1998). Social influence: Social norms, conformity, and compliance. In D. T. Gilbert, S. T. Fiske, & G. Lindzey (Eds.), *Handbook of social psychology* (4th ed., Vol. 2, pp. 151–192). New York: McGraw-Hill.

Clark, M. S., & Mills, J. (1979). Interpersonal attraction in exchange and communal relationships. *Journal of Personality and Social Psychology, 37,* 12–24.

Clark, M. S., & Mills, J. (1993). The difference between communal and exchange relationships: What it is and is not. *Personality and Social Psychology Bulletin, 19,* 684–691.

Cline, V. B., Croft, R. G., & Courrier, S. (1973). Desensitization of children to television violence. *Journal of Personality and Social Psychology, 27,* 360–365.

Clinton, W. (1998, January 27). State of the Union address.

Coch, L., & French, J. R. P., Jr. (1948). Overcoming resistance to change. *Human Relations, 1,* 512–532.

Cochran, S. D., Mays, V. M., Ciarletta, J., Caruso, C., & Mallon, D. (1992). Efficacy of the theory of reasoned action in predicting AIDS-related sexual risk reduction among gay men. *Journal of Applied Social Psychology, 22,* 1481–1501.

Cohen, J. (1992). A power primer. *Psychological Bulletin, 112,* 155–159.

Cohn, D. (1992, March 1). Per-can fees catch on as area's trash mounts. *Washington Post,* p. 1.

Colvin, R. C., & Block, J. (1994). Do positive illusions foster mental health? An examination of the Taylor and Brown formulation. *Psychological Bulletin, 116,* 3–20.

Comstock, G., Chaffee, S., Katzman, N., McCombs, M., & Roberts, D. (1978). *Television and human behavior.* New York: Columbia University Press.

Cook, P. J., & Ludwig, J. (1998). The burden of "acting White": Do Black adolescents disparage academic achievement? In C. Jencks & M. Phillips (Eds.), *The Black-White test score gap* (pp. 375–400). Washington, DC: Brookings Institute.

Cook, S. W. (1979). Social science and school desegregation: Did we mislead the Supreme Court? *Personality and Social Psychology Bulletin, 5,* 420–437.

Cook, T. D., & Campbell, D. T. (1979). *Quasi-experimentation: Design & analysis issues for field settings.* Chicago: Rand McNally.

Cook, T. D., Campbell, D. T., & Perrachio, L. (1990). Quasi experimentation. In M. Dunnette & L. Hough (Eds.), *Handbook of industrial and organizational psychology* (2nd ed., pp. 491–576). Palo Alto, CA: Consulting Psychologists Press.

Cook, T. D., & Shadish, W. R. (1994). Social experiments: Some developments over the past fifteen years. *Annual Review of Psychology, 45,* 545–580.

Cooley, C. H. (1956). *Human nature and the social order.* New York: Free Press.

Cooper, H. (1993). In search of a social fact. A commentary on the study of interpersonal expectations. In P. Blanck (Ed.), *Interpersonal expectations: Theory, research, and application* (pp. 218–226). Paris, France: Cambridge University Press.

Copple, C., Cline, M., & Smith, A. (1987). *Paths to the future: Long-term effects of Head Start in the Philadelphia School District.* Washington, DC: Department of Health and Human Services.

Crick, N. R., & Dodge, K. A. (1994). A review and reformulation of social information-processing mechanisms in children's social adjustment. *Psychological Bulletin, 115,* 74–101.

Crocker, J., & Major, B. (1989). Social stigma and self-esteem: The self-protective properties of stigma. *Psychological Review, 96,* 608–630.

Crocker, J., Major, B., & Steele, C. (1998). Social stigma. In D. T. Gilbert, S. T. Fiske, & G. Lindzey (Eds.), *Handbook of social psychology* (4th ed., pp. 504–553). Boston: McGraw-Hill.

Croizet, J., & Claire, T. (1998). Extending the concept of stereotype threat to social class: The intellectual underperformance of students from low socioeconomic backgrounds. *Personality and Social Psychology Bulletin, 24,* 588–594.

Currie, J., & Thomas, D. (1995). Does Head Start make a difference? *American Economic Review, 85* (3), 341–364.

Dabbs, J. M., Jr., Carr, T. S., Frady, R. L., & Riad, J. K. (1995). Testosterone, crime, and misbehavior among 692 male prison inmates. *Personality and Individual Differences, 18,* 627–633.

David, H. (1994). Reproductive rights and reproductive behavior. *American Psychologist, 49,* 343–349.

Deci, E. L., & Ryan, R. M. (1985). *Intrinsic motivation and self-determination in human behavior.* New York: Plenum.

Deffenbacher, J., Lynch, R., Oetting, E., & Kemper, C. (1996). Anger reduction in early adolescents. *Journal of Counseling Psychology, 43,* 149–157.

deGroot, G. (1994). Do single-sex classes foster better learning? *APA Monitor, 25*(7), 60–61.

Department of Sanitation. (1998). *Fresh Kills landfill.* New York, NY. (Available online at *http://www.ci.nyc.ny.us/nyclink/html/dos/home.html*).

DeRidder, L. M. (1993). Teenage pregnancy: Etiology and educational interventions. *Educational Psychology Review, 5,* 87–107.

Derlega, V., Metts, S., Petronio, S., & Margulis, S. T. (1993). *Self-disclosure.* Newbury Park, CA: Sage.

Deslauriers, B., & Everett, P. (1977). Effects of intermittent and continuous token reinforcement on bus ridership. *Journal of Applied Psychology, 62,* 369–375.

Deutsch, M. (1969). Conflicts: Productive and destructive. *Journal of Social Issues, 25*(1), 7–41.

Deutsch, M. (1980). Socially relevant research: Comments on "applied" versus "basic" research. In R. F. Kidd & M. J. Saks (Eds.), *Advances in applied social psychology* (Vol. 1, pp. 97–112). Hillsdale, NJ: Erlbaum.

Deutsch, M., & Krauss, R. M. (1965). *Theories in social psychology.* New York: Basic Books.

DeVillar, R. (1994). The rhetoric and practice of cultural diversity in U.S. schools: Socialization, resocialization, and quality schooling. In R. DeVillar, C. Faltis, & J. Cummins (Eds.), *Cultural diversity in schools: From rhetoric to practice* (pp. 25–56). New York: State University of New York Press.

Devine, P. G. (1989). Stereotypes and prejudice: Their automatic and controlled components. *Journal of Personality and Social Psychology, 56*, 5–18.

Dines, G., & Humez, J. M. (Eds.). (1995). *Gender, race, and class in media: A text-reader*. Thousand Oaks, CA: Sage.

Dollard, J., Doob, L., Miller, N. E., Mowrer, O. H., & Sears, R. (1939). *Frustration and aggression*. New Haven: Yale University Press.

Donaldson, S. I., Graham, J. W., & Hansen, W. B. (1994). Testing the generalizability of intervening mechanism theories: Understanding the effects of adolescent drug use prevention interventions. *Journal of Behavioral Medicine, 17*, 195–216.

Donaldson, S. I., Graham, J. W., Piccinin, A. M., & Hansen, W. B. (1995). Resistance-skills training and onset of alcohol use: Evidence for beneficial and potentially harmful effects in public schools and in private Catholic schools. *Health Psychology, 14*, 291–300.

Dreyden, J. I., & Gallagher, S. A. (1989). The effects of time and direction changes on the SAT performance of academically talented adolescents. *Journal for the Education of the Gifted, 12*, 187–204.

Dunlap, R. E., Gallup, G., & Gallup, A. (1993). Global environmental concern: Results from an international pubic opinion survey. *Environment, 35*, 7–15, 33–39.

Eagly, A. H. (1992). Uneven progress: Social psychology and the study of attitudes. *Journal of Personality and Social Psychology, 63*(5), 693–710.

Eagly, A. H., & Chaiken, S. (1993). *The psychology of attitudes*. Fort Worth, TX: Harcourt, Brace, Jovanovich.

Ellison, C. G., & Powers, D. A. (1994). The contact hypothesis and racial attitudes among Black Americans. *Social Science Quarterly, 75*, 385–400.

Ensminger, M., & Slusarcick, A. (1992). Paths to high school graduation or dropout: A longitudinal study of a first-grade cohort. *Sociology of Education, 65* (2), 95–113.

Environmental Protection Agency. (1998a). *Municipal solid waste factbook*. Washington, DC: EPA.

Environmental Protection Agency. (1998b). *Characterization of municipal solid waste in the United States: 1997 Update*. Washington, DC: EPA.

Erikson, R., Wright, G., & McIver, J. (1993). *Statehouse democracy*. New York: Cambridge University Press.

Eron, L.D. (1986). Interventions to mitigate the psychological effects of media violence on aggressive behavior. *Journal of Social Issues, 42*(3), 155–169.

Eron, L. D. (1987). The development of aggressive behavior from the perspective of a developing behaviorism. *American Psychologist, 42*, 435–442.

Eron, L. D., & Huesmann, L. R. (1990). The stability of aggressive behavior—

Even unto the third generation. In M. Lewis & S. M. Miller (Eds.), *Handbook of developmental psychopathology* (pp. 147–156). New York: Plenum.

Eron, L. D., & Slaby, R. G. (1994). Introduction. In L. D. Eron, J. H. Gentry, & P. Schlegel (Eds.), *Reason to hope: A psychosocial perspective on violence and youth* (pp. 1–24). Washington, DC: American Psychological Association.

Everett, C., & Everett, S. V. (1994). *Healthy divorce.* San Francisco, CA: Jossey-Bass.

Everett, P., & Watson, B. (1987). Psychological contributions to transportation. In D. Stokols & I. Altman (Eds.), *Handbook of Environmental psychology* (Vol. 2, pp. 987–1008). New York: Wiley.

Felmlee, D., Sprecher, S., & Bassin, E. (1990). The dissolution of intimate relationships. *Social Psychology Quarterly, 53,* 13–30.

Ferguson, R. E. (1998). Teachers' perceptions and expectations and the Black-White test score gap. In C. Jencks & M. Phillips (Eds.), *The Black-White test score gap* (pp. 273–317). Washington, DC: Brookings Institute.

Festinger, L. (1957). *A theory of cognitive dissonance.* Evanston, IL: Row, Peterson.

Festinger, L. (1964). *Conflict, decision, and dissonance.* Stanford, CA: Stanford University Press.

Fiedler, F. (1999, January 21). Thai project. Email correspondence on the Society for Personality and Social Psychology listserve.

Filsinger, E. E., & Thoma, S. J. (1988). Behavioral antecedents of relationship stability and adjustment: A five year longitudinal study. *Journal of Marriage and the Family, 50,* 785–795.

Finks, P. D. (1984). *The radical vision of Saul Alinsky.* New York: Paulist Press.

Fish, J. M. (1995). Why psychologists should learn some anthropology. *American Psychologist, 50,* 44–45.

Fishbein, M., & Ajzen, I. (1975). *Belief, attitude, intention, and behavior: An introduction to theory and research.* Reading, MA: Addison-Wesley.

Fishbein, M., Guenther-Grey, C., Johnson, W. D., Wolitski, R. J., McAlister, A., Rietmeijer, C. A., & O'Reilly, K. (1996). Using theory-based community intervention to reduce AIDS risk behaviors: The CDC's AIDS Community Demonstration Projects. In S. Oskamp & S. C. Thompson (Eds.), *Understanding and preventing HIV risk behavior: Safer sex and drug use* (pp. 177–206). Newbury Park, CA: Sage.

Fishbein, M., Middlestadt, S. E., & Hitchcock, P. J. (1994). Using information to change sexually transmitted disease-related behaviors: An analysis based on the theory of reasoned action. In R. J. DiClemente, & J. Peterson (Eds.), *Preventing AIDS: Theories and methods of behavioral interventions* (pp. 61–78). New York: Plenum.

Fishbein, M., & Rhodes, F. (1997). Using behavioral theory in HIV prevention. In N. H. Corby & R. J. Wolitski (Eds.), *Community HIV prevention: The Long Beach AIDS Community Demonstration Project* (pp. 21–30). Long Beach, CA: University Press.

Fisher, J. D., & Fisher, W. A. (1992). Changing AIDS-risk behavior. *Psychological Bulletin, 111,* 455–474.

Fisher, J. D., & Fisher, W. A. (1996). The information-motivation-behavioral skills model of AIDS risk behavior change: Empirical support and application. In S. Oskamp & S. C. Thompson (Eds.), *Understanding and preventing HIV risk behavior: Safer sex and drug use* (pp. 100–130). Newbury Park, CA: Sage.

Fisher, R. J. (1993). Developing the field of interactive conflict resolution: Issues in training, funding, and institutionalization. *Political Psychology, 14,* 123–138.

Fiske, S. T. (1998). Stereotyping, prejudice, and discrimination. In D. T. Gilbert, S. T. Fiske, & G. Lindzey (Eds.), *Handbook of social psychology* (4th ed., pp. 357–414). Boston: McGraw-Hill.

Fiske, S. T., & Taylor, S. E. (1991). *Social cognition* (2nd ed.). New York: McGraw-Hill.

Forsterling, F. (1985). Attributional retraining: A review. *Psychological Bulletin, 98,* 495–512.

Frey, K., & Sylvester, L. (1997). *Research on the Second Step program: Do student behaviors and attitudes improve? What do teachers think about the program?* Seattle: Committee for Children.

Frieberg, P. (1991). Separate classes for black males? *APA Monitor, 22*(5), 1, 7.

Friedlander, D., & Burtless, G. (1995). *Five years after: The long-term effects of welfare-to-work programs.* New York: Russell Sage Foundation.

Friedman, J., & Weinberg, D. H. (Eds.). (1983). *The great housing experiment.* Beverly Hills, CA: Sage.

Friedrich-Cofer, L., & Huston, A. C. (1986). Television violence and aggression: The debate continues. *Psychological Bulletin, 100,* 364–371.

Gaertner, S. L., & Dovidio, J. F. (1986). The aversive form of racism. In J. F. Dovidio & S. L. Gaertner (Eds.), *Prejudice, discrimination, and racism* (pp. 61–89). Orlando, FL: Harcourt Brace Jovanovich.

Gaertner, S. L., Rust, M. C., Dovidio, J. F., Bachman, B. A., Anastasio, P. A. (1994). The contact hypothesis: The role of a common ingroup identity on reducing intergroup bias. *Small Group Research, 25,* 224–249.

Gaines, S. O., Jr., & Reed, E. S. (1995). Prejudice: From Allport to DuBois. *American Psychologist, 50,* 96–103.

Gardner, G. T., & Stern, P. C. (1996). *Environmental problems and human behavior.* Boston: Allyn & Bacon.

Geen, R. G. (1998). Aggression and antisocial behavior. In D. T. Gilbert, S. T. Fiske, & G. Lindzey (Eds.), *Handbook of social psychology* (4th ed., Vol. 2, pp. 317–356). New York: McGraw-Hill.

Geller, E. S. (1981). The energy crisis and behavioral science: A conceptual framework for large scale intervention. In A. W. Childs & G. B. Melton (Eds.), *Rural psychology.* New York: Plenum.

General Accounting Office. (1987). *School dropouts: Survey of local programs* (Report no. GAO/HRD 87–108). Washington, DC: GAO.

Gerbner, G. (1993). *Women and minorities in television: A study in casting fate.* Philadelphia: Annenberg School for Communication, University of Pennsylvania.

Gerbner, G., Gross, L., Morgan, M., & Signorielli, N. (1994). Growing up with television: The cultivation perspective. In J. Bryant & D. Zillmann (Eds.), *Media effects: Advances in theory and research* (pp. 17–42). Hillsdale, NJ: Erlbaum.

Gerbner, G., Morgan, M., & Signorielli, N. (1994). *Television violence profile no. 16: The turning point from research to action.* Philadelphia: Annenberg School for Communication, University of Pennsylvania.

Gibbons, F. X., & Gerrard, M. (1995). Predicting young adults' health risk behavior. *Journal of Personality and Social Psychology, 69,* 505–517.

Gibbons, F. X., Gerrard, M., Lando, H. A., & McGovern, P. G. (1991). Social comparison and smoking cessation: The role of the "typical smoker." *Journal of Experimental Social Psychology, 27,* 239–258.

Gibbons, F. X., Gerrard, M., & McCoy, S. B. (1995). Prototype perception predicts (lack of) pregnancy prevention. *Personality and Social Psychology Bulletin, 21,* 85–93.

Gonzalez, L. (1994). Effectiveness of bilingual education: A comparison of various approaches in an elementary school district. In R. DeVillar, C. Faltis, & J. Cummins (Eds.), *Cultural diversity in schools: From rhetoric to practice* (pp. 233–262). New York: State University of New York Press.

Gore, A. (1992). *Earth in the balance: Ecology and the human spirit.* Boston: Houghton Mifflin.

Gottman, J. M. (1994). *What predicts divorce? The relationship between marital processes and marital outcomes.* Hillsdale, NJ: Erlbaum.

Greenberg, M., & Ruback, R. B. (1992). *After the crime: Victim decision making.* New York: Plenum.

Greenpeace. (1995, July-September). North Sea victory over Shell. 4(3), p. 1.

Gregory, D. (1997). Shame. In D. N. Sattler & V. Shabatay (Eds.), *Psychology in context: Voices and perspectives* (pp. 144–147). New York: Houghton Mifflin.

Gribbon, J., & Gribbon, M. (1993). *The holes in the sky.* New York: Bantam.

Grossman, D. C., Neckerman, H. J., Koepsell, T. D., Liu, P. Y., Asher, K. N., Beland, K., Frey, K., & Rivara, F. P. (1997). Effectiveness of a violence prevention curriculum among children in elementary school: A randomized controlled trial. *Journal of the American Medical Association, 277,* 1605–1611.

Grube, J. W., Mayton, D. M., II, & Ball-Rokeach, S. J. (1994). Inducing change in values, attitudes, and behaviors: Belief system theory and the method of value self-confrontation. *Journal of Social Issues, 50(4),* 153–173.

Grych, J. H., & Fincham, F. D. (1992). Interventions for children of divorce: Toward greater integration of research and action. *Psychological Bulletin, 111,* 434–454.

Guerra, N., Tolan, P., & Hammond, W. R. (1994). Prevention and treatment of adolescent violence. In L. Eron, J. Gentry, & P. Schlegel (Eds.), *Reason to hope: A psychological perspective on violence and youth* (pp. 383–404). Washington, DC: American Psychological Association.

Gurman, E. (1994). Debriefing for all concerned: Ethical treatment of human subjects. *Psychological Science, 5,* 139.

Guttmann, J. (1993). *Divorce in psychosocial perspective: Theory and research.* Hillsdale, New Jersey: Lawrence Erlbaum.

Hahn, B. A. (1993). Marital status and women's health: The effect of economic marital acquisitions. *Journal of Marriage and the Family, 55,* 495–504.

Hammond, K. R., & Adelman, L. (1976). Science, values, and human judgment. *Science, 194,* 389–396.

Harackiewicz, J. M., Sansone, C., Blair, L. W., Epstein, J. A., & Manderlink, G. (1987). Attributional processes in behavior change and maintenance: Smoking cessation and continued abstinence. *Journal of Personality and Social Psychology, 55,* 372–378.

Harris, M. (1993). Issues in studying the mediation of expectancy effects: A taxonomy of expectancy situations. In P. Blanck (Ed.), *Interpersonal expectations: Theory, research, and application* (pp. 350–378). Paris, France: Cambridge University Press.

Harris, M., & Rosenthal, R. (1985). Mediation of the interpersonal expectancy effect: 31 meta-analyses. *Psychological Bulletin, 97,* 363–386.

Hatfield, E. (1988). Passionate and compassionate love. In R. J. Sternberg & M. L. Barnes (Eds.), *The psychology of love* (pp. 191–217). New Haven: Yale University Press.

Hatfield, E., & Rapson, R. L. (1993). *Love, sex, and intimacy.* New York: HarperCollins.

Hatfield, E., Traupmann, J., Sprecher, S., Utne, M., & Hay, J. (1985). Equity in intimate relations: Recent research. In W. Ickes (Ed.), *Compatible and incompatible relationships* (pp. 91–117). New York: Springer.

Hausman, J., & Wise, D. (Eds.). (1985). *Social experimentation.* Chicago: University of Chicago Press.

Hearold, S. (1986). A synthesis of 1043 effects of television on social behavior. In G. Comstock (Ed.), *Public communication and behavior* (Vol. 1). Orlando, FL: Academic Press.

Heider, F. (1958). *The psychology of interpersonal relations.* New York: Wiley.

Heller, K. (1990). Social and community intervention. *Annual Review of Psychology, 41,* 141–168.

Henshaw, S. K., Kenney, A. M., Somberg, D., & VanVort, J. (1992). *U.S. Teenage Pregnancy Statistics.* Alan Guttmacher Institute.

Herrnstein, R. A., & Murray, C. (1994). *The bell curve.* New York: Grove.

Homans, G. C. (1961). *Social behavior: Its elementary forms.* New York: Harcourt, Brace, & Wrold.

Horner, E. (1998). *Almanac of the 50 states.* Palo Alto, CA: Information Publications.

Hornstein, H. A. (1975). Social psychology as social intervention. In M. Deutsch & H. A. Hornstein (Eds.), *Applying social psychology: Implications for research, practice, and training* (pp. 211–234). Hillsdale, NJ: Erlbaum.

Horwitt, S. D. (1989). *Let them call me rebel: Saul Alinsky, his life and legacy.* New York: Knopf.

House, J. S., Landis, K. R., & Umberson, D. (1988). Social relationships and health. *Science, 241,* 540–545.

Huesmann, L. R., Eron, L. D., Klein, R., Brice, P., & Fischer, P. (1983). Mitigating the imitation of aggressive behaviors by changing children's attitudes about media violence. *Journal of Personality and Social Psychology, 44,* 899–910.

Hurley, E. (1998, May). *White House conference on recycling: A commentary.* *http://j-src.com/wh-conf.htm.* Global Recycling Network.

Huston, T. L., & Chorost, A. F. (1994). Behavioral buffers on the effect of negativity on marital satisfaction: A longitudinal study. *Personal Relationships, 1,* 223–239.

Huston, T. L., & Vangelisti, A. L. (1991). Socioemotional behavior and satisfaction in marital relationships. *Journal of Personality and Social Psychology, 61,* 721–733.

Ivanhoe, L. F. (1996). Updated Hubbert curves analyze world oil supply. *World Oil, 217,* 91–102.

Ivanhoe, L. F. (1997). Get ready for another oil shock. *Futurist, 31,* 20–35.

Jamner, M. S., Wolitski, R. J., Corby, N. H., & Fishbein, M. (1998). Using the theory of planned behavior to predict intention to use condoms among female sex workers. *Psychology and Health, 13,* 187–205.

Jencks, C., & Phillips, M. (1998). The Black-White test score gap: An introduction. In C. Jencks & M. Phillips (Eds.), *The Black-White test score gap* (pp. 1–54). Washington, DC: Brookings Institute.

Jensen, A. R. (1969). How much can we boost IQ and scholastic achievement? *Harvard Educational Review, 39,* 1–123.

Jocklin, V., McGue, M., & Lykken, D. T. (1996). Personality and divorce: A genetic analysis. *Journal of Personality and Social Psychology, 71,* 288–299.

Jones, E. E. (1998). Major developments in five decades of social psychology. In D. T. Gilbert, S. T. Fiske, & G. Lindzey (Eds.), *The handbook of social psychology* (4th ed., Vol. 1, pp. 3–57). New York: Oxford University Press.

Jones, E. E., & Davis, K. E. (1965). From acts to dispositions: The attribution process in person perception. In L. Berkowitz (Ed.), *Advances in experimental social psychology* (Vol. 2, pp. 220–266). New York: Academic Press.

Jones, L. (1989). Teacher expectations for black and white students in contrasting classroom environments. Unpublished master's thesis. University of California, Berkeley.

Josephson, W. D. (1987). Television violence and children's aggression: Testing the priming, social script, and disinhibition prediction. *Journal of Personality and Social Psychology, 54,* 778–788.

Judd, C. M., & McClelland, G. H. (1998). Measurement. In D. T. Gilbert, S. T. Fiske, & G. Lindzey (Eds.), *Handbook of social psychology* (4th ed., Vol. 1, pp. 180–232). New York: McGraw-Hill.

Jussim, L. (1993). Accuracy of interpersonal expectations: A reflection-construction analysis of current and classic research. *Journal of Personality, 61,* 637–668.

Jussim, L., & Eccles, J. (1995). Naturally occurring interpersonal expectancies. *Review of Personality and Social Psychology, 15,* 74–108.

Jussim, L., Eccles, J., & Madon, S. (1996). Social perception, social stereotypes, and teacher expectations: Accuracy and the quest for the powerful self-fulfilling prophecy. *Advances in Experimental Social Psychology, 28,* 281–388.

Kamen-Siegel, L., Rodin, J., Seligman, M. E. P., & Dwyer, J. (1991). Explanatory style and cell-mediated immunity in elderly men and women. *Health Psychology, 10,* 229–235.

Kann, L., Kinchen, S. A., Williams, B. I., Ross, J. G., Lowry, R., Hill, C. V., Grunbaum J. A., Blumson, P. S., Collins, J. L., & Kolbe, L. J. (1998, August). Youth risk behavior surveillance—United States, 1997. *CDC Surveillance Summary (NE9), 47*(3), 1–89

Karau, S. J., & Williams, K. D. (1995). Social loafing: Research findings, implications, and future directions. *Current Directions in Psychological Science, 4,* 134–140.

Katz, D., & Braly, K. (1933). Racial stereotypes of one hundred college students. *Journal of Abnormal and Social Psychology, 28,* 280–290.

Katz, J. (1996). Provisions of the welfare bill. *Congressional Quarterly, 54,* 2192–2196.

Kelley, H. H. (1972). Causal schemata and the attribution process. In E. E. Jones, D. E. Kanouse, H. H. Kelley, R. E. Nisbett, S. Valins, & B. Weiner (Eds.), *Attribution: Perceiving the causes of behavior* (pp. 151–174). Morristown, NJ: General Learning Press.

Kelman, H. C. (1967). Human use of human subjects: The problem of deception in social psychological experiments. *Psychological Bulletin, 67,* 1–11.

Kelman, H. C. (1995). Contributions of an unofficial conflict resolution effort to the Israeli-Palestinian breakthrough. *Negotiation Journal, 11,* 33–41.

Kennedy, E. M. (1993). The Head Start Transition Project: Head Start goes to elementary school. In E. Zigler & S. Styfco (Eds.), *Head Start and beyond: A national plan for extended childhood intervention* (pp. 97–110). New Haven: Yale University Press.

Kenrick, D. T., & Sheets, V. (1993). Homicidal fantasies. *Ethology and Sociobiology, 14,* 231–246.

Kerner Commission. (1968). *Report of the National Advisory Commission on Civil Disorders.* New York: Dutton.

Kiesler, C. A. (1980). Psychology and public policy. In L. Bickman (Ed.), *Applied social psychology annual* (Vol. 1, pp. 49–67). Beverly Hills, CA: Sage.

Kifner, J. (1998, March 29). From wild talk and friendship to five deaths in a schoolyard. *New York Times,* A1, A30.

Kinder, D. R., & Sears, D. O. (1981). Prejudice and politics: Symbolic racism versus racial threats to the good life. *Journal of Personality and Social Psychology, 40,* 414–431.

Kinsey, A. C., Pomeroy, W. B., & Martin, C. E. (1948). *Sexual behavior in the human male*. Philadelphia: Saunders.

Kinsey, A. C., Pomeroy, W. B., Martin, C. E., & Gebhard, P. H. (1953). *Sexual behavior in the human female*. Philadelphia: Saunders.

Kleck, G. (1991). *Point blank: Guns and violence in America*. Chicago: Aldine.

Knoke, D. (1990). *Organizing for collective action: The political economies of associations*. New York: Aldine de Gruyter.

Kraus, S. J. (1995). Attitudes and the prediction of behavior: A meta-analysis of the empirical literature. *Personality and Social Psychology Bulletin, 21*(1), 58–75.

Krauss, B. J., Wolitski, R. J., Tross, S., Corby, N. H., & Fishbein, M. (1999). Getting the message: HIV information sources of women who have sex with injecting drug users—a two-site study. *Applied Psychology: An International Review*.

Kuklinski, M. (1992). The longitudinal influence of perceived differential teacher treatment. Unpublished master's thesis. University of California, Berkeley.

Lacerta Group. (1998). *Recycling magnetic media*. Boston: Lacerta.

Lancourt, J. E. (1979). *Confront or concede: The Alinsky citizen-action organizations*. Lexington, MA: Lexington.

LaPiere, R.T. (1934). Attitudes vs. actions. *Social Forces, 13*, 230–237.

Latane, B., & Darley, J. M. (1970). *The unresponsive bystander: Why doesn't he help?* New York: Appleton-Century-Crofts.

Laumann, E. O., Gagnon, J. H., Michael, R. T., & Michaels, S. (1994). *The social organization of sexuality: Sexual practices in the United States*. Chicago: University of Chicago Press.

Lee, J. (1997). Racism doesn't grow up. In D. N. Sattler & V. Shabatay (Eds.), *Psychology in context: Voices and perspectives* (pp. 212–215). New York: Houghton Mifflin.

Lee, J. A., DeLeon, P. H., Wedding, D., & Nordal, K. (1994). Psychologists' role in influencing Congress: The process and the players. *Professional Psychology—Research & Practice, 25*, 9–15.

Leeming, F., Dwyer, W., Porter, B., & Cobern, M. (1993). Outcome research in environmental education: A critical review. *Journal of Environmental Education, 24*, 8–21.

Lepore, L., & Brown, R. (1997). Category and stereotype activation: Is prejudice inevitable? *Journal of Personality and Social Psychology, 72*, 275–287.

Levenson, R. W., & Gottman, J. M. (1985). Physiological and affective predictors of change in relationship satisfaction. *Journal of Personality and Social Psychology, 49*, 85–94.

Levin, J., & McDevitt, J. (1993). *Hate crimes: The rising tide of bigotry and bloodshed*. New York: Plenum.

Levine, M., Toro, P. A., & Perkins, D. V. (1993). Social and community interventions. *Annual Review of Psychology, 44*, 525–558.

Levy-Leboyer, C. (1988). Success and failure in applying psychology. *American Psychologist, 43*, 779–785.

Lewin, K. (1948). *Resolving social conflicts.* New York: Harper.

Lewin, K. (1951). *Field theory in social science* (D. Cartwright, Ed.). New York: Harper. (Originally published, 1944.)

Lewis, F. M., & Daltroy, L. H. (1990). How causal explanations influence health behavior: Attribution theory. In K. Glanz, F. M. Lewis, & B. K. Rimer (Eds.), *Health behavior and health education: Theory, research, and practice* (pp. 92–114). San Francisco: Jossey-Bass.

Liebert, R. M., & Schwartzberg, N. S. (1977). Effects of mass media. *Annual Review of Psychology, 28,* 141–173.

Liebert, R. M., & Sprafkin, J. (1988). *The early window: Effects of television on children and youth* (3rd ed.). New York: Pergamon.

Lindblom, C. (1990). *Inquiry and change: The troubled attempt to understand and shape society.* New Haven: Yale University Press.

Linz, D., Malamuth, N., & Beckett, K. (1992). Civil liberties and research on the effects of pornography. In P. Suedfeld & P. Tetlock (Eds.), *Psychology and social policy* (pp. 149–164). New York: Hemisphere.

Lipsey, M. W., & Wilson, D. B. (1993). The efficacy of psychological, educational, and behavioral treatment: Confirmation from meta-analysis. *American Psychologist, 48,* 1181–1209.

Lorenz, K. (1966). *On aggression.* New York: Harcourt, Brace, & World.

Lott, B., & Maluso, D. (Eds.). (1995). *The social psychology of interpersonal discrimination.* New York: Guilford.

Lumsden, M., & Wolfe, R. (1996). Evolution of the problem-solving workshop: An introduction to social-psychological approaches to conflict resolution. *Peace and Conflict: Journal of Peace Psychology, 2,* 37–67.

Lynch, J. J. (1977). *The broken heart: The medical consequences of loneliness.* New York: Basic Books.

Madon, S., Jussim, L., & Eccles, J. (1997). In search of the powerful self-fulfilling prophecy. *Journal of Personality and Social Psychology, 72,* 791–809.

Markman, H. J., Floyd, F., Stanley, S., & Storaasli, R. (1988). The prevention of marital distress: A longitudinal investigation. *Journal of Clinical and Counseling Psychology, 56,* 210–217.

Markman, H. J., & Hahlweg, K. (1993). The prediction and prevention of marital distress: An international perspective. *Clinical Psychology Review, 13,* 51–56.

Markman, H. J., Renick, M. J., Floyd, F., Stanley, S., & Clements, M. (1993). Preventing marital distress through communication and conflict management training: A four and five year follow-up. *Journal of Clinical and Counseling Psychology, 62,* 1–8.

Martens, W. J. M. (1998). *Health and climate change: Modeling the impacts of global warming and ozone depletion.* London: Earthscan.

Marx, G. T. (1970). Racism and race relations. In M. Wertheimer (Ed.), *Confrontation: Psychology and the problems of today* (pp. 100–102). Glenview, IL: Scott, Foresman.

Masters, W. H., & Johnson, V. E. (1966). *Human sexual response.* Boston: Little, Brown.

Mayo, C., & La France, M. (1980). Toward an applicable social psychology. In R. F. Kidd & M. J. Saks (Eds.), *Advances in applied social psychology* (Vol. 1). Hillsdale, NJ: Erlbaum.

McAneny, L., & Saad, L. (1994, May). America's public schools: Still separate? Still unequal? *Gallup Poll Monthly,* No. 344, pp. 23–29.

McCarthy, E. D., Langer, T. S., Gersten, J. C., Eisenberg, J. G., & Orzeck, L. (1975). Violence and behavior disorders. *Journal of Communication, 25*(4), 71–85.

McConahay, J. B. (1986). Modern racism, ambivalence, and the Modern Racism Scale. In J. F. Dovidio & S. L. Gaertner (Eds.), *Prejudice, discrimination, and racism* (pp. 91–125). Orlando, FL: Harcourt Brace Jovanovich.

McIntyre, J. J., & Teevan, J. J., Jr. (1972). Television violence and deviant behavior. In G. A. Comstock & E. A. Rubinstein (Eds.), *Television and social behavior (Vol. 3): Television and adolescent aggressiveness* (pp. 383–435). Washington, DC: Government Printing Office.

McKey, R. H., Condelli, L., Ganson, H., Barrett, B., McConkey, C., & Plantz, M. (1985). *The impact of Head Start on children, family, and communities: Final report of the Head Start Evaluation, Synthesis and Utilization Project* (DHHS Pub. No. OHDS 85–31193). Washington, DC: Government Printing Office.

McLeod, J. M., Atkin, C. K., & Chaffee, S. H. (1972). Adolescents, parents and television use: Self-report and other-report measures from the Wisconsin sample. In G. A. Comstock & E. A. Rubinstein (Eds.), *Television and social behavior (Vol. 3): Television and adolescent aggressiveness* (pp. 239–313). Washington. DC: Government Printing Office.

McMillen, M. (1997). *Dropout rates in the United States, 1996.* National Center for Education Statistics. Department of Education (NCES 98–250). (Available online at *http://nces.ed.gov/pubs98/dropout.*)

Meadows, D. H., Meadows, D. L., & Randers, J. (1992). *Beyond the limits.* Post Mills, VT: Chelsea Green.

Melton, G. B. (1995). Bringing psychology to Capitol Hill: Briefings on child and family policy. *American Psychologist, 50,* 766–770.

Metalsky, G. I., Halberstadt, L. J., & Abramson, L. Y. (1987). Vulnerability to depressive mood reactions: Toward a more powerful test of the diathesis-stress and causal mediation components of the reformulated theory of depression. *Journal of Personality and Social Psychology, 52,* 386–393.

Metalsky, G. I., Laird, R. S., Heck, P. M., & Joiner, T. E., Jr. (1995). Attribution theory: Clinical applications. In W. O'Donohue & L. Krasner (Eds.), *Theories of behavior therapy: Exploring behavior change* (pp. 385–413). Washington, DC: American Psychological Association.

Michael, R. T., Gagnon, J. H., Laumann, E. O., & Kolata, G. (1994). *Sex in America: A definitive study.* Boston: Little, Brown.

Montagu, A. (1951). *Statement on race.* New York: Schuman.

Moore, D. W., & Newport, F. (1994, January). Public strongly favors stricter gun control laws. *Gallup Poll Monthly*, No. 340, pp. 18–24.

Myrdal, G. (1944). *An American dilemma: The Negro problem and modern democracy.* New York: Harper.

National Center for Education Statistics. (1998). *Violence and discipline: Problems in U.S. public schools: 1996–97* (NCES 98-030). Washington, DC: Department of Education.

National Commission on the Causes and Prevention of Violence. (1964). *To establish justice, to insure domestic tranquility: Final report.* Washington, DC: Government Printing Office.

National Education Summit. (1996, March). *Policy statement.* (Available from *http://www.summit96.ibm.com*).

National Institute of Mental Health. (1982). *Television and behavior: Ten years of scientific progress and implications for the eighties.* Washington, DC: Government Printing Office.

Neisser, U., et al. (1996). Intelligence: Knowns and unknowns. *American Psychologist, 51,* 77–101.

Nettles, M. T. (1988). *Toward undergraduate student equality in American higher education.* New York: Greenwood.

Neuman, S. (1991). *Literacy in the television age: The myth of the TV effect.* Norwood, NJ: Ablex.

New York Times. (1998, March 29). From wild talk and friendship to five deaths in a schoolyard. *New York Times*, A1.

Nixon, N., & Nixon, B. (1991). *People with AIDS.* Boston: Godine.

Nolen-Hoeksema, S., Girgus, J. S., & Seligman, M. E. P. (1986). Learned helplessness in children: A longitudinal study of depression, achievement, and explanatory style. *Journal of Personality and Social Psychology, 51,* 435–442.

Nolen-Hoeksema, S., Girgus, J. S., & Seligman, M. E. P. (1992). Predictors and consequences of childhood depressive symptoms: A 5-year longitudinal study. *Journal of Abnormal Psychology, 101,* 405–422.

Norman, R. (1975). Affective-cognitive consistency, attitudes, conformity, and behavior. *Journal of Personality and Social Psychology, 32,* 83–91.

Norris, F., & Thompson, M. (1995). Applying community psychology to the prevention of trauma and traumatic life events. In J. Freedy & S. Hobfoll (Eds.), *Traumatic stress: From theory to practice* (pp. 49–71). New York: Plenum.

O'Brien, T., & Zoumbaris, S. (1993). Consumption behaviors hinge on financial self-interest. *American Psychologist, 48,* 1091–1092.

Olweus, D. (1979). Stability of aggression reaction patterns in males: A review. *Psychological Bulletin, 86,* 852–875.

Opotow, S. (1990). Moral exclusion and injustice: An introduction. *Journal of Social Issues, 46*(1), 1–20.

Oskamp, S. (1991). *Attitudes and opinions* (2nd ed.). Englewood Cliffs, NJ: Prentice Hall.

Oskamp, S. (1995). Applying social psychology to avoid ecological disaster. *Journal of Social Issues, 51*(4), 217–239.

Oskamp. S., Burkhardt, R., Schultz, P., Hurin, S., & Zelezny, L. (1998). Predicting three dimensions of residential curbside recycling: An observational study. *Journal of Environmental Education, 29,* 37–42

Ottaway, R. N. (1983). The change agent: A taxonomy in relation to the change process. *Human Relations, 36,* 361–392.

Pallak, M. (1990). Public policy and applied social psychology: Bridging the gap. In J. Edwards, R. S. Tindale, L. Heath, & E. Posavac (Eds.), *Social influence: Processes and prevention* (pp. 327–338). New York: Plenum.

Peabody, G. L. (1971). Power, Alinsky, and other thoughts. In H. A. Hornstein, B. B. Bunker, W. W. Burke, M. Gindes, & R. J. Lewicki (Eds.), *Social intervention: A behavioral science approach.* New York: Free Press.

Pedro-Carroll, J. (1997). The children of divorce intervention program: Fostering resilient outcomes for school-aged children. In G. W. Albee & T. P. Gullotta (Eds.), *Primary prevention works* (pp. 213–238). Thousand Oaks, CA: Sage.

Peterson, C. (1988). Explanatory style as a risk factor for illness. *Cognitive Therapy and Research, 12,* 117–130.

Peterson, C., & Bossio, L. M. (1991). *Health and optimism.* New York: Free Press.

Peterson, C., Colvin, D., & Lin, E. H. (1992). Explanatory style and helplessness. *Social Behavior and Personality, 20,* 1–14.

Peterson, C., Maier, S. F., & Seligman, M. E. P. (1993). *Learned helplessness: A theory for the age of personal control.* New York: Oxford University Press.

Peterson, C., Schulman, P., Castellon, C., & Seligman, M. E. P. (1992). CAVE: Content analysis of verbatim expressions. In C. P. Smith (Ed.), *Motivation and personality: Handbook of thematic content analysis* (pp. 383–392). New York: Cambridge University Press.

Peterson, C., & Seligman, M. E. P. (1984). Causal explanations as a risk factor for depression: Theory and evidence. *Psychological Review, 91,* 347–374.

Peterson, C., Seligman, M. E. P., & Vaillant, G. E. (1988). Pessimistic explanatory style is a risk factor for physical illness: A thirty-five-year longitudinal study. *Journal of Personality and Social Psychology, 55,* 23–27.

Peterson, C., Seligman, M. E. P., Yurko, K. H., Martin, L. R., & Friedman, H. S. (1998). Catastrophizing and untimely death. *Psychological Science, 9,* 127–130.

Peterson, C., Semmel, A., von Bayer, C., Abramson, L. Y., Metalsky, G. I., & Seligman, M. E. P. (1982). The Attributional Style Questionnaire. *Cognitive Therapy and Research, 6,* 287–299.

Pettigrew, T. F. (1998). Intergroup contact theory. *Annual Review of Psychology, 49,* 65–85.

Pettigrew, T. F., & Meertens, R. W. (1995). Subtle and blatant prejudice in western Europe. *European Journal of Social Psychology, 25,* 57–75.

Pfister, G. (1975). Outcomes of laboratory training for police officers. *Journal of Social Issues, 31*(1), 115–121.

Phillips, D. (1991). With a little help: Children and child care. In A. Huston (Ed.), *Children in poverty: Child development and public policy* (pp. 158–189). New York: Cambridge University Press.

Pimentel, D., Harman, R., Pacenza, M., Pacarsky, J., & Pimentel, M. (1994). Natural resources and an optimum human population. *Population and Environment, 15,* 347–369.

Podell, S., & Archer, D. (1994). Do legal changes matter? The case of gun control laws. In M. Costanzo & S. Oskamp (Eds.), *Violence and the law* (pp. 37–62). Thousand Oaks, CA: Sage.

Prilleltensky, I. (1990). Enhancing the social ethics of psychology: Toward a psychology at the service of social change. *Canadian Psychology, 31,* 310–319.

Prochaska, J. O., DiClemente, C. C., & Norcross, J. C. (1992). In search of how people change: Applications to addictive behaviors. *American Psychologist, 47,* 1102–1114.

Prothrow-Stith, D., & Weissman, M. (1991). *Deadly consequences.* New York: HarperCollins.

Ramirez, J. D. (1986). Comparing structured English immersion and bilingual education: First-year results of a national study. *American Journal of Education, 56,* 122–148.

Reed, G. M., Kemeny, M. E., Taylor, S. E., Wang, H. Y. J., & Visscher, B. R. (1994). Realistic acceptance as a predictor of decreased survival time in gay men with AIDS. *Health Psychology, 13,* 299–307.

Reed, T. E. (1969). Caucasian genes in American Negroes. *Science, 165,* 762–768.

Reisch, M., & Wenocur, S. (1986). The future of community organization in social work: Social activism and the politics of profession building. *Social Service Review, 60,* 70–93.

Reitzes, D. C., & Reitzes, D. C. (1986). Alinsky in the 1980s: Two contemporary Chicago community organizations. *Sociological Quarterly, 28,* 265–283.

Renick, M. J., Blumberg, S. L., & Markman, H. J. (1992). The Prevention and Relationship Enhancement Program (PREP): An empirically-based preventive intervention program for couples. *Family Relations, 41,* 141–147.

Reno, R. R., Cialdini, R. B., & Kallgren, C. A. (1993). The trans-situational influence of norms. *Journal of Personality and Social Psychology, 64,* 104–112.

Resnick, M. D, Bearman, P. S., Blum, R. W., Bauman, K. E., Harris, K. M., Jones, J., Tabor, J., Beuhring, T., Sieving, R. E., Shew, M., Ireland, M., Bearinger, L. H., & Udry, J. R. (1997). Protecting adolescents from harm. Findings from the National Longitudinal Study on Adolescent Health. *Journal of the American Medical Association, 279,* 823–832.

Rettew, D., & Reivich, K. (1995). Sports and explanatory style. In G. M. Buchanan & M. E. P. Seligman (Eds.), *Explanatory style.* Hillsdale, NJ: Erlbaum. (pp. 173–185)

Reuter, P. (1979). Easy sport: Research and relevance. *Journal of Social Issues, 35*(3), 166–182.

Robinson, J. P., & Bachman, J. G. (1972). Television viewing habits and aggression. In G. A. Comstock & E. A. Rubinstein (Eds.), *Television and social behavior* (Vol. 3): *Television and adolescent aggressiveness* (pp. 372–382). Washington, DC: Government Printing Office.

Rokeach, M. (1971). Long-range experimental modification of values, attitudes, and behavior. *American Psychologist, 26,* 453–459.

Rokeach, M. (1979). Value theory and communication research. In D. Nimmo (Ed.), *Communication yearbook* (Vol. 3, pp. 7–28). New Brunswick, NJ: Transaction Books.

Rosenstock, I. M. (1974). The health belief model and preventive health behavior. *Health Education Monographs, 2,* 354–385.

Rosenthal, R., & Jacobson, D. (1968). *Pygmalion in the classroom.* New York: Holt, Rinehart & Winston.

Rosenthal, R., & Rubin, D. (1978). Interpersonal expectancy effects: The first 345 studies. *Behavioral and Brain Sciences, 1,* 377–415.

Ross, L. (1977). The intuitive psychologist and his shortcomings: Distortions in the attribution process. In L. Berkowitz (Ed.), *Advances in experimental social psychology* (Vol. 10, 174–221). New York: Academic Press.

Ross, S. I., & Jackson, J. M. (1991). Teachers' expectations for Black males' and Black females' academic achievement. *Personality and Social Psychology Bulletin, 17,* 78–82.

Rothman, A. J., Salovey, P., Turvey, C., & Fishkin, S. A. (1993). Attributions of responsibility and persuasion: Increasing mammography utilization among women over 40 with an internally oriented message. *Health Psychology, 12,* 39–47.

Salovey, P., Rothman, A. J., & Rodin, J. (1998). Health behavior. In D. T. Gilbert, S. T. Fiske, & G. Lindzey (Eds.), *The handbook of social psychology* (4th ed., Vol. 2, pp. 633–683). Boston: McGraw-Hill.

Sata, L. S. (1975). Laboratory training for police officers. *Journal of Social Issues, 31*(1), 107–114.

Schaller, M., Crandall, C. S., Stangor, C., & Neuberg, S. L. (1995). What kinds of social psychology experiments are of value to perform? Comment on Wallach and Wallach (1994). *Journal of Personality and Social Psychology, 69,* 611–618.

Scheier, M. F., Matthews, K. A., Owens, J. F., Magovern, G. J., Sr., Lefebvre, R. C., Abbott, R. A., & Carver, C. S. (1989). Dispositional optimism and recovery from coronary artery bypass surgery: The beneficial effects on physical and psychological well-being. *Journal of Personality and Social Psychology, 57,* 1024–1040.

Schram, S. (1995). *Words of welfare: The poverty of social science and the social science of poverty.* Minneapolis: University of Minnesota Press.

Schultz, P. W. (1999). Changing behavior with normative feedback interventions: A field experiment of curbside recycling. *Basic and Applied Social Psychology, 21,* 25–36.

Schultz, P. W., Baker, N., Phaller, A., & Watkins, R. (1999, April). *Prejudice and the automatic activation of stereotypes about Hispanics.* Paper presented at Western Psychological Association meeting, Irvine, CA.

Schultz, P. W., & Oskamp, S. (1996). Effort as a moderator of the attitude-behavior relationship: General environmental concern and recycling. *Social Psychology Quarterly, 59,* 375–383.

Schultz, P. W., Oskamp, S., & Mainieri, T. (1995). Who recycles and when: A review of personal and situational factors. *Journal of Environmental Psychology, 15,* 105–121.

Schultz, P. W., & Schultz, L. A. (1996). Students and handguns: Attitudes, behaviors, and policies in an urban high school. *Proteus, 13,* 57–60.

Schultz, P. W., & Zelezny, L. (1999). A value basis for environmental attitudes: A multi-national study. *Journal of Environmental Psychology.*

Schulz, R., & Hanusa, B. H. (1978). Long-term effects of control and predictability-enhancing interventions: Findings and ethical issues. *Journal of Personality and Social Psychology, 36,* 1194–1201.

Schwartz, W. (1995). *New information on youth who drop out: Why they leave and what happens to them.* New York: ERIC Clearinghouse on Urban Education.

Schwarzer, R. (1994). Optimism, vulnerability, and self-beliefs as health-related cognitions: A systematic overview. *Psychology and Health, 9,* 161–180.

Schweinhart, L. J., Barnes, H. V., & Weikart, D. P. (1993). *Significant benefits: The High/Scope Perry Preschool Study through age 27.* Ypsilanti, MI: High/Scope.

Sears, D. O. (1986). College sophomores in the laboratory: Influences of a narrow data base on social psychology's view of human nature. *Journal of Personality and Social Psychology, 51,* 515–530.

Segerstrom, S. C., Taylor, S. E., Kemeny, M. E., Reed, G. M., & Visscher, B. R. (1996). Causal attributions predict rate of immune decline in HIV-seropositive gay men. *Health Psychology, 15,* 485–493.

Seligman, M. E. P., & Schulman, P. (1986). Explanatory style as a predictor of productivity and quitting among life insurance agents. *Journal of Personality and Social Psychology, 50,* 832–838.

Shaffer, D. R., Pegalis, L. J., & Bazzini, D. G. (1996). When boy meets girl (revisited): Gender, gender-role orientation, and prospect of future interaction as determinants of self-disclosure among same- and opposite-sex acquaintances. *Personality and Social Psychology Bulletin, 22,* 495–506.

Sheaff, L., & Talashek, M. (1995). Ever-pregnant and never-pregnant teens in a temporary housing shelter. *Journal of Community Health Nursing, 12,* 33–45.

Sheley, J., McGee, Z., & Wright, J. (1992). Gun-related violence in and around inner-city schools. *American Journal of Diseases of Childhood, 146,* 677–682.

Sherif, M. (1935). A study of some social factors in perception. *Archives of Psychology,* No. 187.

Shireman, W. K. (1993). Solid waste: To recycle or to bury California? In T. Palmer (Ed.), *California's threatened environment: Restoring the dream* (pp. 170–181). Washington, DC: Island Press.

Sieber, J. E., Iannuzzo, R., & Rodriguez, B. (1995). Deception methods in psychology: Have they changed in 23 years? *Ethics and Behavior, 5,* 67–85.

Sieber, S. D. (1981). *Fatal remedies: The ironies of social intervention.* New York: Plenum.

Sigelman, L., & Welch, S. (1993). The contact hypothesis revisited: Black-White interaction and positive racial attitudes. *Social Forces, 71,* 781–795.

Simmons, I. G. (1991). *Earth, air, and water: Resources and environment in the late 20th century.* London: Edward Arnold.

Singer, D. G., Zuckerman, D. M., & Singer, J. L. (1980). Teaching elementary school children television viewing skills: An evaluation. *Journal of Communication, 30,* 84–93.

Slaby, R. (1995). *Early violence prevention: Tools for teachers of young children.* Washington, DC: National Association for the Education of Young Children.

Snyder, M. (1987). *Public appearances, private realities: The psychology of self-monitoring.* New York: Freeman.

Snyder, M., & Tanke, E. D. (1976). Behavior and attitude: Some people are more consistent than others. *Journal of Personality, 44,* 501–517.

Soliday, E., & Stanton, A. (1995). Deceived versus nondeceived participants' perceptions of scientific and applied psychology. *Ethics and Behavior, 5,* 87–104.

Spencer, S. J., Steele, C. M., & Quinn, D. (1999). Stereotype threat and women's math performance. *Journal of Experimental Social Psychology, 35,* 4–28.

St. Lawrence, J. S., Brasfield, T. L., Jefferson, K., & Alleyne, E. (1995). Theoretical models applied to AIDS prevention. In A. J. Goreczny (Ed.), *Handbook of health and rehabilitation psychology* (pp. 555–582). New York: Plenum.

Stack, S. (1990). New micro-level data on the impact of divorce on suicide, 1959–1980: A test of two theories. *Journal of Marriage and the Family, 52,* 119–127.

Stack, S., & Eshleman, J. R. (1998). Marital status and happiness: A 17-nation study. *Journal of Marriage and the Family, 60,* 527–537.

Stanfield, R. (1996). This reform may not be the answer. *National Journal, 28,* 1664.

Stanley, S., Markman, H., Peters, M., & Leber, D. (1995). Strengthening marriages and preventing divorce. *Journal of Family Relations, 44,* 392–402.

Staples, B. (1997). Black men and public space. In D. N. Sattler & Shabatay, V. (Eds.), *Psychology in context: Voices and perspectives* (pp. 294–297). New York: Houghton Mifflin.

Steele, C. M. (1997). A threat in the air: How stereotypes shape intellectual identity and performance. *American Psychologist, 52,* 613–629.

Steele, C. (1998). Stereotyping and its threat are real. *American Psychologist, 53,* 680–681.

Steele, C. M., & Aronson, J. (1995). Stereotype threat and the intellectual test performance of African Americans. *Journal of Personality and Social Psychology, 69,* 797–811.

Steele, C., & Aronson, J. (1998). Stereotype threat and the test performance of academically successful African Americans. In C. Jencks et al. (Eds.), *The Black-White test score gap* (pp. 401–427). Washington, DC: Brookings Institute.

Steele, C. M., Spencer, S., Nisbett, R., Hummel, M., Harber, K., Schoem, D., & Carter, K. (1998). African American college achievement: A "wise" intervention. Unpublished manuscript, Stanford University.

Steger, W., & Bowermaster, J. (1990). *Saving the earth: A citizen's guide to environmental action.* New York: Knopf.

Steinberg, L., Blinde, P. L., & Chan, K. S. (1984). Dropping out among language minority youth. *Review of Educational Research, 54,* 113–132.

Stern, P. C. (1992). Psychological dimensions of global environmental change. *Annual Review of Psychology, 43,* 269–302.

Sternberg, R. J. (1988). Triangulating love. In R. J. Sternberg & M. L. Barnes (Eds.), *The psychology of love* (pp. 119–138). New Haven: Yale University Press.

Sternberg, R. J. (1997). Construct validation of a triangular love scale. *European Journal of Social Psychology, 27,* 313–335.

Stewart, A. J., Copeland, A. P., Chester, J. E., & Barenbaum, N. B. (1997). *Separating together: How divorce transforms families.* New York: Guilford.

Stone, J., Aronson, E., Crain, A. L., Winslow, M. P., & Fried, C. B. (1994). Inducing hypocrisy as a means of encouraging young adults to use condoms. *Personality and Social Psychology Bulletin, 20,* 116–128.

Stone, J., Cooper, J., Wiegand, A. W., & Aronson, E. (1997). When exemplification fails: Hypocrisy and the motive for self-integrety. *Journal of Personality and Social Psychology, 72,* 54–65.

Strenta, A. C., Elliott, R., Adair, R., Scott, J., & Matier, M. (1993). Choosing and leaving science in highly selective institutions. Report submitted to A. P. Sloan Foundation.

Stuckert, R. P. (1964). Race mixture: The African ancestry of White Americans. In P. B. Hammond (Ed.), *Physical anthropology and archaeology: Selected readings* (pp. 192–197). New York: Macmillan.

Surgeon General's Scientific Advisory Committee on Television and Social Behavior. (1972). *Television and growing up: The impact of televised violence* (Report to the Surgeon General, U.S. Public Health Service). Washington, DC: Government Printing Office.

Sweeney, P. D., Anderson, K., & Bailey, S. (1986). Attributional style in depression: A meta-analytic review. *Journal of Personality and Social Psychology, 50,* 974–991.

Taylor, S. E. (1998). The social being in social psychology. In D. T. Gilbert, S. T. Fiske, & G. Lindzey (Eds.), *The handbook of social psychology* (4th ed., Vol. 1, pp. 58–98). New York: Oxford University Press.

Taylor, S. E., & Brown, J. D. (1988). Illusion and well-being: A social psychological perspective on mental health. *Psychological Bulletin, 103,* 193–210.

Taylor, S. E., & Brown, J. D. (1994). Positive illusions and well-being revisited: Separating fact from fiction. *Psychological Bulletin, 116,* 21–27.

Taylor, S. E., Kemeny, S. E., Aspinwall, L. G., Schneider, S. G., Rodriguez, R., & Herbert, M. (1992). Optimism, coping, psychological distress, and high-risk sexual behavior among men at risk for acquired immunodeficiency syndrome (AIDS). *Journal of Personality and Social Psychology, 63,* 460–473.

Terry, D. J., Gallois, C., & McCamish, M., (Eds.)(1993). *The theory of reasoned action: Its application to AIDS-preventive behaviour.* Oxford, England: Pergamon.

Thomas, M. H., Horton, R. W., Lippincott, E. C., & Drabman, R. S. (1977). Desensitization to portrayals of real-life aggression as a function of exposure to television violence. *Journal of Personality and Social Psychology, 35,* 450–458.

Toch, H., & Lizotte, A. (1992). Research and policy: The case of gun control. In P. Suedfeld & P. Tetlock (Eds.), *Psychology and social policy* (pp. 223–240). New York: Hemisphere.

Treisman, U. (1985). *A study of mathematics performance of Black students at the University of California, Berkeley.* Unpublished manuscript.

Tucker, J. S., Friedman, H. S., Schwartz, J. E., Criqui, M. H., Tomlinson-Keasey, C., Wingard, D., & Martin, L. R. (1997). Parental divorce: Effects on individual behavior and longevity. *Journal of Personality and Social Psychology, 73,* 381–391.

U.S. Bureau of the Census. (1975). *Historical statistics of the United States: Colonial times to 1970.* Washington, DC: Department of Commerce, Bureau of the Census.

U.S. Bureau of the Census. (1997). *Statistical abstracts of the United States, 1997.* Washington, DC: Department of Commerce, Bureau of the Census.

U.S. Department of Health, Education, and Welfare. (1971). *The institutional guide to DHEW policy on protection of human subjects* (DHEW Publication No. (NIH) 72–102). Washington, DC: Government Printing Office.

U.S. Environmental Protection Agency. (1992, August). *The consumer's handbook for reducing solid waste* (EPA530-K-92–003). Washington, DC: EPA.

United Nations. (1995). *Demographic yearbook.* New York: Department for Economic and Social Information and Policy Analysis, UN Secretariat.

United Nations. (1998). *World population projects to 2150.* New York: Department of Economic and Social Affairs, United Nations Secretariat.

Ventura, S. J., Taffel, S. M., Mosher, W. D., & Henshaw, S. (1992). Trends in pregnancies and pregnancy rates, United States 1980–1988. *Monthly Vital Statistics Report, 41,* 6.

Vincent, T. A. (1990). A view from the hill: The human element in policy making on Capitol Hill. *American Psychologist, 45,* 61–64.

Vooijs, M., & Van der Voort, T. (1993). Learning about television violence: The impact of a critical viewing curriculum on children's attitudinal judgments of crime series. *Journal of Research and Development in Education, 26,* 133–142.

Waas, G. A. (1988). Social attributional biases of peer-rejected and aggressive children. *Child Development, 59,* 969–992.

Wager, J. T. (1995–1996). Double exposure. *Nucleus, 17*(4), 1–3, 12.

Walsh, M. (1993). Highway vehicle activity trends and their implications for global warming: The U.S. in an international context. In D. Greene & D. Santini (Eds.), *Transportation and global climate change* (pp. 1–48). Berkeley, CA: ACEEE Books.

Wasting Opportunities. (1990, December 22). *The Economist,* p. 14.

Weiner, B. (1979). A theory of motivation for some classroom experiences. *Journal of Educational Psychology, 71*, 3–25.

Weiner, B. (1986). *An attributional theory of motivation and emotion.* New York: Springer-Verlag.

Weiner, J. J., & Wright, F. E. (1973). Effects of undergoing arbitrary discrimination upon subsequent attitudes toward a minority group. *Journal of Applied Social Psychology, 3*, 94–102.

Weinstein, N. D., & Klein, W. M. (Eds.). (1996). Special issue: Unrealistic optimism about personal risk. *Journal of Social and Clinical Psychology, 15*, 1–142.

Weinstein, R. S. (1996). High standards in a tracked system of schooling: For which students and with what educational supports? *Educational Researcher, 25*, 16–19.

Weinstein, R. S. (1998). Promoting positive expectations in schooling: In N. Lambert & B. L. McCombs (Eds.), *How students learn: Reforming schools through learner-centered education* (pp. 81–111). Washington, DC: American Psychological Association.

Weinstein, R. S., Madison, S., & Kuklinski, M. (1995). Raising expectations in schooling: Obstacles and opportunities for change. *American Educational Research Journal, 32*, 121–160.

Weinstein, R. S., & McKnown, C. (in press). Expectancy effects in "context": Listening to the choices of students and teachers. In J. Brophy (Ed.), *Teachers' and students' expectations* (Vol. 7). New York: JAI.

Weinstein, R. S., Soule, C. R., Collins, F., Cone, J., Melhorn, M., & Simantocci, K. (1991). Expectations and high school change: Teacher-researcher collaboration to prevent school failure. *American Journal of Community Psychology, 19*, 333–402.

Weiss, L., & Wolchik, S. (1998). New beginnings: An empirically-based intervention program for divorced mothers to help their children adjust to divorce. In J. M. Briesmeister & C. E. Schaefer (Eds.), *Handbook of parent training: Parents as co-therapists for children's behavior problems* (2nd pp. 445–478). New York: Wiley.

Wertheimer, L. K. (1998, Sept. 10). Dropping back in. *Dallas Morning News*, A1.

Wheelan, S. A., Pepitone, E. A., & Abt, V. (Eds.). (1990). *Advances in field theory.* Newbury Park, CA: Sage.

Wheeler, C. G. (1993, October). 30 years beyond "I have a dream." *Gallup Poll Monthly*, No. 337, pp. 2–10.

White, L. K. (1990). Determinants of divorce: A review of research in the eighties. *Journal of Marriage and the Family, 52*, 904–912.

Whyte, W. F., Greenwood, D. J., & Lazes, P. (1991). Participatory action research: Through practice to science in social research. In W. F. Whyte (Ed.), *Participatory action research* (pp. 19–55). Newbury Park, CA: Sage.

Wildavsky, A. (1979). *Speaking truth to power: The art and craft of policy analysis.* Boston: Little, Brown.

Willig, A. (1985). A meta-analysis of selected studies on the effectiveness of bilingual education. *Review of Educational Research, 55*, 269–317.

Wirthlin Worldwide. (1998). *From this day forward: The 1998 Michigan marriage report.* Virginia. (Available online at: *http://www.mfforum.com/marriage/table. html*)

Wittig, M. A., & Bettencourt, B. A. (Eds.). (1996). Social psychological perspectives on grassroots organizing [Special issue]. *Journal of Social Issues, 52*(1), 1–220.

Wittig, M. A., & Grant-Thompson, S. (1998). The utility of Allport's conditions of intergroup contact for predicting perceptions of improved racial attitudes and beliefs. *Journal of Social Issues, 54*(4), 795–812.

Wolchik, S. A., West, S. G., Westover, S., Sandler, I. N., Martin, A., Lustig, J., Tein, J. Y., & Fisher, J. (1993). The Children of Divorce Parenting Intervention: Outcome evaluation of an empirically based program. *American Journal of Community Psychology, 21,* 293–331.

Wolitski, R. J., and the CDC AIDS Community Demonstration Project Research Group. (1999). Community-level HIV intervention in five cities: Final outcome data from the CDC AIDS Community Demonstration Projects. *American Journal of Public Health.*

Wood, W., Wong, F. Y., & Chachere, J. G. (1991). Effects of media violence on viewers' aggression in unconstrained social interaction. *Psychological Bulletin, 109,* 371–383.

World Health Organization. (1997). *Weekly epidemiological record.* Geneva, Switzerland.

World Health Organization. (1998). *Report on the global HIV/AIDS epidemic.* Geneva, Switzerland.

World Scientists' Warning to Humanity. (1992, November). (Available online at: *http://www.mit.edu:8001/people/teal/ucs_warning.html*)

Yee, A. H., Fairchild, H. H., Weizmann, F., & Wyatt, G. E. (1993). Addressing psychology's problems with race. *American Psychologist, 48,* 1132–1140.

Zigler, E., & Muenchow, S. (1984). How to influence social policy affecting children and families. *American Psychologist, 39,* 415–420.

Zigler, E., & Muenchow, S. (1992). *Head Start: The inside story of America's most successful educational experiment.* New York: Basic Books.

Zigler, E., Styfco, S., & Gilman, E. (1993). The national Head Start program for disadvantaged preschoolers. In E. Zigler & S. Styfco (Eds.), *Head Start and beyond: A national plan for extended childhood intervention* (pp. 1–42). New Haven: Yale University Press.

Zill, N., Morrison, D. R., & Coiro, M. J. (1993). Long-term effects of parental divorce on parent-child relationships, adjustment, and achievement in young adulthood. *Journal of Family Psychology, 7,* 91–103.

Zillmann, D. (1992). Pornography research, social advocacy, and public policy. In P. Suedfeld & P. Tetlock (Eds.), *Psychology and social policy* (pp. 165–189). New York: Hemisphere.

Zillmann, D. (1994). Cognitive-excitation interdependencies in the escalation of anger and angry expression. In M. Potegal & J. F. Knutson (Eds.), *The dynamics of aggression.* Hillsdale, NJ: Erlbaum.

Zuckerman, M. (1990). Some dubious premises in research and theory on racial differences. *American Psychologist, 45,* 1297–1303.

AUTHOR INDEX

SUBJECT INDEX

Acid rain, 170
Accuracy of expectations, 141
Action research, 197–198
Activism, 13–14, 197–200
  activist organizations, 204–206
Advocacy role, 199
Agitators, 199–200
Aggression, 106. *Also see* Violence
  biology of, 107
  frustration and, 108
  stability of, 111
AIDS, 4, 55, 148–153, 157–164
  prevalence, 149–150
  risky behaviors, 150–153, 157–161
AIDS Community Demonstration
  Project, 156–161
Alinsky, Saul, 200–204
  conflict tactics, 201–203
  outcomes of his organizing,
    203–204
American Psychological Association,
  32–33, 35, 209
Anger management, 114
Applied social psychology:
  definition, 6
  features, 6–11
  problem orientation, 6–7
  problems, 14–16
  roles and activities, 12–14,
    197–200
Attitude, 63, 76–78, 153–154
  and behavior, 154–157, 161–164,
    175–177
  dimensions of, 153
  environmental, 175
Attribution:
  applications to health psychology,
    46
  causal, 42
  consequences of, 44–45
  controllability, 44–46
  definition, 42, 110
  dispositional, 42
  external, 43, 56, 177
  factors in, 43
  for success or failure, 44–45, 56
  fundamental attribution error, 43
  globality, 44, 46–47, 53, 56
  internal, 42, 44–47, 56
  locus, 44–45
  negative, 101
  reattribution training, 56–58
  situational, 43
  stability, 44–47, 56
  theory, 42–46
Attributional style, 46–58
  catastrophizing, 53
  measurement of, 47–48
  mechanisms underlying, 54–56
  optimistic, 55–56
  pessimistic, 46–47, 49–56

reattribution training, 56–58
Augmentation, 43
Authority, 179

Baseline survey, 158, 181
Basic science, 6–7
Behavioral intentions. *See* Intentions
Bilingual education, 134–135
Black students, 133–134
Bottle bills, 177
Brown v. Board of Education, 5

Carrying capacity, 170
Causal relations, 24–25, 27–31, 42,
  207
CAVE technique, 47–48, 51
CFCs, 171
Change agentry, 12, 197
Chavez, Cesar, 190–191
Children:
  effects of divorce on, 91–95
  preventing violence in, 122–123
  social adjustment of, 109–111
Coercive role, 199–200
Cognitive dissonance, 162–164
  and condom use, 162–164
  definition, 162
  hypocrisy, 162–164
Collaborative role, 198
Commitment, 87–89, 162–164
Commons dilemma, 184
Communal relationship, 97
Community organizing, 200–204
Competence training, 5
Condom use, 160–161
Conflict:
  resolution, 113
  tactics, 199–203
Confounding, 31
Consequences, unintended, 15–16
Consistency, 178
Consultation, 12, 197
Contact hypothesis, 79
Control. *See* Perceived control
Correlation:
  coefficient, 23
  correlational method, 23–24
  correlational studies of aggression,
    118–120
Cost-benefit comparisons, 11
Counter-attitudinal advocacy, 121
Crime, 119–120
Critical viewing skills, 120–121
Cultivation effect, 117–118

Deception, 34
Delayed treatment design, 94–95
Delinquency, 119–120
Demand-withdrawal interaction, 98
Depression, 49–50
Desensitization, 118

Diffusion of responsibility, 9
Disclosure, 89
  reciprocity, 89
Discounting, 43
Discrimination, 62–64, 76–79. *Also
  see* Prejudice
  definition, 63, 76–77
Disidentification, 71
Disincentives, 177
Disinhibition, 118
Dissonance. *See* Cognitive dissonance
Divorce, 86, 90–101
  effects on children, 91–95
  infidelity in, 98–99
  intergenerational transmission,
    95
  prediction of, 95–99
  prevention of, 99–101
  rates, 91

Effect size, 26
Emotions, 97
  reciprocity of, 97
Empathy training, 113–114
Environmental destruction, 5,
  168–174
  steps to avoid, 184–185
Environmental organizations, 185,
  205–206
Equity, 97
Ethical issues, 32–35, 207–209
  debriefing, 34
  deception, 34
  guidelines, 33, 209
  harmful consequences, 32
  in influencing public policy,
    207–209
  informed consent, 34
  use of findings, 34–35
Ethnic group, 64–65
Evaluation, 12, 101, 114–116, 121,
  132–134, 209
Evaluation apprehension, 70
Evidence, strength of, 15
Exchange relationship, 97
Expectations, 136, 138–144
  accuracy of, 141
  effect on performance, 139–140
  for minority students, 141–142
  raising, 142–144
  shown by teacher behaviors, 140
Experimental method:
  features, 25–26
  studies of aggression, 118
  large-scale social experiments,
    191–195
Experimenting society, 191–192
Expert role, 197–198
Explanatory style. *See* Attributional
  style

244